ONCE MORE, WITH FEELING

I0811897

ONCE MORE, WITH FEELING

Five Affecting Plays

Edited by Erin Hurley

Playwrights Canada Press
Toronto

Once More, With Feeling © 2014 by Erin Hurley
Bliss (*Félicité*) copyright © Olivier Choinière, translation copyright © 2008 Caryl Churchill. Published by arrangement with Nick Hern Books, London (www.nickhernbooks.co.uk), and Theatre Communications Group, New York (www.tcg.org).
Nanay (Mother): A Testimonial Play copyright © 2014 Caleb Johnston and Gerladine Pratt.
RAGE copyright © 2014 Michele Riml.
The Glass Box copyright © 2014 Theatre Terrific.
The Salon Automaton copyright © 2014 Nathalie Claude, translation copyright © 2014 Nathalie Claude and Moynan King.
The copyright of the individual introductory contibutions remains with the respective authors.

No part of this book may be reproduced, downloaded, or used in any form or by any means without the prior written permission of the publisher, except for excerpts in a review or by a licence from Access Copyright, www.accesscopyright.ca.

For professional or amateur production rights, please contact the publisher.

LIBRARY AND ARCHIVES CANADA CATALOGUING IN PUBLICATION
Once more, with feeling : five affecting plays / edited by Erin Hurley.

Includes bibliographical references.
Contents: The salon automaton / by Nathalie Claude -- Rage / by Michele Riml -- The glass box / by Theatre Terrific -- Bliss / by Olivier Choinière ; translated by Caryl Churchill -- Nanay : a testimonial play / by Caleb Johnston & Geraldine Pratt.
ISBN 978-1-77091-217-5 (pbk.)

1. Canadian drama (English)--21st century. I. Hurley, Erin, editor

PS8315.1.O53 2014 C812'.608 C2013-908494-0

We acknowledge the financial support of the Canada Council for the Arts, the Ontario Arts Council (OAC)—an agency of the Government of Ontario, which last year funded 1,681 individual artists and 1,125 organizations in 216 communities across Ontario for a total of $52.8 million—the Ontario Media Development Corporation, and the Government of Canada through the Canada Book Fund for our publishing activities.

Canada Council for the Arts Conseil des arts du Canada

ONTARIO ARTS COUNCIL CONSEIL DES ARTS DE L'ONTARIO

Canada

Ontario
Ontario Media Development Corporation

For Hugh,
Heart, mind, and spirit,
With love

Contents

ONCE MORE, WITH FEELING!

Erin Hurley

"Once more, with feeling!" Many will know this command as the title of a musical episode of the 1990s cult television hit, *Buffy the Vampire Slayer*.[1] This echo is appealing not only for how it foregrounds musical expression as an elevated mode of emotional expression—conventionally, in musicals, characters sing and dance when they can no longer express themselves adequately through ordered speech—but also for its invocations of popular culture, fandom, and celebrity, those fundamentally elevated modes of solicitation to felt attachment (to forms and people), and of investment on the part of fans to the same. The attractions and pitfalls of such mood enhancers are at issue in a number of the plays anthologized in these pages. In Olivier Choinière's *Bliss* (*Félicité* in its original French), four Walmart employees enact the facing pages of a tabloid that tell of a superstar diva's temporary retirement from show business juxtaposed with the story of a fan's horrific abuse by her family. Their stories are connected by the intensity of feeling-response to their situations and their persons, and by the sometimes healing/sometimes hurting relationships between a celebrity and her public. Theatre Terrific's *The Glass Box* also capitalizes on the desirous dynamics of celebrity culture to tell its story of the

1 Somewhat more obscurely, it is also the title of a 1958 Broadway comedy by Harry Kurnitz about a harpist and her conductor husband that was then made into a movie directed by Stanley Donen in 1960.

asymmetrical attribution of sexual feelings—and of feeling sexy—across bodies of different types and abilities. Here, the characters are the actor-devisors of the piece—Susanna Uchatius, Watson Moy, and Kyla Harris—who, in turn, take on the personae of Sophia Loren, Brad Pitt, and Cleopatra (Cleo). Sophia and Cleo are "in rehab" after having a doubled "accident"—Sophia's accidents are aging and a regretted missed sexual opportunity, Cleo's are falling in love with Antony and a spinal-cord injury. Brad is their emotional counterpoint in his sweet romanticism, modelled on the image of Pitt as a "good guy" and "nice person," which are also sexy attributes. Through a talk-show format set of questions and answers—again an invitation to make private lives public for others' pleasurable (and judgmental) consumption—the three characters and their personae re-evaluate their sexual worth.

Despite the fruitful connections to the dynamics of celebrity, however, it is more likely that this command—once more, with feeling—arises out of musical culture itself and a set of rehearsal and performance practices that will be familiar to theatre artists as well. "Once more, with feeling!" demands another attempt at performance by those who are simply "marking" their way through a piece. It asks them to treat the rehearsal context as a "real performance," a context in which they play full out, in which they "mean it" instead of just executing the notes (or lines or movements) in a perfunctory manner. It commands, then, an investiture of self and of feeling into the technical, which makes the technical something "more." It is precisely this challenge that organizes Nathalie Claude's play for one flesh-and-blood actress and three automata, *The Salon Automaton*, in which an Edwardian woman hosts a weekly "salon" (à la Natalie Barney) of three guests—automata of her own creation. The plot consists of a series of tests of the automatons' capacities—e.g., breathing, eating and drinking, interpreting data—the climax of which is the test for appropriately expressed emotion. That climax also proves the limit of the automatons' abilities; they fail in their attempt at investing their emotional expression of sadness—what they know they should be performing—with convincing feeling. And this failure comes despite the Hostess's training of them in some of the basics of emotionally fulsome theatrical performance. At its opening, the Hostess leads her automata through a set of warm-up exercises to performance, including exercises of breathing, articulation, and vocal production. The metatheatrical frame is consolidated in the clues of the salon's repeated performance. For example, shards of broken glass litter the corners of the room, remnants of their breakage in weeks past and indicator for the inevitable moment of smashed champagne flutes in the particular iteration of the salon to which the theatre audience is privy. In this, the automatons' final "rehearsal" of their salon, they are enjoined by the Hostess to play it "for real."

Who cares? And what do they care about? are questions explored poignantly and in all-too-timely a fashion in Michele Riml's award-winning play for young audiences, *RAGE*. A two-hander that sets a female high-school guidance counsellor in a loaded conversation with one of her charges, a teenage boy with the eponymous nickname, *RAGE* stages the encounter between the heightened emotionality and affective turmoil of adolescence and the ideological duplicity of a middle-aged woman whose beliefs are shaken. But it is also a lesson in dialogic argument on questions of peace and violence, of resistance and apathy, and of commitment through action to ideals. If Laura, the guidance counsellor, is revealed to lack such follow-through (or, in the terms articulated above, to lack such investment of self and feeling into the technical), Rage, alas, displays his commitment to fully invested and executed performance. The prop of a gun is at once the symbol of Rage's emotional volatility and its mode of expression.

The issue of care and its associated labours is front and centre in the verbatim theatre piece *Nanay (Mother)*, created by cultural geographers Geraldine Pratt and Caleb Johnston with the Philippine Women Centre of BC. It lays bare what sociologist Arlie Hochschild has called the "heart transplant" from the global South to the global North that characterizes contemporary dependent care work in countries like Canada. This set of monologues derived verbatim from interviews with Filipinas working in child-, elder-, or other forms of dependent-care in Canada as part of the Live-In Caregiver Program count the costs of such labour, including alienation from family of origin, sometimes degrading conditions of work and living, and emotionally fraught relationships with those for whom they are paid to care. Focusing on the employer-employee dyad more than the care worker/cared-for relation, *Nanay* also reveals something of the socio-political and economic contexts in Canada that create such a delegation of affective labour that is costly, though asymmetrically, on both sides of that equation.

And so, affect, feeling, and emotion are the red thread that brings together the plays in this collection. You might well ask if this would not be the red thread in any play collection. The answer, as far as I'm concerned, is that it could indeed be yes. Because making, managing, distributing, and provoking feeling of all kinds is a key element of what theatre does, of why it matters.[2] As Nicholas Ridout has argued, theatre is an affect-producing machine, a "vibratorium" that engages audiences intimately and collectively through its sensate lures.[3] Moreover, there has to be something that captures attention or makes an impression on an audience to keep it in its proverbial seats. This attention-capturing or impression-making is not the exclusive province of emotion, even if they often derive from feeling or emotional display; for audiences can be moved (altered) by calculated, rational argument or, on the contrary, left unimpressed (unaffected) by a particularly cool aesthetic. But this being moved, being influenced, or, in contemporary parlance, being "impacted" by another in a way that changes something about the self is precisely the province of what philosophers Gilles Deleuze and Félix Guattari, following Baruch Spinoza, call "affect" in *A Thousand Plateaus*. Deleuze defines affect as the variation of a body in its encounter with another. Note that that body need not be human, nor even sensate. Thus, a hammer may affect a nail in their smashing encounter and a chair may affect a sitter, inviting the sitter to take up a certain, limited range of positions by virtue of the chair's organization (back, seat, legs) in relation to the sitter's physiology (another set of back, seat, and legs) and the sitter's abilities (of motion, arrangement, and the like). It is in this widened, philosophically inflected sense that one might argue for plays being "affecting." And I think the five collected in this

2 See Erin Hurley, *Theatre & Feeling* (Basingstoke: Palgrave Macmillan, 2010).

3 Nicholas Ridout, *Stage Fright, Animals, and Other Theatrical Problems* (Cambridge: Cambridge UP, 2006), and "Welcome to the Vibratorium" *The Senses & Society* 3.2 (2008), 221–31.

volume are; their various organizations of backs, seats, and legs (that is, in Aristotelian terms, in their plot, character, language, "thought" [argument], and spectacle) combine with audience affordances (their sensory capacities, their cultural and theatrical histories, their comfort/discomfort in their places, etc.) to make a mutual impression of play on audience and audience on play. This is one of the reasons that a play—whether read or performed—is never the same twice. It is not just that performance is only ever imperfect in its repetitions, it is also that the "bodies" put in relation by the theatrical (or reading) event are never the same two times in a row.

In my selections, then, I've looked for plays that highlight different kinds of affecting encounters and, as such, make different kinds of impressions. I might argue that *RAGE* makes its strongest impression thematically in its content, but its explosive content is also pressurized by the dramaturgical structure of the two-hander and the enclosed office space in which it transpires. The almost surrealist organization of *Bliss*, with its slipping in and out of incantatory exclamations, brutal imagery, a mix of presentational and realist stylistic elements (notably address) can be disorienting and tumultuous. The cynicism of the piece—and the intellectual and moral shabbiness of the society it takes as its object—is delivered without affective indirection in a series of gut-punching passages. In Claude's *Salon Automaton*, the technical elements of production hold particular fascination. Indeed, Claude's contribution to this volume thematizes such a fascination, exploiting the creaky mechanics of Edwardian automatons for a certain creepiness factor in her drawing-room tragicomedy.

Genre also makes an impression. Whether reading "women's weepies" or the purgative structures of realism,[4] feminist critics in particular have paid attention to the ways in which generic conventions shape narrative expectation and provoke, or even condition, affective response and intensity. And so I also purposefully chose a range of different genres of theatre (documentary, devised, tightly scripted, TYA, etc.) to encourage examining how the

4 See Robyn Warhol, *Having a Good Cry: Effeminate Feelings and Pop-Culture Forms* (Ohio State UP, 2003), and Jill Dolan, *The Feminist Spectator as Critic*, second revised edition (Ann Arbor: U of Michigan P, 2012).

affect-producing machine that is the theatre uses a range of technologies to produce those affects. What kinds of feeling-technologies undergird Theatre for Young Audiences or documentary theatre, for instance? Nicholas Hanson's introduction to *RAGE* suggests that TYA tends to utilize the "hotter" affects as a way of both connecting to their audiences and, as importantly, allowing for the demonstration of emotional intensity that their audiences often associate with "good acting." But what about a genre like documentary theatre, with its legible, fact-based foundation and its normative direct address to the audience who, in turn, act as a witnessing or judging public? Is its less overt use of emotion management part of an effort to impress its topics more firmly on the "real world," where the kind of emotional intensity—performed or experienced—that theatre can provide is precisely not the norm?

These are generalizations, of course. We'd need more than one volume of five plays to responsibly tease out their various generic, thematic, and technical lures, prompts, and traces of affect. I offer these five affecting plays nonetheless as provocations for further investigation of the different forces and impressions within the gamut of Canadian theatrical performance, a place to begin—and to begin again, once more, with feeling.

Bonne lecture!

BLISS (FÉLICITÉ)

Olivier Choinière
translated by
Caryl Churchill

BLISS: THROUGH THE LOOKING GLASS

Stéphanie Nutting

Who is more real
The person who is looking
Or the reflection in the mirror
—Olivier Choinière, *Chien savant*

Olivier Choinière is no stranger to controversy. He has been accused of "hacking" a Molière play at the elite Théâtre du Nouveau Monde by distributing headphones to specific audience members and delivering a running commentary, thereby grafting his own performance onto the live show.[1] He has raised the ire of at least one theatre critic who called another of his plays, *Venise-en-Québec*, a "freak show,"[2] proving that the thinly veiled allegory of what arguably points to a myopic and stagnant Quebec had hit a nerve. Indeed, the same play that earned its author the status of finalist for the Governor General's Literary Award in 2006 had in fact polarized the critical

1 See J. Kelly Nestruck, "How Olivier Choinière Committed Theatrical 'Rape,' " *The Globe and Mail*, 1 April 2012, accessed 26 July 2013. http://www.theglobeandmail.com/arts/theatre-and-performance/how-olivier-choiniere-committed-theatrical-rape/article4096773/.

2 Raymond Bertin, "Le *freak show* du Théâtre d'Aujourd'hui: *Venise-en-Québec*," *Jeu: Revue de théâtre* 121.4 (2006): 65–67, accessed 22 July 2013. http://id.erudit.org/iderudit/24351ac.

landscape—many critics loved it but some loathed it. And, while the subject of socio-political stagnation turns out to be a sensitive one, it is worth noting that Quebec society reappears as a topic of scrutiny in his more recent plays as well. *Nom de domaine* (*Domain Name*, 2012) and *Mommy* (2013), both return to the question of Quebec society and foreground, in very different ways, a portrait of a Quebec nostalgic about its past.

But Choinière has also tested the physical and aesthetic limits of theatre as a genre, and performance in general, with his self-guided walking tours of the city of Montreal. *Beauté intérieure* (*Beautiful on the Inside*, 2003) and *Bienvenue à—(une ville dont vous êtes le touriste)* (*Welcome To a—(City Where You Are the Tourist)*) led self-guided "spect-acteurs" equipped with audio sets through some strange and gritty back alleys of Montreal, whereas *Ascension* (*Ascent*, 2006) led solitary walkers equipped with audio sets up to the summit of Mont Royal.[3] Contrary to what one might expect if one were a "tourist," the audio that accompanies these walks is by and large unsettling. Typically, the audio narrative veers steeply away from the external landmarks of the walks themselves, favouring instead stories of intimate violence and degradation, thus sabotaging any notion of entertainment or leisure as locus of pleasure.[4] Indeed, Choinière takes direct aim at the pursuit of pleasure, and more specifically "pleasure" as commodified by patterns of consumerism and entertainment. These two major themes that run through Choinière's oeuvre tie in to *Bliss* in quite a fascinating way and they deserve a closer look.

Bliss was first created in French by the Théâtre de la Manufacture at Théâtre La Licorne in Montreal under the title *Félicité* (2007), directed by Sylvain Bélanger with Jean-Denis Leduc as artistic director. The following year, Caryl Churchill's English translation, which is featured in this anthology, was performed at the Royal Court Theatre in London, UK, with Joe Hill-Gibbins as director. The play has since been performed in Scotland, Switzerland, and Australia; a Spanish translation is forthcoming as well.

3 The English translations of the titles are my own.

4 For an in-depth study of the ways in which Choinière subverts tourism, see Francis Ducharme, "Quand le théâtre joue à se prendre pour du tourisme: les déambulatoires audioguidés d'Olivier Choinière," *L'Annuaire théâtral* 47 (2010): 85–101.

The word "bliss"—the standard English equivalent for "félicité"—is not much of an equivalent, really. It takes the "calm and durable" happiness implied in the French word and ratchets it up to "perfect joy" or even a "state of being in heaven." This fortuitous *step up*, as it were, ultimately heightens the irony that drives the play. One may ask, "What is better than perfect joy and how do we get it?" The short response, from Choinière's ironic perspective, is "nothing" and "tabloids." Or, more accurately, we get it through the arousal of intense interest in the details of celebrities' private lives, which the media carve out and shrink-wrap for our benefit.

It is no accident that the author has chosen the chanteuse Céline Dion as the hyperreal diva for his searing treatment of media-fuelled adulation. The Dion "brand" is not just any brand. Céline Dion elicits strong emotions (both love and hate) in her listeners and audiences to such an extent that virtually no Québécois is indifferent to her. As a cultural phenomenon, she permeates Quebec, a fact that has been deftly analyzed by Erin Hurley, who refers to Dion's "inescapability" as part of the reason that Dion's sound has become the "the keynote or tonic . . . of Québécois pop."[5]

Although the Dion surname is not mentioned in *Bliss*, there is no mistaking the real-life referent, thanks to ample and obvious clues (not the least of which being her signature song from the '90s, "The Power of Love"), but also because all displays of emotion connected to "Céline" are hyperbolic. Indeed, as the main protagonist, a Walmart cashier, flips through tabloids during her break, she is mesmerized by the magazines' focus on Céline's announcement of a hiatus from singing. Her co-workers restage the moment, using gossip language like a camera to zoom in on and crystallize the moment:

> **DISPLAY:** On the big screen: close-up of Céline's face
> **MANAGER:** One tear—with her finger. Fantastic—wonderful

Tears of joy signal a shared affect that seals an alliance between the iconic Céline, her journalists, her biographer, and her photographers:

---

5 Erin Hurley, *National Performance: Representing Quebec from Expo 67 to Céline Dion* (Toronto: U of Toronto P, 2011), 158.

> **COSMETICS:** When Céline appeared at the press conference in jeans and a sweater—a baggy sweater, really—simple. The journalists were on their knees
> **DISPLAY:** The Photographer wanted to take a photo but he was crying too much

Mediated by the language of tabloid gossip, feelings are first frozen into poses and then into images. Yet the way they reverberate within the so-called "dialogue" reminds us that spectacle, as a commodity, is far from static; on the contrary, it is all about the *circulation* of appearances as goods. The French political philosopher, Guy Debord, put it best when he wrote, "The spectacle is not a collection of images, but a social relation among people, mediated by images."[6] Certainly, the quotation that appears as a preamble to Choinière's text leaves no doubt as to the power of Debord's influence on Choinière's world view and his work. The consumption of appearances (including packaged feelings on display) occurs in relation to other people, yet despite all that, the thrall of the aesthetic of surfaces makes us passive and undermines real connections.

Moreover, it seems that the tabloid narrative of bliss, and the contemplative passive gaze it triggers, does not discriminate. The carefully controlled illusions of the star system eventually crack open. Initially contained on the facing page of the gossip magazine, the shocking story of an unknown woman (Isabelle) gradually contaminates the consumption of Céline's domestic bliss. As two diametrically opposed domestic "scenes" unfold, slippage occurs. Horror creeps in.

In terms of subject matter, it is noteworthy that Quebec playwrights, from Michel Tremblay to Michel Marc Bouchard and Daniel Danis, are well known for dissecting family dystopia. Choinière, in line with this theatre culture, returns to this familiar subject matter only to push it to its agonizing brink. But what really is at stake extends well beyond the specifics of Quebec's territory and social history. What Debord calls the *spectacle*—a world vision tied to the

---

6 Guy Debord, *Society of the Spectacle*, trans. Fredy Perlman and Jon Supak (Detroit: Black and Red, 1983), paragraph 4.

production and circulation of representations—affects the intensity with which people experience life. "Everything that was directly lived has moved away into a representation,"[7] declared Debord. Not much has changed since Debord wrote his essay in 1967 except, undeniably, the speed of production and consumption and, of course, the modes of representation—it is significant that the characters in *Bliss* play video games during which they routinely *lose* "lives." If nothing can be "directly lived" in capitalist societies, it follows that *the spectacle* has also seriously changed the ways in which people conceptualize intimacy.

Pornography is an obvious example of how the illusion of intimacy has become commodified. Interestingly, for gossip theorists such as Patricia Spacks, there is an analogy to be drawn between magazine (or television) gossip and publicized sex. As much as "serious" gossip fosters closeness, celebrity gossip does the opposite: "like publicized sex," she writes, "[it] creates loneliness: a sense that people have nothing to do with one another except look and be looked at."[8] In Choinière's dystopia, the glossy language of gossip media is punctuated by obscenities, as if the alienating effects of gossip were not enough to defeat all hope of closeness and intimacy. In a way, the tension between publicity and intimacy points to a spectacular (in the full sense of the word) binary system that, when unpacked, would seem to involve a whole series of opposing terms: reality/fantasy, opulence/squalor, wealth/poverty, romantic love/physical violence, trust/betrayal, bliss/horror. However, those clean categories of contrasts are a little too neat for Choinière. Fantasy is not contained outside of reality and horror is not detached from bliss. Instead, the cascade of meanings and differences is more akin to the famous M.C. Escher painting *Drawing Hands*, where the hand being drawn is also the hand doing the drawing. In other words, there is no "inside" or "outside" to the modern-day illusion, so when the enigmatically named character "ORACLE" looks into the bathroom mirror, she sees an image that is at once her and not her—it even has another name: "I'm looking at you. You're looking at me. We smile at each other."

7 Ibid., paragraph 1.

8 Patricia Spacks, *Gossip* (Chicago: U of Chicago P, 1986), 25.

Bliss was first produced by the Royal Court Theatre at Jerwood Theatre Upstairs, London, UK, between March 28 and April 26, 2008. It featured the following cast and creative team:

Brid Brennan: Cosmetics Salesperson
Haley Carmichael: Oracle
Neil Dudgeon: Manager
Justin Salinger: Display Assistant

Director: Joe Hill-Gibbins
Designer: Jeremy Herbert

CHARACTERS

Cosmetics Salesperson: 1. Acts under another's direction. 2. Applies makeup, disguises, smoothes things over. 3. Woman, late forties.

Manager: 1. Runs things on behalf of someone else. 2. Organizes, forbids, confronts. 3. Man, early fifties.

Display Assistant: 1. Designs and arranges the displays, shows off the merchandise. 2. Records, places, situates. 3. Man, late twenties.

Oracle: 1. Expresses herself with authority, is highly trusted. 2. Announces, decides, settles. 3. Woman, early thirties.

PLACE

The stage, that is *from the other side of the mirror*.

PUNCTUATION

A slash (/) indicates the start of the next speech.

The dash (—) indicates a gesture expressing a thought, an ellipsis, hesitation, or censorship.

A sentence without a full stop (.) indicates that the next speech follows without a pause.

NOTE

Dialogue in small caps indicates a louder voice or a quote from a newspaper.

MANAGER, COSMETICS SALESPERSON, DISPLAY ASSISTANT enter and face the audience. They're wearing blue overalls, except for the MANAGER. They're all wearing name tags with letters and numbers backwards so you can't read them. They're smiling. ORACLE enters and faces the audience. She's not smiling. She's wearing the same blue overalls. On her name tag you can read: 31CARO.

ORACLE: Begin.

COSMETICS: Everyone—breathless

DISPLAY: Your legs—

MANAGER: No one dared breathe

COSMETICS: The silence—at the end of the note; I mean when the last note had died away

MANAGER: Vast

DISPLAY: Then everyone looked up at the same time

MANAGER: The balloons were beginning to fall

COSMETICS: RAINING balloons

MANAGER: But she stayed where she was, microphone in her hand, mouth open—eyes scrunched up

COSMETICS: And it's as if—she was still singing

DISPLAY: That's right: as if the roar of the crowd was coming out of her mouth

MANAGER: Thousands of spectators—in her mouth

COSMETICS: People were yelling, balloons still raining down on them—on her, standing there

MANAGER: Mouth open—eyes scrunched up

DISPLAY: And then flash—all at once, from all over

MANAGER: Wonderful

DISPLAY: As if everyone wanted to keep the same memory.

COSMETICS: After that, she lowered her arms, she opened her eyes, she smiled—yes, she smiled and she said: "Thank you"
ORACLE: No—before
COSMETICS: Before what?
ORACLE: Before she said it
MANAGER: You're right—before that, she put her hand on her heart and said: "Thank you," but / without saying thank you
DISPLAY: WITHOUT saying thank you
MANAGER: Just mouthing the words "Thank you"
DISPLAY: Yes, because people—
COSMETICS: But she did end up saying "Thank you," I mean really
DISPLAY: But it took— That's why she said: "Stop. It's too much."
COSMETICS: YES, then after that: "I love you lots!"—with her arm
DISPLAY: Then: "I love you too," because everyone was shouting: "I LOVE YOU"
MANAGER: "WE LOVE YOU, CÉLINE!"
COSMETICS: Then Céline crying
DISPLAY: On the big screen: close-up of Céline's face
MANAGER: One tear—with her finger. Fantastic—wonderful
DISPLAY: But everyone kept on: "CÉLINE! CÉLINE!"
COSMETICS: That's when Céline said: "Thank you from the bottom of my heart," bending her head, then softly, the first notes of—obviously! For an encore Céline sang "The Power of Love," still crying
MANAGER: Her cheeks—soaking wet
COSMETICS: And everyone was crying. After the encore: "DON'T GO, / CÉLINE!"
DISPLAY: CÉLINE on television—in every house
COSMETICS: In the living room: everyone crying
DISPLAY: Next day—newspapers, magazines: "GOODBYE, CÉLINE," in big letters
ORACLE: Not "GOODBYE," "SEE YOU LATER"
MANAGER: "SEE YOU LATER"—yes, that's right—Céline just wanted a break.
COSMETICS: When Céline appeared at the press conference in jeans and a sweater—a baggy sweater, really—simple. The journalists were on their knees
DISPLAY: The Photographer wanted to take a photo but he was crying too much

COSMETICS: Céline and René sat down. Céline smiled—simple. And the press officer had a word with the Journalist and the Journalist asked if—no—earlier, the Journalist said: "Hello, Céline," and Céline said: "Hello, lovely. How's your throat?" Céline knew the Journalist had been ill, she'd been briefed—no—she / just knew

MANAGER: And what did the Journalist ask?

COSMETICS: The Journalist asked: "How long's the break for, Céline?" And René replied

MANAGER: It's not René who replied, it's Céline—she replied: "I don't know yet" and after that René said: "Maybe two—three years"

DISPLAY: That's right: "Maybe five, maybe seven"

COSMETICS: "Or maybe not, maybe just a month, who knows," but, "If Céline took a break for a month it would feel like ten years, if she came back after ten years it would be as if she'd never left," thought the Journalist

MANAGER: Céline said: "I want to take some time for myself, with my family," then gazing upward: "One thing I do know, I'll always be with you"

COSMETICS: And the Journalist felt she was speaking to her—for her—that it was just to her she was saying that

DISPLAY: When Céline got up from the press table, the Photographer felt she turned towards him; it was for him she was turning her head, stroking her belly

COSMETICS: Céline was pregnant

ORACLE: Céline didn't say she was pregnant

MANAGER: No, not at the press conference, it was a fucking journalist who

COSMETICS: The Journalist didn't say anything, I mean she just THOUGHT Céline was pregnant—maybe, even if deep down she knew

MANAGER: Someone talked, someone took a photo, a photo of her lying in bed

DISPLAY: It wasn't one of the Photographer's photos

MANAGER: René made them withdraw the magazine with the photo—all the magazines, from all the newsagents and all the shops. Céline wanted it to be INTIMATE.

DISPLAY: It was in the plane—René's private jet, *The Céline*, that the Photographer—knew. It was unbelievable! The Photographer had always dreamt

of flying in *The Céline*, and it was there, up in the sky, Céline asked him: "How'd you like to be my motherhood photographer?" and the Photographer cried
MANAGER: She wanted to take the time to experience it together, peacefully
COSMETICS: The Journalist had obtained an exclusive interview with Céline in *The Céline*, and when they landed Céline said: "Why don't you come and spend some time at the house?" She didn't need to say any more
MANAGER: She wanted it to be at home, just the family
COSMETICS: So when Céline took the Journalist's hand and looked at her with—her eyes, she knew what Céline was going to tell her and the Journalist cried
MANAGER: And when the Californian Doctor said: "Céline, you'll have to remain in bed," Céline didn't feel like a prisoner, quite the opposite, she said to herself: "I'm going to stay in bed and I'm going to read, read all the fan letters I haven't had time to read," and all day long she lay there in the bedroom, a wonderful bedroom
DISPLAY: The light was—extraordinary
MANAGER: Even bigger than the bedroom when she was married, the second time
COSMETICS: Maybe not bigger
MANAGER: She wanted it just as big
DISPLAY: It wasn't bigger but it seemed bigger—because of the desert
COSMETICS: The desert?
DISPLAY: The bedroom was at the back of the house—looked out onto the desert. The view—unbelievable
COSMETICS: And the garden—the / Babylonian garden
DISPLAY: Babylonian
MANAGER: The Las Vegas house: a real castle
DISPLAY: The Photographer took photos
COSMETICS: That bedroom—maybe not quite as big as the second marriage bedroom—was where she invited the Journalist
MANAGER: No journalist has been in Céline's bedroom. Céline said to René: "I don't want anyone—except my friends and family." Journalists just saw PHOTOS / of the bedroom

COSMETICS: Not all the journalists, THE Journalist
ORACLE: The Biographer
MANAGER: Okay, the Biographer, because journalists, journalists in general, they come to press conferences or they can fuck off
COSMETICS: The Biographer
MANAGER: Even when they come to press conferences—you've got to watch out who you ask to press conferences. You remember the French journalist / who
COSMETICS: You don't ask just anyone
MANAGER: Exactly—the French journalist who said to René: "Céline? You mean Louis-Fernand Céline?"
COSMETICS: "Ferdinand"—oh god, yes
MANAGER: "Louis-Ferdinand Céline?"
DISPLAY: Who is Louis-Ferdinand Céline?
COSMETICS: An actor
MANAGER: And René said: "No, not Louis-Ferdinand, but Céline, THE CÉLINE, the one and ONLY," then everyone laughed and the stupid fucking French journalist shut his fucking stupid French gob.
COSMETICS: I say "journalist" because at first she couldn't believe she'd been made THE official Biographer, I mean that Céline had given her a gift like that. When she said: "I want people to know the truth," she was so beautiful—radiant. The Biographer replied: "Céline, spiteful people are unhappy people."
DISPLAY: She was so beautiful—radiant, lying in that vast bed, her hair spread out on the pillows—a mountain of pillows and her on top
MANAGER: Wonderful
DISPLAY: And the Photographer asked René to lie down beside her, in his golden pyjamas
MANAGER: It wasn't pyjamas. It was traditional / dress
DISPLAY: Traditional dress, but I said pyjamas because it was so—simple, so lovely to see them, to suddenly see the man and the woman, like any other couple waking up, "CÉLINE AND RENÉ HAVE A LIE-IN," said the caption. Parents-to-be who love each other and are looking forward to their baby
COSMETICS: Céline said: "I want my child to know how much he was loved and wanted and looked forward to; how much his father loved his mother

and his mother loved his father; how much the whole family loved each other and were looking forward to his arrival." And the Biographer cried
DISPLAY: The Photographer saw before him the teenager who sang for the pope; he saw before him THE VOICE OF GOD, the most beautiful voice in the world; the Photographer had in his viewfinder success and international triumph, but when success and international triumph said to him: "How do you want me?" as if she'd never done it before, almost blushing as if it was the first time, then the Photographer saw before him THE LITTLE GIRL FROM CHARLEMAGNE, the childhood friend he'd been at school with, and the Photographer cried.
MANAGER: René came in one morning with some magazines from Quebec. Céline adored reading magazines from Quebec. When René came into the bedroom, Céline said: "Darling, come and kiss me."
ORACLE: No—she says: "Thanks for the flowers. They smell good."
COSMETICS: What flowers?
ORACLE: The flowers René sent
MANAGER: / René never
ORACLE: BECAUSE he went out early to play golf AND he wasn't going to be there when Céline woke up. The Chambermaid puts them in a vase
DISPLAY: What Chambermaid?
ORACLE: The black Chambermaid
MANAGER: René didn't hire a black chambermaid
ORACLE: ONE of the chambermaids out of a whole lot of chambermaïds; René can't be expected to know all the chambermaids. The black Chambermaid puts the flowers on the chest of drawers, next to the mirror, with a card signed: "With Love, René," and goes to give Céline a letter
COSMETICS: What letter?
ORACLE: A fan letter
COSMETICS: But it's usually the secretary who gets / the letters
ORACLE: Too late. Céline says: "Give it to me."
COSMETICS: What does the letter say?
ORACLE: The letter says: "Dear Céline, I think about you a lot. Like you, I'm always in bed. My illness stops me getting up. My family look after me. When

I'm sad they play me your music. I like the song "Everywhere I See You" very much. It's like me talking but you singing. I hope I'll get better one day so I can see one of your concerts live. Love you lots, Isabelle." Before leaving, the Chambermaid asks Céline for her autograph.

MANAGER: "There's two kinds of employee," thinks René

ORACLE: Céline signs an autograph for her—in French

MANAGER: "There's the ones that ask for autographs and the ones that don't—simple as that"

ORACLE: The black Chambermaid goes out of the room backwards—big smile—disappears.

DISPLAY: Then the Bodyguard doesn't see anyone leave?

ORACLE: The Bodyguard's in the staff kitchen—having lunch.

DISPLAY: He might hear—I don't know—the door opening or shutting

ORACLE: If the Bodyguard heard the door he'd think it was the Biographer who'd just gone in

COSMETICS: Isn't the Biographer in the bedroom ALREADY?

ORACLE: NO—the Biographer hasn't arrived yet. Céline's all alone—crying.

MANAGER: René comes into the bedroom with some magazines from Quebec—where you can see the photos of Céline and René in the bedroom and read the articles about Céline's pregnancy, but when René sees Céline crying, René thinks: "Bad news."

COSMETICS: Céline's crying about the letter; I mean she found it so beautiful—touching

MANAGER: It's when Céline says: "Thanks for the flowers. They smell good," when he sees the flowers, that's when he thinks: "Bad news." He's really scared, because René never sent Céline any flowers. He goes to look at the flowers by the mirror. An enormous bunch because of the reflection. He picks up the card, "With love, René." His accountant has already told him his signature's easy to imitate. He doesn't say anything about it to Céline; he goes out of the bedroom with the card—goes to see Céline's personal Bodyguard

DISPLAY: The Bodyguard doesn't understand, he didn't see anyone

MANAGER: René says: "Go check the flowers."

DISPLAY: The Bodyguard comes into the room and goes to look at the flowers, even though it's not his job—bends over them. Céline says: "They smell good," but the flowers hardly smell at all and anyway they're a long way from the bed. The Bodyguard says to himself: "How could she smell the flowers from way over there?"

MANAGER: The Californian Doctor has forbidden Céline to get out of bed. "It's dangerous. Céline could lose her baby." René gets out his mobile to call the florist and find out who they sold the flowers to, but there's no number on the card because it's not a florist's card, it's a label from Walmart

COSMETICS: When the Biographer comes into the bedroom, Céline says: "I've had such a beautiful letter—really touching; I'd like to reply, I really want to write to her." There's no return address on the envelope, there's nothing at all on the envelope because there isn't an envelope, there's just the letter. Céline says to the Biographer: "I want to know all about Isabelle," smiling through her tears

ORACLE: No—crying

COSMETICS: Crying?

ORACLE: Howling—with pain

MANAGER: René runs into the bedroom

ORACLE: René's nowhere near the bedroom; he's outside—the other end of the garden

MANAGER: René's calling the DOCTOR

ORACLE: The Doctor's already in the bedroom—with the Biographer and the Bodyguard. Céline's howling

DISPLAY: The Bodyguard goes nearer

MANAGER: The Doctor's running to the bed

ORACLE: Céline's covers are stained with blood—between her thighs

MANAGER: They lift up the covers

COSMETICS: The Biographer closes her eyes—takes Céline's hand—René plunges his head / between her thighs

MANAGER: The DOCTOR

COSMETICS: I mean the DOCTOR—the CALIFORNIAN Doctor plunges his head between Céline's thighs

DISPLAY: Céline's cries are like a song. You'd think she was singing. The Bodyguard backs away

MANAGER: The Doctor shouts: "SHE'S LOSING HER BABY."

COSMETICS: The Biographer picks up the phone—to call an ambulance

MANAGER: The Doctor hangs up the phone. He snarls: "Imbecile! She can't move."

DISPLAY: The Bodyguard bumps into the chest of drawers and things fall off the top: CDs, a camera

COSMETICS: The Biographer doesn't know what to do; she starts wiping the blood—on the phone

MANAGER: "CALL RENÉ!"

DISPLAY: The Bodyguard sees in the Doctor's blood-red hands Céline's blood-red baby

COSMETICS: It's not even a baby, it's hardly a baby, it's—the Biographer can't look, the Biographer goes out, the Nurse comes in—it's a big red prawn. Céline's personal Nurse takes the big red prawn out of the Doctor's hands

DISPLAY: The Bodyguard can't look

COSMETICS: The Nurse doesn't know what to do with it

ORACLE: The flash goes off

COSMETICS: What flash?

ORACLE: The flash from the camera.

MANAGER: Who's taking PHOTOS?

DISPLAY: NO ONE!

COSMETICS: The Nurse throws the big prawn down the toilet—flush!—gets a towel, wets it, wrings it—washes Céline, changes Céline

DISPLAY: The Bodyguard puts back the camera, the CDs—he's shaking

MANAGER: The Californian Doctor calls René—he says: "René, I'm so sorry. The baby's dead." René's shaking—his legs won't hold him anymore; he's come all the way across the garden. He runs into the house, holding himself up on the walls, makes it to the bedroom, his eyes—burning with tears. René wants to tear his heart out; Céline keeps saying: "DOCTOR, WHERE'S MY BABY? MY BABY?"

COSMETICS: Finally Céline goes to sleep. The Nurse stays with her—the rest of the day—all night. Next morning, Céline wakes up with a big smile, then she says to the Nurse: "Mum, I'm so glad you came to see me." Céline's sick, she's / not well

MANAGER: She just needs to see her family, to have them around her. René calls Céline's Mother and her brothers and sisters—her Father. He tells them to come. He doesn't say why, he just tells them to come, and when the family get to Vegas next day, René takes Céline's Mother in his arms and cries

COSMETICS: René doesn't have to say anything, Céline's Mother knows

MANAGER: René cries on her shoulder. Behind Céline's Mother is Céline's Father. René looks at Céline's Father, smiling, shy, awkward, overcome by René, Vegas, by the marble, the soft tops, the sunshine, the garden, the desert, the palm trees. How can the Father smile? His daughter's lost her baby—their baby, and René closes his eyes, hugs Céline's Mother tight as if to stop himself from

COSMETICS: Céline's Mother says to René: "I know what it's like; I lost my first one." The Mother goes into the house, goes straight to the Nurse to find out how Céline is. The Nurse says: "Take care of her." Céline's Mother doesn't need anyone telling her that. She knows perfectly well how to look after her daughter.

DISPLAY: The Bodyguard squeezes up to let Céline's Brother come in. Céline's Brother is surprised that the Bodyguard is as—small as him. The Brother sits on the bed and hugs his sister, Céline, who he hasn't seen for ages, except on stage or in photos, and she looks younger than in her photos—or thinner, he can't tell which. He doesn't know what to say. He just feels awkward, awkward at being alone with her, and she's smiling—the others still haven't come—the rest of the family. She strokes his arm, she says: "I think about the sick children and I don't feel so bad," but he can't look at her anymore—he looks away, has a look round. Unbelievable. He'd imagined a much bigger bedroom—that's it: the room looked bigger in the pictures. If he'd brought some magazines from Quebec he could have compared. He stares at the flowers, the flowers by the mirror. He gets up—the bunch looks twice as big because of the mirror. He bends over the flowers. The flowers don't smell. They're plastic.

COSMETICS: When Céline's Mother goes into the kitchen, the famous kitchen in the Vegas house, the kitchen she's only seen in pictures—in the magazines, she sees dirty dishes spilling all over the worktop. Céline's Mother's annoyed to see dirty dishes on the worktop; I mean that no one had thought of putting them in the dishwasher. Céline's Mother picks up a dirty plate to put it in the dishwasher but she can't find a dishwasher. Where is the dishwasher? Where are the staff, the maid, the cook? She calls René; she's going out of the kitchen calling René; she starts wandering down the corridors calling René; she starts thinking: "The man I gave my daughter to"; she's thinking about her daughter; she thinks: "I haven't been to see my daughter yet"

MANAGER: Céline says to her Father: "Don't cry, Pops. It could have been worse." Céline's Father doesn't understand what she means. What could have been worse? "There are people with nothing, nothing at all"—she repeats: "Nothing at all," and Céline's Father understands less than ever. His son's at the other end of the bedroom. He doesn't say anything; he stays there without moving. You'd think he was hiding something behind his back. Where are the others? His brothers and sisters? And then Céline's Father sees what the Brother was hiding behind his back; he puts it up to his face: a camera—he's going to take a photo, it's really not a good moment. Céline's Father says to Céline's Brother: "Put on a record," and the Brother backs off

DISPLAY: The Brother puts the camera down—a throwaway camera he bought at a tax-free shop. He puts it on the chest of drawers; he's glad to get rid of it, he feels silly for having bought it. He wipes his hands on his thighs and picks up a CD, the first one he finds, one of Céline's early singles. He picks up another one, a Céline double album, because there's only Céline CDs in Céline's bedroom.

ORACLE: She says: "Put some Céline on for me."

MANAGER: The song begins and Céline cuddles up against her Father. Céline's Father daren't take his daughter in his arms. She puts her head on his knees. She says: "Stroke my hair like when I was sick."

COSMETICS: Céline's Mother hears the music, a song she knows—which her daughter sings—used to sing; she walks towards the music

MANAGER: Céline's sucking her thumb and humming like when she was little, which used to make her Father say: "One day she'll be a singer"

ORACLE: "One day she'll suck cocks."

COSMETICS: Cé— Céline's Mother stops at the door
MANAGER: Her Father daren't move, his arms by his sides
COSMETICS: The Mother listens to Céline singing, hears the music—her husband, her son
MANAGER: Céline's hugging him tight now—presses against him as if she'd like to go back inside him, give him the strength to hug her
DISPLAY: Céline's Brother's looking at the photos, the newspaper cuttings, the posters of Céline on Céline's bedroom wall; her Brother wants to sink through the floor
COSMETICS: Céline's mother puts her hand on the doorknob
MANAGER: Someone could, someone's going to, someone wants to, Céline's Father wants to sink through the floor
ORACLE: Doorbell.
COSMETICS: Céline's Mother freezes, turns round, walks down the corridor, goes towards the front door—stops. She's waiting for someone to open it—someone who lives there—staff. Céline's Mother calls out: "IS SOMEONE GOING TO OPEN THE DOOR?"
ORACLE: Doorbell.
COSMETICS: "NOBODY'S GOING TO ANSWER?" you'd think there was nobody home
ORACLE: Doorbell. It's the Neighbour.
COSMETICS: What neighbour?
ORACLE: The next-door Neighbour.
COSMETICS: Céline's Mother didn't know Céline and René had neighbours. She looks out of the colossal window, the window where you see the colossal avenue of palm trees. She sees a black woman outside the front door
ORACLE: She knocks on the door with her fist.
COSMETICS: Céline's Mother didn't know there were blacks in that neighbourhood. The Mother decides to answer even so. She practises: "What can I do for you? What can I do for you?" She opens the door—realizes she still has the dirty plate in her hand—too late—she's already opening the door. She hides the dirty plate behind her back.
ORACLE: The Neighbour says: "Good morning. I'm the Neighbour."

COSMETICS: Maybe not black after all, maybe it's seeing her against the light—her face in the shadow
ORACLE: The Neighbour says: "Is Isabelle there?"
COSMETICS: Who?
ORACLE: Isabelle.
COSMETICS: The Mother says: "Does she work here?"
ORACLE: The Neighbour says: "I know she's there, I can hear music."
COSMETICS: The Mother says: "Sorry, I can't help you," and the Mother slowly closes the door
ORACLE: The Neighbour looks her in the eye.

ORACLE looks at COSMETICS SALESPERSON.

COSMETICS: The Mother feels the Neighbour's eyes—goes on shutting the door. The Neighbour keeps staring at her, holding the door back with her gaze, stopping her shutting it with her eyes—WHAT EYES. The Neighbour steps forward, her face comes out of the shadow and her eyeballs come out of their sockets, swivelling in all directions—quivering at the end of their optic nerves. "Are you going to close or not, BLOODY DOOR!" Pushes as hard as she can

ORACLE looks at the audience.

The door shuts, clicks, locks—lock the door, put the security chain on, go back to the kitchen. But when the Mother sees her husband at the table from behind, in his vest, hair on his neck, elbow lifted, head tilted back—like this—drinking a beer, a cigarette in his other hand, when she sees the ash on the floor, the plate—the dirty plate she had in her hand, which she's still holding—slips out of her fingers, and breaks on the dirty kitchen's dirty floor.
MANAGER: WHAT ARE YOU LOOKING AT ME FOR? PICK IT UP.
COSMETICS: The Mother doesn't pick it up, she's running to the bedroom, the floor creaks under her feet—hand on the doorknob, ear to the door: no more music. The Mother goes into—her daughter's bedroom. She can't see her, it's dark, but she can hear her breathing. The Mother goes to the window and

opens the curtains. Outside it's snowing—in the desert. The Mother closes the curtains, her eyes get used to the gloom, she can make out her daughter—her body on the bed. She's asleep. The Mother thinks: "I haven't kissed my daughter yet"; she goes nearer; she's bending over her—wanting to kiss her, but her daughter has her eyes wide open—she's dribbling saliva, her mouth is stuck to the pillow. Why isn't she asleep? The Mother's annoyed, her daughter needs her rest. She certainly shouldn't be sleeping on her stomach. She turns her onto her back

ORACLE: And does up her ankles again to the bars of the bed.

COSMETICS: In the kitchen

MANAGER: YOU GOING TO PICK UP THE FUCKING PLATE?

COSMETICS: The Mother doesn't answer. Goes to the sink, gets another plate

MANAGER: NOT THAT ONE, FUCKING STUPID! THE ONE YOU BUST.

COSMETICS: ARE YOU HUNGRY?

MANAGER: The Father doesn't answer.

COSMETICS: YOU EATEN?

MANAGER: WHAT AM I SUPPOSED TO EAT? YOUR FUCKING

COSMETICS: She doesn't give him time to talk about her fucking pizza, the Mother chucks the plate at his head—Frisbee. He ducks, the plate gets stuck in the wall—crack!—just above his head. The plate doesn't break, because it's not a plate, it's a saucepan lid. He gets up

MANAGER: The Father gets up, the chair falls over: WHAT'S YOUR FUCKING PROBLEM?

COSMETICS: No time to escape, she's already got hold of the broom. No time to protect himself—smack!—breaks the broom on his head; I mean the broom doesn't break

MANAGER: The Father falls on the ground, his hand on his forehead: CRAZY CUNT

COSMETICS: STILL HUNGRY? She keeps hitting him, short little blows, but hard. He's crying

MANAGER: Not crying. WHAT'S THE FUCKING MATTER WITH YOU?

COSMETICS: He's bleeding on the ripped vinyl—perfect. The broom—the Mother puts the end of the handle under his nose. He doesn't move

MANAGER: He doesn't move, the kitchen light's swinging—the Mother's shadow on the cupboards—gigantic

COSMETICS: WHO WAS THE LAST ONE IN THE BEDROOM?

MANAGER: HOW AM I SUPPOSED TO

COSMETICS: YOU WAS IN THE KITCHEN, COULDN'T YOU HEAR?

MANAGER: DIDN'T HEAR NOTHING

COSMETICS: YOU HEARD NOTHING, THAT'S BECAUSE IT WAS YOU!

MANAGER: WHAT YOU TRYING TO SAY?

COSMETICS: SHE'S SICK, FOR FUCK'S SAKE! HADN'T YOU NOTICED? SHE MUST NOT GET UP

MANAGER: I DIDN'T MOVE HER

COSMETICS: RIGHT, YOU WANT TO TELL ME WHAT SHE'S DOING ON HER STOMACH?

DISPLAY: The Brother comes into the kitchen—he keeps out of the way

MANAGER: GET YOUR ARSE OVER HERE, YOU CUNT

DISPLAY: He doesn't move

MANAGER: YOU BEEN BACK IN THE BEDROOM?

DISPLAY: WHEN?

MANAGER: DON'T MEAN YESTERDAY, DO I

DISPLAY: The Brother backs off

COSMETICS: The Mother goes after him. IT'S YOU WHAT UNDID HER?

DISPLAY: I DIDN'T TOUCH HER

COSMETICS: YOU'D BETTER FUCKING NOT HAVE OR IT'S YOU GOING TAKE HER TO HOSPITAL

MANAGER: The Mother has her back turned. The Father seizes his chance—gets up, grabs the broom

COSMETICS: DROP THAT

MANAGER: YOU DROP THAT. Snatches the broom from her, pushes her with his foot—falls on her arse—big arse. Wonderful

COSMETICS: The Mother looks at him. GO ON! HIT ME! WHILE YOU GOT THE CHANCE

DISPLAY: The broom's in the air, the Father yells

MANAGER: He hits the fridge—twice, the broom doesn't break. SHIT

COSMETICS: He tries to break the broom on his knee—SISSY!—doesn't even crack

DISPLAY: He rests the broom on the worktop and tries to break it with his foot, but the broom slips

MANAGER: FOR CHRIST'S SAKE! The Father drops the broom—picks up a chair

COSMETICS: He lifts up the chair, catches the light bulb on the ceiling—his shadow on the floor

MANAGER: He throws the chair against the wall

DISPLAY: The chair bounces off, falls upright, doesn't break—Ikea

COSMETICS: She starts laughing

DISPLAY: Unbelievable

MANAGER: The Father grabs the Mother by her hair and drags her to the broken plate

COSMETICS: A little bit of the plate gets stuck in her hand. She yells

MANAGER: The Father rubs her face in the pieces. I SAID PICK IT UP! She's wailing

COSMETICS: Not wailing. She's struggling.

DISPLAY: The Brother jumps on the Father

MANAGER: On his back. The Father swings round and smashes the Brother against the fridge

COSMETICS: THE FRIDGE! All the magnets fall off

MANAGER: The Father takes a swing at him

DISPLAY: Smashes the Brother to the ground

MANAGER: The Father gets him in a hold—the vice. The Brother's head between his knees and he squeezes

DISPLAY: The Father finds this funny

MANAGER: Because he's seeing his head upside down—his mouth upside down. It's like a goblin face. His hair's a beard. His chin's a pointy head

DISPLAY: The Brother's shouting

MANAGER: With creases for a mouth and a mouth in his forehead

COSMETICS: A long dribble of slobber

DISPLAY: Father spits in the Brother's mouth

MANAGER: The Brother's choking—wailing

DISPLAY: Not wailing, catching his breath—he gets free

MANAGER: No, it's the Father lets him go.

COSMETICS: The three of them, sitting in the kitchen—not a word—breathing. Clang! The saucepan lid comes away from the wall—out of the crack, falls on the floor, rolls

DISPLAY: The lid rolls clear of the wall, the chair. It makes smaller and smaller circles, turning on itself faster and faster—trrr!—and it stops.

COSMETICS: She gets up and picks it up

MANAGER: Gets up and goes for a piss

DISPLAY: Gets up, TV—Nintendo—*Super Mario*

COSMETICS: Kitchen—living room. She watches her son playing. He's good. YOU GET SOME?

DISPLAY: Pause—Mario's hovering. Gives her the bag

COSMETICS: THE CARD

DISPLAY: Gives her the credit card. Mario falls over and kicks the tortoise

COSMETICS: Empties the bag on the table, makes four lines with the card, rolls up a ten, sniffs a line

MANAGER: In the living room—mobile, beer, cold pizza. The Father's got the box on his lap, throwing crusts at the Brother

DISPLAY: FOR CHRIST'S SAKE. Level three—ice slides.

MANAGER: GOT SOME MAGAZINES?

DISPLAY: NOTHING ABOUT CÉLINE.

MANAGER: CAMERA?

DISPLAY: I GOT ONE THROWAWAY LEFT. Lost concentration—loses a life

COSMETICS: GIVE ME THAT. Mario's sliding, surfing—it's all turns. The handset's clicking. OKAY! The Mother's never got that far before—pause. Another line, scrape—gulp it down. Unpause, continue

MANAGER: BONUS. She never takes her bonus

DISPLAY: SECRET PASSAGE

COSMETICS: SHUT YOUR FACES! Mario breaks off his glide, skate-skate, steams ahead, back on his tracks—one hundred and eighty—up against the wall of ice

DISPLAY: Sees himself in it and goes right through

MANAGER: Light through the window. Their shadows are stretching, writhing

DISPLAY: Running through the room, over the walls—turning round
MANAGER: The snowplow crosses the desert of—of the empty parking lot.
ORACLE: Close your eyes.

MANAGER, COSMETICS SALESPERSON, and DISPLAY ASSISTANT close their eyes.

Now, imagine what sort of life you'd have had if you'd always been in bed. Imagine the life of Isabelle, Céline's fan, lying in her bedroom, her sick girl's bedroom, curtains always drawn—light years away from her idol's bedroom in Las Vegas. Imagine yellowing paint, carpet coming unstuck, dusty curtains; imagine the chest of drawers, the broken mirror, the plastic flowers to give some colour. Imagine the posters, photos, articles about Céline which decorate the walls, and stuck against one wall, pushed into a corner, Isabelle's bed, which is too small but takes up all the room in the bedroom. Imagine Isabelle, lying on her mattress, dreaming of Céline, because all she can do to fight her illness is dream of Céline. Céline is her only hope, even though Isabelle's not going to get better. Isabelle's in the last stage of her illness. The only thing keeping her alive is Céline—photos, articles, songs by Céline. Céline is her whole life and in her life everything is Céline. Isabelle is a fan of Céline, but without Céline Isabelle wouldn't be a fan, so she'd be nothing. She'd just be a body without a name. If I said: "Céline's dead" Isabelle would begin to decompose, or better still if I said: "Céline's like Father Christmas, she's not really true," then Isabelle would—burst, spatter over the walls—explode, and when you've imagined all that, when you've managed to feel the smell of the room, the broken springs of the mattress—stained mattress, no covers for Isabelle, when the springs are starting to make you feel ill, you put your fingers inside yourself
COSMETICS: Isabelle's Mother opens her eyes: WHAT? The blue of the TV, the line of coke—hears a noise, goes out of the living room, goes into the bedroom. Her daughter—sweating, having a fit. IT'S STARTING AGAIN!
MANAGER: The Father opens his eyes: the blue of the TV
COSMETICS: Shouldn't have just tied up her feet
DISPLAY: The Brother hears the Mother calling

COSMETICS: COME AND HELP. She's been playing in it—her hands all bloody

MANAGER: The Father comes into the bedroom. His daughter's crying but without crying, mouth open—eyes scrunched up

COSMETICS: HOLD HER

DISPLAY: The Brother comes into the bedroom

MANAGER: Her Father gets hold of her wrists—from behind, because she's trying to bite him. He holds her wrists with one hand, gets her chin with the other, she bites his finger SHIT

COSMETICS: DON'T SWEAR! She's struggling

MANAGER: PUT ON A CD

DISPLAY: The Brother runs to the CDs, in the dark—bumps into the chest of drawers

COSMETICS: PHOTOS OF CÉLINE FIRST

DISPLAY: On the chest of drawers—picks up the throwaway camera

COSMETICS: WHERE THEY GONE?

MANAGER: LOOK UNDERNEATH. She's trying to lick him

COSMETICS: Picks up an old magazine from under the bed, opens it to the centre page: "CÉLINE AND RENÉ HAVE A LIE-IN"

DISPLAY: Looks for a good angle—too dark

MANAGER: LOOK. She doesn't want to—shakes her head

COSMETICS: Turns the page

DISPLAY: Click—turns on the flash

COSMETICS: Reads the caption: "CÉLINE'S LOOKING FOR A NAME FOR HER BABY."

MANAGER: Opens her eyes with his fingers

DISPLAY: The flash goes off by itself

COSMETICS: "I WANT MY CHILD TO KNOW HOW MUCH HE WAS LOOKED FORWARD TO, WANTED"

DISPLAY: She focuses

COSMETICS: "HOW MUCH HIS FATHER LOVED HIS MOTHER AND HIS MOTHER LOVED HIS FATHER"

MANAGER: Her arms relax

COSMETICS: "HOW MUCH THE WHOLE FAMILY LOVED EACH OTHER AND WERE LOOKING FORWARD TO HIS ARRIVAL."

MANAGER: LOOK. She stares at the picture and smiles. The Father can let go of her wrists

COSMETICS: The Mother signals to the Brother to come closer. "I AM A FULFILLED WOMAN."

MANAGER: She straightens herself up, getting into the same pose as in the magazine

COSMETICS: "CÉLINE WEARS CHANEL."

DISPLAY: The Brother puts his eye to the viewfinder

ORACLE: He sees his Father from behind—his back completely covered with hair

MANAGER: TAKE A PICTURE. QUICK

DISPLAY: Click! The flash goes off

ORACLE: Her mother has her eyes half-closed, caught with something like the beginning of a smile

MANAGER: TAKE ANOTHER

DISPLAY: Click—

COSMETICS: "CÉLINE HAS FILM PROJECTS."

ORACLE: You'd think she was reading her a bedtime story—to send her to sleep

DISPLAY: Click!

ORACLE: What's odd isn't her smile. It's the fact that her Mother's breasts are bare.

COSMETICS: The Mother moves back

DISPLAY: The flash goes off

ORACLE: From the position of his arm, you can tell the Father's just taking off his belt.

MANAGER: The Father gets up

COSMETICS: PUT ON A CD

ORACLE: You never see the Brother. He's taking the pictures.

DISPLAY: The Brother turns round. I'M GOING TO PUT A CD ON

ORACLE: You can't see her very well. Her face is blurred

COSMETICS: PRESS "PLAY"

ORACLE: The white marks either side of the bed are her feet

MANAGER: "PLAY"—PRESS "PLAY"

ORACLE: You can't see her eyes—her mouth is like a dark stain
COSMETICS: ARE YOU PLAYING IT OR WHAT?
ORACLE: That's how you can tell she has her eyes shut and she's crying, mouth open—eyes screwed up
MANAGER/COSMETICS/DISPLAY: "PLAY"!

The song "Partout Je Te Vois (Everywhere I See You)" bursts out. MANAGER, COSMETICS SALESPERSON, DISPLAY ASSISTANT *are all crying, mouths open, eyes screwed up.*

ORACLE: Go on.
COSMETICS: The skin on her back
DISPLAY: Her cheeks— Her wrists, big as this
MANAGER: Her belly swollen up like a balloon
DISPLAY: Like a pregnant woman, or rather
MANAGER: No. Malnutrition or
COSMETICS: She could hardly walk
DISPLAY: She couldn't walk. They dragged her
COSMETICS: The Receptionist had seen plenty of rubbish people 'specially since she moved to Sherbrooke. But this—that one, with her—dress
DISPLAY: "A skeleton," thought the Security Guard
COSMETICS: At the desk—war. Her Mother said she had indigestion "again." Her Father said she was faking—he was smiling
MANAGER: How could her Father smile?
COSMETICS: It was clear she hadn't eaten for a long time or been washed. They brought her to hospital because they "couldn't stand her anymore."
DISPLAY: You'd think her parents resented her being ill.
COSMETICS: The Receptionist told them to go and sit down. She heard the Mother say: "Happy now? Star of the show?"
DISPLAY: Unbelievable
MANAGER: Not a word from her. She was looking straight ahead—into space
DISPLAY: Her Brother was taking photos in the waiting room—with a throw-away camera

COSMETICS: The Receptionist couldn't hear herself think
DISPLAY: You couldn't hear anything except the irritating little sound of the throwaway camera which the Brother kept clicking and clicking. A family of lunatics
MANAGER: When the Doctor called her name, they didn't get up—no one reacted at all, not even Isabelle
COSMETICS: The Nurse had to
MANAGER: Not the Nurse, the Receptionist
COSMETICS: The Nurse who was ALSO doing reception—
ORACLE: The Nurse-Receptionist
COSMETICS: The Nurse-Receptionist had to go and find them—took Isabelle's arm, but they didn't want to let go of her
DISPLAY: They didn't want to let her go
MANAGER: They didn't want her to be examined all by herself. The Doctor shut his eyes as if to stop himself from
DISPLAY: The Security Guard had to threaten them—the only language people like that understand.
MANAGER: Isabelle's body on the examination table—a stain on the white paper. The Doctor didn't even examine her
COSMETICS: I mean you only had to look at her: suffering, violence, poverty
MANAGER: The Doctor went straightaway to tell the parents he was keeping her in—they could go home
COSMETICS: The Mother was angry as if she thought someone was playing a trick on her
MANAGER: The Father: "What's she doing that to us for?"
DISPLAY: The Brother was crying—the Security Guard had confiscated his camera. He'd "see it tomorrow" if he was good
COSMETICS: The Nurse-Receptionist checked with the Father that she had the right telephone number—his mobile, so she could reach them in an emergency, knowing perfectly well she wouldn't call them even in an emergency. "The last people to call in an emergency," thought the Nurse-Receptionist
DISPLAY: The Security Guard ordered them to go home.

MANAGER: During the examination, the Doctor asked Isabelle where she'd got the bruises, if something had happened—an accident. She didn't say anything—she didn't answer, as if she didn't understand. The infection was advanced. Isabelle's belly was hard and purple. You could see huge veins running under her skin. Dropsy? Neurofibrositis?
COSMETICS: Probably the result of a home abortion—which she'd done to herself or—more likely
MANAGER: But the Doctor didn't mention abortion to Isabelle. He'd wait for the results—till she saw the Psychiatrist.
COSMETICS: In the bath, Isabelle hid her sex with her hands—protecting herself. Rubbing her back, the Nurse thought: "Indigestion doesn't make your ankles bleed." Isabelle didn't want to eat or drink anything, or open her mouth. The Nurse gave her medicine intravenously
DISPLAY: When the Security Guard came into the room, Isabelle was asleep. He put the throwaway camera on the bedside table, next to the mirror and the flowers—where you couldn't miss it.
COSMETICS: Isabelle slept for twelve hours. The Nurse had made sure to shut the curtains. Next day, the Nurse came in pushing her trolley slowly without making a sound. When she opened the curtains, Isabelle was already up—I mean her eyes were wide open. The Nurse asked her if she'd / slept well
ORACLE: The Nurse-Receptionist stops speaking when she sees Isabelle.
COSMETICS: Why?
ORACLE: Her belly
COSMETICS: What about her belly?
ORACLE: Isabelle's belly's got bigger.
DISPLAY: The Psychiatrist comes into the room. When he sees Isabelle's belly, he can't understand why the Nurse-Receptionist isn't already running out—to call the Doctor
COSMETICS: She DOESN'T WANT to frighten her. She's not crying—doesn't seem to be in pain. The Nurse-Receptionist gives the Psychiatrist a meaningful look and goes out calmly
DISPLAY: The Psychiatrist puts the table over the bed, even though it's not his job. He says: "Good morning," as if nothing was wrong. Isabelle doesn't reply—

nothing at all. He puts the tray on the table and puts a pillow behind her back. Isabelle lets him do it and does nothing herself—she smiles. Nervous shock? Schizophrenia? The Psychiatrist picks up the teaspoon and the fruit salad

ORACLE: Isabelle takes the Psychiatrist's pen out of his shirt pocket.

DISPLAY: The Psychiatrist is pleased. Isabelle's trying in her own way to make contact—she wants to play

ORACLE: She wants to write.

DISPLAY: The Psychiatrist takes a piece of paper—his pad—and gives it to her

ORACLE: Isabelle's writing.

DISPLAY: What?

ORACLE: A letter.

DISPLAY: What does she say in her letter?

ORACLE: The Psychiatrist doesn't have time to read it; the Nurse comes from behind and takes the letter

COSMETICS: The Nurse takes the letter and reads it

ORACLE: Not the Nurse

COSMETICS: The Nurse-RECEPTIONIST

ORACLE: Not her, a different one. The Night Nurse

DISPLAY: / What's that?

MANAGER: Since when?

ORACLE looks at DISPLAY ASSISTANT.

ORACLE: The Psychiatrist sees the Night Nurse's hand taking the letter; he sees her night arm

DISPLAY: The Psychiatrist shuts his eyes

ORACLE: His eyes can't shut, his eyes can still just see, they go up the Nurse's arm

DISPLAY: Turns his head

ORACLE: Can't—sees her uniform

DISPLAY: Doesn't look

ORACLE: LOOKS at the name tag on the uniform, the name, the BACKWARDS LETTERS

DISPLAY: DOESN'T LOOK

ORACLE: TOO LATE. The Psychiatrist has to read my name: ORACLE. He has to see my eyes, which are looking at him, looking right into his eyes. I'm moving away, making off with the letter, sliding like a shadow—towards the mirror. I take the hospital flowers—the plastic flowers—take the throwaway camera. I stop in front of the mirror. I'm looking at you. You're looking at me. We smile at each other—disappear.

ORACLE faces the audience.

MANAGER: The Doctor comes into the room
COSMETICS: The Nurse-Receptionist comes into the room
MANAGER: The Doctor freezes
DISPLAY: The Psychiatrist can't move—his eyes are riveted to the mirror
COSMETICS: The Nurse puts a hand to her mouth
DISPLAY: The Psychiatrist sees their reflections, frozen. He turns—at last he can turn—slowly turns his head towards Isabelle
MANAGER: The Doctor goes up to the bed
COSMETICS: The Nurse behind him
MANAGER: Isabelle's belly is enormous
COSMETICS: You'd think—it was swelling up
MANAGER: The Doctor's seen the X-rays. The dropsy was concealing a cancer—an enormous tumour. The Doctor has in his head a negative of a tumour getting bigger—while you look at it
COSMETICS: Isabelle isn't crying—I mean she doesn't seem to be in pain
MANAGER: Isabelle's smiling. She gives a pen to the Psychiatrist
DISPLAY: The Psychiatrist takes his pen back
MANAGER: The Doctor puts his hand on Isabelle's belly—delicately. He says: "How are you feeling today?"
ORACLE: And then you say: "I feel good. Always do."
DISPLAY: But Isabelle's lips don't move—they stay closed.
COSMETICS: Who says: "I feel good. Always do"?
MANAGER: The Doctor doesn't use his stethoscope; he puts his ear directly on Isabelle's belly

ORACLE: The Doctor hears: "Me."
MANAGER: The voice—the voice is coming from inside her belly
ORACLE: And then you say: "I'm called Caro. I'm the biggest fan."
MANAGER: The Doctor slowly lifts Isabelle's pyjama jacket
COSMETICS: The belly—inside—completely black
DISPLAY: The Psychiatrist can't look
MANAGER: Swollen—black liquid
DISPLAY: But his eyes keep trying to find, trying despite himself, are FORCED TO TRY AND FIND. Between her thighs, there's something missing—sex, anus
ORACLE: Isabelle's got no hole, no crack. No way out except her mouth because everything's coming out of her mouth, which is opening after all. Isabelle can, after all. She can after all speak; she wants to speak—too late. Her air's cut off, her vocal cords are blocked, her mouth's filling up, overflowing, opening with a river of black bile which bursts out horizontally and falls, splattering the white sheets. Isabelle's vomiting, completely, endlessly emptying her belly. The bile overflows and runs onto the white floor and spreads through the hospital room. The Doctor, the Nurse, and the Psychiatrist skate towards the door, fall over, get up, fall over again, howling and burning. They melt, turn black, and disappear under the overwhelming wave of sick. Isabelle vomits till she's empty, on and on, her mouth open, her eyes popping out, her navel touching her spine. Inside her, something's turning inside out—like a glove. Something's coming up and out and on and on: a long scarf of joined-up handkerchiefs—like a conjuring trick. Liver, kidneys, stomach, intestines—dedaah!—with her lungs, which are collapsing, and her heart, which is fluttering, on the end. Hanging out of her mouth: her esophagus, which has come out backwards. She takes her esophagus in her fingers and instinctively wants to pull, but she tells herself: "Swallow, swallow." She wants to swallow her heart; she gets hold of her heart and opens her mouth, but her shoulder comes adrift and all the rest follows. Her left arm's turning back on itself as she vomits it out. The bones are breaking away from the muscles and they fall—a little white heap at her feet—till her arm's hanging from her mouth, empty, inside out. She goes up to the mirror and looks at the inside of her arm, the veins and nerves, like the finger of a big red plastic glove turned inside out. Flush! Someone's flushed

the toilet but she doesn't wonder who's there, she's just trying to swallow her left arm before anyone comes. "Swallow, swallow," but she vomits her right arm, which empties itself and turns inside out, followed by her left leg—she falls on the floor—and her right leg—slides on her back. On her back with four tubes of meat coming out of her mouth, she thinks: "God, I must look so silly," and vomits her rib cage and spine, which knock out her teeth and jaw on the way through. With a pop! her skull bursts—grey matter's running down like wet cement. Her head turns inside out—a floppy wig, and comes out backwards through her mouth, and once she's spat out the pieces of skull she can vomit her pelvis and the rest of the spine down to the coccyx, which comes out of her mouth, and her mouth turns inside out and vomits itself. You're not wondering how anyone can live without a skeleton, you're just wondering if anyone's seen you, and you find a way of holding yourself up on your floppy inside-out legs and of finding your optic nerves in the folds of your inside-out face with your floppy inside-out hands and pulling on them so you can get your eyes out. Even if your eyeballs are swivelling in all directions, you can see the white of the sink, the tap, the running water. Take your fingers out of your mouth, lift your head, look in the mirror. You can see your name tag in the mirror, read the letters of your name, preceded by your employee number: 31CARO. Backwards that says: ORACLE. I'm looking at you. You're looking at me. We smile at each other. Quick, Caro. Hide the plastic flowers in your backpack.

COSMETICS: I come out of the toilet.

ORACLE: In the mirror you see the Cosmetics Salesperson come out of the toilet.

COSMETICS: I look at Caro: poor little cow.

ORACLE: Dry your mouth, turn off the tap.

COSMETICS: I go up to her—to the next sink. I say: "Not feeling better?"

ORACLE: Through the Tannoy on the ceiling: Céline, hard to make out.

COSMETICS: I turn on the tap for no reason—wash my hands. I see her bag down by her feet. I say: "What are you doing after work?" Imagine an evening with Caro: death.

ORACLE: You're about to say: "I'm going to listen to Céline's latest DVD," but you don't have time, the music breaks off right in the middle of the chorus.

"Thirty-one to checkout number eight." You dry your hands on your overalls though there is a hand dryer, but the Cosmetics Salesperson's using the hand dryer

COSMETICS: The hot air isn't very hot; I'm rubbing my hands hard—I watch her go out. I say: "Come and eat with us at lunch"—out of guilt.

ORACLE: Open the door—the chorus is drowned out by the noise of the store. Go and put your bag in the staff room, go down the corridor, come out onto the floor: section seven, "Men's Underwear." Céline is playing a bit louder. The Display Assistant's talking to the new girl, pretending not to see you. He's thinking of something to say to make her laugh. The new girl laughs anyway, maybe because she saw a bit of intestine sticking out under your overall

DISPLAY: Caro goes by, doing up her overall. I pretend not to see her—pick a piece of paper up off the floor even though it's not my job. Unbelievable. She spends her whole time in the toilet—her whole break.

ORACLE: "The hardest thing about work is other people—hearing what they think." You wonder if there's a kind of work where people are all alone—really all alone. Lighthouse keeper. Section twelve, "Boots and Shoes," the words of the song "Everywhere I See You" are loud and clear. A salesman whistles the tune while he gets a pair of shoes ready—takes off the paper. Watch out, at the end of thirteen: the Manager's looking at you with his arms folded

MANAGER: There are two kinds of employees: the ones who work and the ones who pretend to work—simple as that.

ORACLE: You bend your head—hurry, but it's hard to hurry when your legs are floppy and inside out.

MANAGER: I stare at her without saying anything. Always works.

ORACLE: The cashier at checkout number seven still has the phone in her hand—wiping it, and hangs up. The click cuts into the song while Céline's holding the note at the end. Go to your checkout, take off the "CHECKOUT CLOSED" sign, and wait. The cashier at checkout number seven sighs and says: "Move along to the next checkout, please," almost crying. The customers did understand, they were just trying to work out if it's worth changing queues and risking losing their place.

MANAGER: Basically there are two kinds of employees: the ones who steal and the ones who don't steal.
ORACLE: The second-to-last person in the queue finally makes a move—too late, the last one's quicker. He throws himself at your checkout—gets in front. You say: "Do you have your Walmart card?" telling him off.
MANAGER: I watch thirty-one talking to her customer: doesn't smile enough.
ORACLE: Credit card—doesn't work: wrong PIN number. The customer's head's somewhere else—not concentrating.
MANAGER: I go behind checkout eight. Her shoes comply with regulations.
ORACLE: The customer who was pushed out of the way puts down his blender. He takes a Céline DVD off the rack—a look and a smile.
MANAGER: The customer pays cash.
ORACLE: You say: "Thank you, have a nice day."
MANAGER: "Have a nice day and thank you for shopping at Walmart," but I don't take thirty-one up on it. I say: "Caro, come and see me in my office. When you have a moment." Meaning: "At the beginning of your lunch hour."
DISPLAY: I'm going towards the checkouts and I see the Manager standing behind Caro: endless training.
MANAGER: I see the Display Assistant looking for something to do. I go back to the centre aisle and walk to twenty-one, "Toy Section."
DISPLAY: I catch up with the Manager and walk behind him—almost running. I'm waiting for orders.
ORACLE: Section twenty-one swallows them up. The centre aisle is empty. You've no customers at your checkout. You look at number seven. She's got her back to you; she's talking to number six, five's talking to four, three to two; who's one talking to? No time to talk to anyone, she's always busy; it's the checkout for "Two articles or less." A night job. Security Guard—at the shopping centre. You'd be really alone there. You'd walk down the corridors. There'd be no one to see you. The shop-window dummies wouldn't frighten you. You'd say on your radio: "Checking at Walmart." You'd take out your keys, you'd open the revolving doors, and once you were inside you'd take off your cap and your uniform. You wouldn't need to hide in the toilet anymore.

You'd walk through all the sections completely naked. You'd get yourself some flowers from seventeen, "Interior Decoration." You'd go up the escalator to the second floor. You'd choose a bed in a demonstration room with a mirror and a chest of drawers. You'd put on a DVD—never the same one. One night it'd be the concert at the Stade de France, another time it'd be— A customer appears in front of you and makes you jump. She says: "Hello, lovely," but without looking at you. She rummages in her handbag with her head down. You can't see her eyes because she's wearing dark glasses. You look for her purchases—can't see any, what did she buy? But then you spot the bottle of perfume—something expensive—the perfume called Céline Perfume. You pick up the bottle of perfume, beep! it goes through; you're about to tell her the price but the right money's already on the counter and the whole meaning of the song "Incognito" is suddenly revealed to you. You don't have to look, you know it's her. She puts one hand on your inside-out hand and there's just her and you in an empty, silent Walmart. She says: "I've been looking for you for a long time," and you're crying and you can't stop. You push the money gently back towards her and she understands that this is the moment when you can give her back all the love she's given you. Between sobs you say: "I'm your biggest fan." She looks at you then with your eyes starting out of your head and your eyeballs swivelling round and she smiles. She loves you, ugly as you are. She picks up a *Live in Las Vegas* DVD from the checkout rack and takes out a pen and signs it. She gives you the DVD and puts the money in her purse, the bottle of perfume in her handbag, saying: "Thank you," but without saying thank you, just mouthing the words "Thank you," and she goes and meets her Bodyguard at the Walmart entrance—and disappears. On the DVD she's written "Céline" diagonally and just above it "See you soon." Number seven asks what's so funny, taking an interest for once, but you go: "You wouldn't understand," and wipe away a tear. It's time. Hide the DVD, close your checkout, put up the sign "CHECKOUT CLOSED," and walk down the centre aisle without hurrying. Our secret.

MANAGER: She comes into my office without knocking—and smiling.

ORACLE: You know what the Manager's going to say: your shoes don't comply with regulations. But he doesn't know what it's like living without a skeleton.

MANAGER: She sits down without being told.

ORACLE: But when he learns that Céline in person came to your checkout

MANAGER: I'm waiting for her to realize.

ORACLE: He'll understand—he'll understand why you didn't make her pay for the bottle of perfume. He'll congratulate you even.

MANAGER: She's just realized.

ORACLE: What's your bag doing on the Manager's desk?

MANAGER: I say: "Open it."

ORACLE: Don't open it.

MANAGER: And I say: "There are things I can understand and things I can't understand. If an employee doesn't feel good and it affects their work to a certain extent, I can understand that. But if an employee who doesn't feel good and whose work is GREATLY affected by their state of mind then goes on to steal, that I can't understand."

ORACLE: In your bag: your lunch and the plastic flowers with their label.

MANAGER: "I don't understand and I don't want to understand." No pity. I stare at the plastic flowers.

ORACLE: How could he understand?

MANAGER: How can she smile?

ORACLE: Céline understands you. She looked for you. She found you. She wrote: "See you soon." She's waiting for you. You have the DVD to prove it—NO—don't show it to him. Say nothing about it—our secret. Pick up your bag

MANAGER: I pick up something on my desk—an order form. "You're not coming back tomorrow."

ORACLE: Get up, put on your backpack, go out of the Manager's office—out of the office, back through section seven, "Men's Underwear," into the corridor, past the toilets. Into the staff room. The Display Assistant is sitting at the table reading the paper. The Cosmetics Salesperson is waiting by the microwave. Put your bag on the rack

COSMETICS: I saw her do it—put the flowers in her backpack.

ORACLE: Take out your lunch

DISPLAY: I look up: Caro.

ORACLE: Act just like it's lunch break

COSMETICS: Personally I don't give a fuck.
ORACLE: Act like nothing's wrong
COSMETICS: Plastic flowers, not a big deal.
DISPLAY: Not eating her lunch in the toilets? Something must have happened.
COSMETICS: I could have kept my big mouth shut.
ORACLE: Like an ordinary day.
COSMETICS: But the truth is I can't stand her—the sight of her.
ORACLE: Even if Céline did appear at your checkout the day her latest DVD's come out, don't say anything—our secret, just the two of us. It would make them miserable—they'd be jealous
DISPLAY: "Caro" isn't short for Caroline. Her parents really called her that, just "Caro."
COSMETICS: There's something—dead about her eyes.
ORACLE: Hide the album signed "See you soon—Céline" at the bottom of your bag
DISPLAY: One look at her and I feel sick. With her half-name.
ORACLE: Take your lunch, turn round, look the Cosmetics Salesperson right in the eye
COSMETICS: I say: "Welcome to our humble abode!" That wasn't necessary.
ORACLE: Go and sit opposite the Display Assistant
DISPLAY: I'm still reading the paper, even though I want to shout: "WHAT HAVE YOU GOT TO SMILE ABOUT, YOU POOR SPASTIC?"
ORACLE: And look. Look at the front page of the paper. At the top you can see a picture of an American actress with her mouth open. In the middle, a picture of an Iraqi father holding his dead son in his arms—and his mouth is open too, but his eyes are scrunched up. You'd think they were two contestants on *Star Academy*
COSMETICS: I wait two seconds after the beep and take my lasagna out of the microwave and go and sit next to her—out of guilt.
DISPLAY: I hate it when someone reads the paper at the same time as me. I turn the page with a flick.
COSMETICS: I say to Caro: "What did you make yourself for lunch?"

ORACLE: On the second page, you can see a big publicity shot of Céline. "WIN A TRIP TO LAS VEGAS TO SEE CÉLINE." You see Céline putting makeup on in front of a mirror in her dressing room

COSMETICS: She doesn't answer—want to hit her.

DISPLAY: I put the paper on the table so she can read it too. I say: "FUCK."

COSMETICS: I say: "What?"

DISPLAY: "FUCK," referring to the article, but it was for Caro—stupid fuck.

ORACLE: The Display Assistant has put the paper on the table. It's hard to read the headline on page three because the words are upside down.

MANAGER: Why didn't I tell her to leave right away? She'll use her last afternoon to steal something else or break something—have her revenge.

ORACLE: ACCUSED is easy enough to make out because of the two Cs

COSMETICS: I say: "Is it the girl from Sherbrooke who died of cancer of the ovaries?" as if there'd been one who died of lung cancer, one of prostate cancer, one had her leg cut off, and so on.

MANAGER: Not in the toilets—a bad sign.

ORACLE: "ACCUSED OF AGGRESSION"—"AGGRESSION" backwards is "NOISSERGGA." That doesn't mean anything.

DISPLAY: I say: "It wasn't just the father, it was the whole family."

COSMETICS: I say: "Let's have a look."

MANAGER: Not in the children's play area either.

ORACLE: "ORACLE" means something.

DISPLAY: I look at the photo of the victim when she was little. Her smile—unbearable.

COSMETICS: "Let's have a look."

DISPLAY: I give the paper to the Cosmetics Salesperson.

ORACLE: You can see it upside down, read the headline, see the picture, the picture of the Father, who's walking along with his head down. The Cosmetics Salesperson unfolds the paper but it's a trap. On the left-hand page the publicity photo: Céline putting on makeup in her dressing room. On the right-hand page, the picture of the Father outside the court. He's going past a little frozen crowd shouting: "MONSTER! MURDERER!" He's about to go into the courtroom

MANAGER: I go into the staff room
ORACLE: The courtroom.
MANAGER: What courtroom?
ORACLE: The Father's going into the courtroom—the trial
MANAGER: The Father doesn't go in, / he steps back

ORACLE looks at MANAGER.

ORACLE: The Father has to go in, he's under escort
MANAGER: WHAT'VE I DONE? NOT DONE / NOTHING
ORACLE: THE MOTHER TALKED
COSMETICS: THE MOTHER DIDN'T SAY NOTHING!

ORACLE takes the throwaway camera out of her overalls.

ORACLE: The jury were horrified by the photos.

ORACLE looks at the audience.

COSMETICS: The Mother told the judge—she didn't want a second child
MANAGER: According to the accused, she told the landlord: "THE CHILD BENEFIT'LL PAY FOR THE COKE"
COSMETICS: They called her Isabelle, but he called her "SPUNKBAG," accused the Mother
MANAGER: "SHE DIDN'T PUT ANY NAPPIES ON HER. SHE LET HER PISS AND SHIT ON THE FLOOR," said the victim's Brother
DISPLAY: The Father said to his SON: "LOOK, SHE'S A GASH," while masturbating her with a Pepsi bottle
COSMETICS: "HE DIDN'T WANT HER TO GO TO SCHOOL," said the Mother
MANAGER: "SHE'S THE ONE THOUGHT OF SHACKLES"
DISPLAY: Usually it was the Father, sometimes the Mother. The Brother took photos. He's the one who put on music—CDs of Céline—to drown her cries

COSMETICS: One day, a neighbour saw Isabelle cross in front of her bedroom window

MANAGER: One of the members of the family had forgotten to tie her up

ORACLE: "But how could Isabelle have survived all those years of torture?" asks the newspaper at the end of the article. Easy.

MANAGER: Lunch break's over.

COSMETICS: I close the paper, pick up the plate, open the dishwasher, put the plate in the dishwasher.

DISPLAY: I rub my hands together, get up.

MANAGER: I must tell Caro to leave.

ORACLE: The hardest thing is hearing people think. The hardest thing is seeing what they see. When Isabelle's finished vomiting, she gets up and walks to the mirror. That's difficult. Isabelle has never walked in her life. She drags herself, slips in the bile, leans on the wall. She hangs on to the chest of drawers, gets in front of the mirror—the mirror in the hospital bedroom, and in the mirror Isabelle looks at herself. From then on, everything's easy. Because in the mirror, Isabelle doesn't see herself. Isabelle sees Céline. In the mirror Isabelle just sees Céline—her dressing room—Céline putting on makeup in her dressing room. She can even see the reflection of the camera behind her. The lunch break's over—start again.

MANAGER, COSMETICS SALESPERSON, and DISPLAY ASSISTANT smile.

DISPLAY: The Cameraman steps back, they're bringing the box

COSMETICS: Céline says "bye bye" in the mirror—to the camera—and curls up in a little ball in the box

DISPLAY: They close the box and roll it under the stage. The camera can't go under the stage to see what's going on under the stage—with René

MANAGER: Under the stage—"bring out the tiger in her"

DISPLAY: That's right

MANAGER: René's walking round Céline miming a whip. Céline roars

ORACLE: No

DISPLAY: After that, Céline gets back in the box. The show begins, the box comes up and Céline

ORACLE: NO. That was for the tour. Céline doesn't appear out of the floor here. Céline comes on from the wings, straight onto the stage of / Caesars Palace

COSMETICS: Caesars Palace—YES—microphone in her hand and she's going to simply, straightforwardly talk to her public. She says: "You can't / imagine

DISPLAY: imagine how happy we are to see you here"

COSMETICS: As if we were in her kitchen, in her home, with her. "It's extraordinary, thank you."

DISPLAY: There—applause. Céline looks down

COSMETICS: "Here we are in this wonderfully beautiful, huge, magnificent theatre"

MANAGER: No—not "huge, magnificent": "INCOMPARABLE"

COSMETICS: "Incomparable"—"We've rehearsed the songs and we're feeling inspired. I'm surrounded by / wonderful people"

MANAGER: "WONDERFUL." Yes

DISPLAY: "We've been so longing to do it live," and at that everyone felt they were with her

COSMETICS: Then, to everyone, holding out her hand: "I want to thank you for making our dream come true. Despite everything that's happening"

DISPLAY: Dot dot dot, tears in her eyes, emotional pause

COSMETICS: "Let's try to hope / for"

MANAGER: There's a sigh after: "LET'S TRY"

DISPLAY: "LET'S TRY" is said with a sigh

COSMETICS: "Let's try—to hope for peace."

MANAGER: And then, for the musicians and dancers: "Let's go, let's have fun!"

DISPLAY: The first bars start to play

ORACLE: And that's when I go into the hospital bedroom and put the flowers on the chest of drawers in front of the mirror. From the other side, you're looking at me. I'm looking at you. We smile at each other. I walk towards the bed to give Isabelle the reply Céline wrote her. Isabelle's staring at the ceiling with her mouth open. I put the letter in Isabelle's limp hand. You go up on the stage and walk towards Céline to give her Isabelle's last letter.

MANAGER, COSMETICS SALESPERSON, and DISPLAY ASSISTANT stop smiling.

Céline opens the letter and reads it. Céline's crying. She looks at you and says: "Thank you," but without saying thank you, just mouthing the words "Thank you." She takes your hand and turns back to the audience. And there you are, really alone—with Céline. And you feel really good.

MANAGER, COSMETICS SALESPERSON, and DISPLAY ASSISTANT scrunch their eyes shut. ORACLE smiles.

Always do.

Long pause. Blackout.

NANAY (MOTHER): A TESTIMONIAL PLAY

Geraldine Pratt
and Caleb Johnston
in collaboration with
the Philippine Women
Centre of BC

STATES OF PRESENCE AND ABSENCE: AN INTRODUCTION TO *NANAY (MOTHER): A TESTIMONIAL PLAY*

Patrick Alcedo

How moving it would have been had I experienced live *Nanay (Mother): A Testimonial Play*, written by Geraldine Pratt and Caleb Johnson and directed by Alex Ferguson, when it first premiered at the 2009 PuSh International Performing Arts Festival in Vancouver. How I wish I did not just read the script and the reviews and consumed Internet websites dedicated to *Nanay*. I would have even followed it across the Atlantic to Berlin where it was restaged for a theatre festival, and later to Edinburgh where a reading of it became part of a conference focusing on family. After all, liveness is at the heart of every theatre. And, as *Nanay* piercingly reminds us, being there with one's warm body is the best way to be present.

Based on interviews conducted over the course of fifteen years among Filipino workers, their families, and Canadian employers, *Nanay* illustrates the power of qualitative research in theatre production. Created in collaboration with the Philippine Women Centre of BC, the play painfully braids the sad plight of Filipino nannies together with the frustration of Canadians in finding care for their own children and elderly parents. Additionally the play comments on the problems behind Canada's Live-In Caregiver Program, the notorious LCP, which is the current iteration of the original Foreign Domestic Movement Program. Since 1981, this twinned program has provided entrance to Canada and the promise of permanent Canadian residency for immigrant caregivers, many of who are overwhelmingly Filipino females, or Filipinas. The program has either directly hired them from the Philippines, or indirectly from somewhere else where they have served as domestic helpers, like Hong Kong and the Middle East. For most Filipinas, these receiving destinations are considered "back doors" for Canada, which despite stricter hiring policies is nonetheless a dream country in which to permanently settle down.

Nanay is about an anxiety around "presence" and "absence" that is triggered by diasporic human movement and the need for love and affection within and outside one's home. I imagine that almost all Canadian employers and Filipino caregivers, some of whom I grew up with in the Philippines or later met in Toronto where I now live, share such anxiety. Although the play brings out anxieties that are unique to the lives of its characters, its narrative is powerfully synecdochic of the experience of international care work by Filipinos and of their Canadian employers. In the case of the latter, the anxiety is over the Filipino nanny, a new "presence" who will suddenly live in their homes to attend to the needs of their loved ones. Will she care for them the way a loving family member really should? Will she protect their child's little body in layers of clothes when the cold Canadian weather takes over or bother to wake up in the middle of the night when their frail, aging parent has to go to the bathroom? Their anxiety is also about the new "absence" that they themselves have created primarily due to economic reasons. Instead of them doing the caring, suddenly it is the foreign nanny who will be left alone with their babies and debilitated parents while they are out earning money to pay household bills and inescapable mortgages.

In the case of the former, the anxiety is induced by the Canadian family they will live with and work for, a new "presence," a family that is obviously not their own, and, in most likelihood, has a starkly different cultural background and set of values from theirs. However, the greater anxiety lies in leaving their own family and children behind, a new "absence" they have to endure to send money back home for their children's education and families' other basic needs. For at least two years, they will have to maintain their LCP status to gain the required length of legal employment, which in turn will allow for petitioning their immediate family back in the Philippines to be finally reunited with them in Canada. Will their children excitedly dig into their packed lunches the way they used to now that it is their husbands who prepare them? Although they used to grumble about it at times, will they actually miss doing those meals early in the morning before everybody wakes up at dawn? Will their husbands not spend their hard-earned money on vices, and, God forbid, not sexually liaise with others when it is way past dusk and their children are fast asleep? And will they themselves not find a special someone when the waiting and its accompanying loneliness become unbearable? Above all, will their love be strong enough for their own families to remain affectionate with each other in spite of the vast distances and stretches of time that separate them?

In *Nanay*, confusing states of "absences" and "presences" uncomfortably criss-cross between Canadian employers and Filipino nannies—states of being that are in perpetual transport, or, better yet, caught in a knotted traffic.

Rather than your typical proscenium or rake theatre, the play was held at what appears to be somebody else's former two-storey house in the original Vancouver production. As expected in any middle-class Canadian home, it had a spacious living room, furnished kitchen, a couple of bedrooms, and a working bathroom. Uncannily linked to websites feeding authentic advertisements for those looking for and wanting to be nannies, two live computer screens broadcast that it was a home-cum-performance space. As a first-generation Filipino immigrant, I would have understood right away the material objects randomly placed in the nannies' room: letters; photos; phone cards; rosaries symbolizing Roman Catholic faith and devotion to the Blessed Virgin Mary; and Skyflakes biscuit crackers, popular snacks and at times emergency meals in the Philippines which are now easily bought at Filipino or "Asian/ Oriental" stores in Canada. These objects tell the story of the way Filipinos live the quotidian in the diaspora.

Upon entering the "theatre," two guides greeted the visitor at the door. One led the audience to the ground floor where the nannies' stories unfolded and the other to the second floor, reserved for employers. I understand their guidance as a reification of a classic structure that divides the dirt below (nannies clean on a daily basis) and the cleanliness above (the employers feel entitled to have), or the subordination under and the power on top. The new experience of walking around instead of sitting down would have put me on edge, going through with other audience members each corner of every room and encountering in the process stories and dialogues coming from characters who performatively inhabit them.

The play's design structure demonstrates astuteness and sophistication in bringing to life labour shortage and immigration challenges specific to Canada, issues that grab my attention as an academic and artist, but also as a foreign worker akin to the nannies in *Nanay*. However, what ultimately drives the play is its characters, intelligently delineated by their professions and stations in life and whose voices are sensitively layered in a composite fashion.

According to the script, before the audience was ushered to the two different floors, they were first introduced to the character Carl, a "nanny agent," an ex-engineer whose dialogue included racist descriptions of Filipinas as "simple people," "servants" who will treat an employer like a "god" and "will lick your home clean." For me, he foreshadows the gloominess that blankets *Nanay*. On the ground, the nannies Ligaya—a name that ironically means "happiness" in the Filipino language Tagalog—and Joanne, a former nurse in the Philippines, were to be found. There was nothing happy about Ligaya's life. Her husband, who worked in the Middle East, suddenly stopped sending money. Thus, she was forced to work abroad to fend for the children she had to leave in the care of her parents. Joanne did not have a rosy life either. Although her family was not as dysfunctional as that of Ligaya's, her situation in Canada was filled with employment woes, one after another, which kept preventing her from legally obtaining her residency status.

On the floor above them were the characters Karen and Denise and the married couple Richard and Stephanie, who were looking for someone to take care of their children. There was also Nadine, in search of a caregiver. Nadine's mother had a stroke and was suffering from Parkinson's disease, leaving their family desperate to find a live-in caregiver. I read their desire to find the best care for their loved ones as admirable, and for most of them their concern about the well-being of the Filipinas they hired was as well. Nadine employed Letty, thirty-two, whose husband was still in the Philippines. Nadine was worried about Letty's loneliness and provided her with Internet service so she could use it to communicate with her husband. The couple Richard and Stephanie seemed genuine about treating their Filipina nanny Marlena as a friend: they asked her to stop calling them "Sir" and "Madam." When a boyfriend from the US and Marlena were expecting a baby, they were concerned about the tenuousness of that relationship and her future in Canada. But my delight in their concern for their caregiver is short-lived, for it angers me to find out how patronizing they actually were to Marlena and how exploitative they were to the "European" nanny they hired afterward.

In a "chapel" the audience met Ari, speaking tongue-in-cheek on behalf of the Canadian government. He justified the generosity and wisdom of the LCP program: that it is a boon to Canadian families and Filipinos wanting Canadian citizenship, that the Philippine government benefits from the staggering $15 billion in remittances Filipinos scattered as workers all over the world wired each year back to the Philippines.

The final character was Michelle, reunited four years ago with her mother, a Filipina nanny, after eight years of waiting in the Philippines. That length of time estranged daughter from mother—the occasional long-distance calls were not enough to bind them. Sadly, rather than the companionship of her mother and her own permanent residency, it was her meagre work at McDonald's that gave her a sense of heaven in Canada.

In addition to exposing Canada's labour and immigration dilemmas, *Nanay* is a dark reminder of the Philippines' failure to provide for their own citizens due to graft and corruption, as notoriously popularized by the late dictator Ferdinand Marcos and his shoe-hungry wife, Imelda, and as practised by generations of Filipino public officials. Ligaya, in the middle of her monologue delivered while mopping the kitchen floor at the Vancouver "theatre," recounted that a major push behind her leaving the Philippines was the nation's hopeless economic state and the dismal peace-and-order situation under the Marcos regime. Despicable practices continue even under the leadership of the current president, Benigno "Pnoy" Aquino III, the son of Benigno "Ninoy" Aquino Jr.—Marcos's assassinated archrival in politics—and the late President Corazon Aquino, who was the heroine of the 1986 People Power

Revolution that ousted the Marcoses. Take for instance the alleged ten billion–peso (roughly $240 million) pork-barrel scam. Known more simply as the "Napoles scam," after accused mastermind Janet Lim-Napoles, this racket saw government-development funds earmarked for programs intended to benefit the marginalized and poor—a population the characters Ligaya and Joanne belong to—systematically diverted to fictitious projects and non-governmental organizations for years in order for some members of congress and the senate to pocket the money.

For anyone lucky enough to have experienced *Nanay* live, whether at that "house/theatre" in Vancouver, at the Berlin festival, or at the Edinburgh conference, or vicariously, like me, through the script and virtual representations, I can imagine that they would have been left with nostalgia for home and a sense of *tristesse*. When they stepped back to their own everyday—after leaving the various performing sites, closing the pages of the script, and turning off their computers—I wish that the lives of the characters would continue to linger with them, as they have for me. If the commiseration, anger, frustration, and hope found in *Nanay* can continue to be unveiled and made present, then it will have contributed significantly to a force in redressing global iniquities.

Nanay premiered at the 2009 PuSh International Performing Arts Festival in Vancouver, and subsequently toured to Berlin, presented at the Hebbel am Ufer Theater as part of an international festival exploring the family. A staged reading of the play was performed in Edinburgh during the annual conference of the Royal Geographical Society and toured to the Philippines in November 2013. The play was directed by Alex Ferguson for every production. With the exception of the placing of the nanny agent scene, the script presented here is the one used for the Vancouver production.

NOTE

This is a hybrid installation-performance event. The audience is led through a series of modules. Based on the notion of making public an archive of private feeling, *Nanay* animates research materials collected by a University of British Columbia professor, some in partnership with the Philippine Women Centre of BC. These materials have been gathered over a fifteen-year period to document the short- and long-term impacts of Canada's Live-In Caregiver Program (LCP). With the exception of the guides' text and the monologue of the Canadian government official, the script is based entirely on the edited verbatim transcripts of interviews conducted with Filipino domestic workers, Canadian employers, "nanny" agents, and Filipino youth. (Square brackets indicate non-verbatim additions.)

WELCOME TO THE ARCHIVE

Audience members are admitted to an archive room. This group should be approximately 48-60 individuals. Two computer stations are set up in the foyer with images projected on one wall. Computers are linked to the websites of actual nanny agencies. As they assemble audience members (possibly under the direction of a cast member in the audience) have the opportunity to browse the resumés and support materials of domestic workers. After an introduction, the audience is broken up into smaller groups and led by guides along one of two routes: the one starting with employers and the other with domestic workers. Each group eventually experiences both routes through the performance/installation.

One group remains downstairs and is broken into two smaller groups to encounter several domestic workers with the aid of a guide; the other heads upstairs to move along the employers' route. Front of House will have handed out survey forms on clipboards to each audience member. The survey forms provide the opportunity for spectators to note down questions and comments they may have for the post-performance talkback.

THE DOMESTIC WORKER ROUTE

Scene 1: Nanny Agent

The agent has a desk, chair, computer, cellphone, pen, and paper.

CARL: My clients are all over the country. The other nanny agencies don't have the girls that I have. You see, if you want a girl—German, Austrian, Danish—call me. Nobody else has them. Show me one agency in [British Columbia] that has a Swiss girl, and I'll eat my hat. I mean, Filipino girls you can get anywhere. Me, I deal with specifics. We do bring Filipinas as well but it's a minor part of our stock, if you want to call it that way. Our main stream is Europe.

These Filipinas are very simple people. They can get pleasure out of very simple things. The same tired, old jokes can be told fifty times, and they laugh. When you talk Filipinos you're talkin' about—if you excuse the word—"servants." So you're dealing with a totally different mentality. She's used to being a servant.

One of the main questions we ask our clients when they're going for an overseas: Would you treat the girl as a member of the family? This means she can eat dinner with you. If you're having a cup of coffee she sits with you to talk. This is a member of the family. Filipinas are not in that category. Because they feel they are a servant. They're coming here to serve. They come in here, the employer is a god. It's a totally different breed. I have nothing against Filipinas, nothing against any nationals. We have people who want Filipinos and we give 'em that, because there's a need for them.

Your average Filipino girl is a quiet, shy personality. She does her job and that's the most important thing. The house has to be clean, spotless. When god is coming home—sorry, the parents are coming home. The kids, they come second.

The phone rings and he answers.

Hello, how can I help you? What do you have? Do you have a separate suite? How many children? How many square feet? How many bathrooms? Do you want housecleaning? Cooking meals? Babysitting in the evenings? How much have you been paying? Okay, I've got two girls that I can send to you right away. One is Czech; she's nineteen. I've got another girl from Thailand in her forties. Yes, they're both intelligent but the Czech girl might be a bit better. She's a little heavy, but it's no problem. How about Saturday? Offer them $700 and then raise it again in three months. Even [if] it's just $50, it's an incentive. Can I get your number? Okay, goodbye.

(addressing audience) She was calling me to help with someone on July 15. So you heard me; I heard what she needs. Usually, [this] computer is not even on my desk. Because this is my computer. *(He points to his head.)* I know the girls I have on hand. You ask other people, they'll tell you the same thing about Filipinos. Depends what you're looking for, what you want. My personal view, if you have a baby and you want someone to lick your home clean: Filipino girl. Go for that. If you have kids three, four years of age, and you want interaction, you want them to go to the park, arts and crafts, do things, you're better off with a European.

And here's another thing. I had to show the government of Canada that I'm worthy of Canada to give me landed immigrant status. This is how I came to this country. I'm an engineer by profession. This is why Canada said, okay, we will take you. Because I'm an engineer. Never mind I ended up not being an engineer.

European [girls] are coming here for a year. They have a job and [after that] they're going home. Filipinos want to stay. But why a girl that is coming from the Philippines, who hardly has high school, who came as a nanny, can apply for landed immigrant status after two years. *(snaps his fingers)* Just like that. Doesn't make any sense. Girls are going to work; they have a contract. Finish the contract. Thank you, goodbye. You don't have a job here, you have nothing to stay here for. I don't mind the girls staying here. I have nothing against them. They're fine. They're very nice people. Nothing wrong. I am questioning the logic behind the government decisions. But why do I have to go through all that to be a landed immigrant when people who are a lot less just get it like that? Why? This is not right.

Scene 2: Stories of Leaving

This monologue is delivered in a back kitchen or small utility room. The character is washing dishes and/or mopping the floor. Her back is turned against the audience. A mirror is mounted on one wall in which audience members—standing in close proximity (perhaps four feet away)—can witness themselves watching. The door to the room is closed. The intention is to communicate some of the factors propelling Filipino women to leave their families to work abroad, as well as their sense of hope and optimism about the prospects of overseas live-in domestic work.

GUIDE: We're going into the kitchen now, to meet Ligaya. She's a mother of four. She was a stay-at-home mom in the Philippines, and grew up in a middle-class family. She came to Canada through the LCP.

LIGAYA: My name is Ligaya. In the Philippines, in my mind, it was always the future of my children. And I was; I was really disappointed with my life. Because I have a husband, and he was working in the Middle East. At that time my son was nine months and Melissa my daughter was one month. I was looking forward to a better future. And then only to find out that, after a half year in—working abroad—he's not anymore sending money. So I said, I think in a few years, if my children are able to stay in the care of my parents, I'm going to work abroad. Because at that time the Philippines is really a corrupt country.

And it's not only that. The prices are getting high, and there're strikes everywhere. And there're brownouts. Yeah, and every time there's a brownout in the middle of the night, somebody said that it's some of the soldiers are being—what's this word?—delivered by the military for fighting the insurgents in Mindanao. That was Marcos's regime. So, okay, I didn't know about those, only from talk.

So, okay, there are times when my children would come home and we didn't have nothing. We had nothing to eat. So I have to—once I had to ask food from the neighbours. My parents . . . they have a better life because my brothers, my father, they have good jobs. Only I hated to ask help from them because there's always a sermon on the table. I don't like it.

So, okay, I'm a very independent person. I'm telling myself I always have the last card. And I always have the last laugh. So I said, "My children, don't worry. When before you reach high school, I will be able to work abroad. And then, we will have a better life. And a better future." And saying that—I didn't mean to say that—but when my son started high school, god has listened to me, to what I said. Because my aunt, who was leaving her job in Hong Kong for the States found her own replacement. And in her mind it was me. So, see? God answered my prayers. She told me that all she had in mind is me. Because she approached my dad and he gave a good signal.

At that time my eldest son was starting high school. And in my mind, I wanted him to start in a private school. So I paid for his entrance exam. After three weeks of worrying about the results of my son's entrance test they posted the results. He was number eight, in the top ten. And I said, "Oh, my son, come, come, your number, look at your name there." And on the other side of the board, it's the tuition fees. And it costs ten thousand pesos. Not only that: the allowance, but everything.

My husband's not sending money, and I said, if I can kill somebody, it would be him. Well, because maybe he has women over there. And he is looking after his own self only. After a few months, I got my working papers for Hong Kong. My husband was mad. He said he wanted me to stay home to take care of the children. And I said, "Well, if you want me to take care of the children then why are you not sending money every month?" And I told him: "I have dreams, big dreams for my children." And he didn't say anything. So what's the point? I said, "Now this time no one can dictate to me."

That's when I said, instead of finding luck in the Philippines, I would just try to find my luck in, you know, in Canada . . . I know that I will just be strong and leave everything, leave my kids in the care of my family.

But I have a fighting spirit, something like that. I'm the eldest. I'm the rebellious one. And I think that is one of the qualities that gives me the spirit, the spirit to be courageous. Like look, I've been through a lot in life, and still I face it squarely. I'm not scared to be, you know, for being poor. And I went abroad. I left my children behind. I told myself I have to win all the battles. I have to fight them squarely and face every problem eye to eye. And yeah, I'm very thankful that my mom taught me this. With all these challenges, I'm a survivor.

Scene 3: Stories of Employment

The audience is led to an adjacent room to listen to JOANNE*'s story of employment in the LCP. The idea is to create an intimate setting where audience members gather in small groups in close proximity to the actor to listen to her testimony. In this instance, a few chairs are set in a circle, in the centre of which is a wire-mesh box with a stuffed bunny inside. Drawn on the far wall behind the actor is a large human-scale calendar (a grid marking three years). Throughout the scene, the actor uses the calendar to indicate the passing of time and the threat of not completing the LCP within three years, the time allowed to qualify for permanent-resident status.*

GUIDE: Now we'll hear from Joanne what it's like to work within the LCP. Joanne was trained as a nurse in the Philippines and left her husband and two children to work in Canada. She races against the federal government's rule that twenty-four months of live-in-care work must be completed within thirty-six months in order to qualify for Canadian permanent residence.

JOANNE: My name is Joanne, married—of course, one husband, and I have two kids. I am a nursing graduate from Emilio Aguinaldo College. In the

Philippines I worked as a community health nurse in my hometown for five years. I came here November 13, 2003, under the Live-In Caregiver Program, the famous LCP. I had no idea about the LCP. I didn't prepare myself for the treatment that would happen to me inside the home. That's why I was shocked.

There was a problem with my first employment contract and I finally started work January 5, 2004. I started working for them without papers. It was not legal. I worked for them "under the table" from January until April, 2004. And so those first five months didn't count towards my twenty-four months needed so that I could apply for my landed-immigrant status. My work permit was approved April 5. But April 2 was my last day; I was told by my male employer that he no longer had work and they would not be able to keep a nanny.

I had been away for the weekend and it was only when I called them to arrange to come home that I learned that they decided they would not continue my contract. So I said, "What's going to happen? My work permit is on its way." In fact, they just told me that they would drop off my stuff. It was them who packed my things. I told them I didn't want them to touch my things because those were my personal stuff. I should be the one packing my personal stuff, my own stuff. I told them. But they just told me, "Oh, just don't worry. Nothing will go missing." I told them, "Yeah, I know that but the thing is, those are mine." So I just left it because I thought if I go there they might call the police. I was worried that I might be set up.

My other complaint with them is my room. I wouldn't consider my room as a bedroom because it is used as a storage area. As part of the LCP I'm supposed to have a real bedroom with a lock. There is a lock. But it's on the outside of the room. So I wouldn't be able to go out of the room. I would be trapped in the bedroom.

After they let me go I was left with no choice. I had to survive. So I went to [Angel Nannies] to find my next employer. I started working for them in May. I remember this date because this is my birthday. I took care of an elderly woman with cancer that started in her leg and then metastasized to her lungs. That was twenty-four-hour care because it was only the two of us. It can be said that my presence was needed. So for four months I worked with no permit; it was under the table. So again this didn't count. [And now ten months have gone by that don't count towards my twenty-four months.] I had followed up my work permit with Immigration and the work permit was approved September 7. Two weeks later my employer died.

I found my next employer, Janice, from Whistler. I want to stress that I was taking care of three kids: seven, four, and three years old. Regarding my working conditions, I wake up at 6:30 in the morning; I end up working sometimes until nine or eleven at night. I worked straight from 6:30 and prepare their breakfast. There are three kids so I dress all of them. I brush their teeth, even the seven-year-old. I help them with everything, even with putting on their shoes, socks, everything I'm supposed to do for them. I prepare their lunch and put it in their lunch bags. Plus if I were not able to locate their scarves, the employer would even get angry at me. Like that. She would say to me, "Do you know how much that cost me? That was so expensive!"

So that's 6:30. I'm the one who brings them to the car. I'm the one who buckles all of them in the van. She takes so long to get ready in the morning. She doesn't even do anything! She just lies down. When all the kids are buckled, we just sit in the car and wait for her. There are times when we drive to the village because she gets a coffee. Sometimes she buys me a coffee at Blenz, which is good because I'm tired by that time. So by the time I get home, it's eleven or 10:30 and I begin my work right away. By twelve, the youngest has to be picked up, and she makes me accompany her again. She brings me because she wants an "*alalay*" servant, just like someone to dial the phone while she drives, someone to hand her her credit card when she buys things. I'm the one to "*talagang achay ka*." I'm really expected to be always moving, ready to serve her.

She doesn't work. It's her husband that works down here in Vancouver. He's a money manager. I'm not really sure what a money manager does. So who only lives in the house are the three kids, me, and the mother. But during the night time—this is what's "nice"—one of the kids, the youngest, wakes up in the middle of the night and crawls into bed with me. Why doesn't she crawl into bed with her mother? The mother said, "Why don't you lock your door then?" So I did it once. But the thing is, the kid is knocking! So I have to wake up in the middle of the night. My sleep is interrupted and I can't fall back to sleep after that. So my work here was also twenty-four-hour care. I would finish ironing eleven p.m. Twelve a.m. she would come to my room; sometimes all the kids are asleep beside me because they don't want to sleep beside their own mother.

Not only did I take care of the three kids and their mother, I also took care of their bunny. The bunny was not part of my contract. I'm the one who has to care for and clean the bunny. I clean the bunny's poo every day. I feed the bunny every day. Everything.

There were many times the mother would go down to Vancouver. It would just be the kids and myself. In fact, she told me, "You're the mother now; I'm not the mother anymore." I'm doing everything. She expects me to review the school work and assignments with the kids. I am even expected to help them with French. What do I know about French? "*Sobra na*!" It's really too much.

I even hand-wash clothing, like sweaters, even hand-washing panties. I'm not embarrassed to say that I had to hand-wash blood-soiled panties! One time, when I sorted her laundry, I noticed the blood-soiled panties. Of course I didn't want to wash them knowing that she wanted me to hand-wash laundry. So I just placed it in her bathroom sink.

I placed it in the sink. I let it soak in there. I expected that she would wash it the next day. But no, it was still there. I just left it again until the next day. But no, it was still there. The panties have been soaking in her sink for two days. She didn't touch it. So what was I to do? I got her point clearly. So I washed it. My work with Janice was twenty-four-hour care. September, October, November, this was all under the table. That's what I can say to describe my experience there.

I really want to continue working, bear a little more sacrifice. You have to understand that sometimes it's really hard to assert yourself to an employer because you don't want to have your employment terminated, right? So sometimes you just say, "Okay." You accept and keep on accepting. It's so hard to object to their demands, especially knowing that my immigration papers are precarious right now. But it is too much to handle. I've already given my best. That's it. But all of them are depending on me . . . If I break down, many others will break down. So I need to be strong. That's the only thing that keeps me going. They're all leaning on me. I need to keep standing. But the thing is, I don't know what step to take next. I really want to go home, but what about the fate of my family.

GUIDE: Joanne was unsuccessful in getting her twenty-four months of employment. She was forced to return to the Philippines in 2006. Okay, could you all follow me?

Scene 4: Stories of Separation

The audience is led into a long, narrow corridor. Both doors are shut. Several speakers are hanging from the ceiling. Long wooden church pews are set up along one wall. On the opposite wall light boxes are mounted, displaying a series of photos. These could be images evocative of the Philippines, faces of domestic workers and their children, or a series of children's faces as they age through time (two, six, ten years old). The intent is to visually represent the period of separation. Images fade into black or to a very low level of light. The soundscape then begins. The intention is to demonstrate how the relationships between families are mediated through various forms of media. We are also attempting to convey a sense of separation, of estrangement, disembodied narrative, and the tensions of caring at a distance. The soundscape is composed of the voices of individuals from different families telling of their experiences of separation. The voices of the mothers and son are the voices of actual migrants rather than those of professional actors.

GUIDE: The median length of time of separation between domestic workers and their children is eight years.

The audio begins to play.

MOTHER 1: I left my family year 1993. My eldest was nine and seven months and second was seven half and the third was—

MOTHER 2: Six. Yeah, I'm Christine. I left my family when my children was four and a half and three.

DAUGHTER: My mother left when I was in grade five so probably that's around 1988.

MOTHER 1: We were all crying when we left.

SON: I think she was in Vancouver.

MOTHER 1: I remember when.

SON: It's so hard to recall 'cause—

MOTHER 1: They were crying so hard 'cause we never separate since they were young and since they were little and that was the first time that I will go away and they understand that I will be away.

SON: So she left afternoon, it was afternoon, she left and she was trying to get our aunts and uncles to like entertain us or something, like take our minds off 'cause we had a sense of her leaving.

MOTHER 1: Four years and eight months I never went home in between these years. It's so I could have a better life in the future. Ummm . . .

DAUGHTER: My mom would take care of me in ways that, she would send money and letters but it's hard to connect when you're just sending letters right? It takes a month before it gets to the Philippines.

MOTHER 1: I did receive letters, like if I sent them letters I'll receive up to two months, I'll receive an answer, and then I can answer that back after six months again. That's the only comfort I have there. You just cry every time you will miss our family . . . It took me a while like six months before I stopped crying when I get there. It was very hard to adjust in a way.

SON: She was writing letters, but we just get to see the letter we don't really get to read it. We just see, "Okay she wrote letters," okay, but to us its just like, "Okay," yeah we were like, we want to know how she is but we didn't know how to show it kind of thing . . . Yeah.

MOTHER 1: Then I uh, then I heard about Canada. So I said, oh it's a safe place for my family. I want to bring my kids to this safer place 'cause our place is really in trouble all the time, especially—especially Midanao. I said, "Oh I think Canada is better, Canada is . . . heaven."

SON: Yeah, six years . . . yeah.

MOTHER 1: I went home 1998, 1999, and err, my children were again crying. When I get, when I get to my place oh they were all cryin' because they were, "We miss you very much." That was very good but—

SON: But, yeah, with one visit we always wondered why, oh, she's like gone for that long; she, and then—

DAUGHTER: Okay, okay, she's back now, we're going to treat her special because she's back but I don't have that deep connection with my mom anymore. I was just happy that she came home during my first year in high school and she could see me sing for the first time.

SON: We were—we're happy 'cause like when she comes home she like, oh, like she brought a lot of stuff, so we're like, "Oh okay, so she must have a lot of money or something." But when you get to see her for two weeks, then she's gone it's like we started questioning, "Oh, she came back to visit but it was like two weeks," and we were like so excited but it's like two weeks, right? And then she had to go again so it was like woah. Like for us as kids we get to know her for a couple of weeks and she has to leave again and you start asking a lot of questions again, but then—

MOTHER 1: It was full of joy at that time because we were together but then my husband—err, my savings at the time didn't really last long, but better communication, because I have the cellphone and they can, err, there was already electricity in our island so there was phone, it was "kind of."

Phone rings.

DAUGHTER: Phone calls? I don't stay on the phone that much because after a few years being separated from my mom all I could talk about was my accomplishments and then after that I don't know what to talk about.

Phone rings again.

MOTHER 1: It feels good if you hear their voices. I just love to call like every day, only I can't spend lots of money with the card. But I do have to budget that so . . . But hearing their voices, it's really a comfort . . .

Phone rings.

DAUGHTER: I've got no connection any more, I kind of forgot, since she separated from me she doesn't know me that much.
MOTHER 1: I work hard, very hard work, but if I call, I feel happy.
SON: Our mum's gone; this mum it was really a stranger to us 'cause we were so young.
MOTHER 1: Fifteen years I was only home for three times and they were all big now. *(She starts to cry.)*
DAUGHTER: And then that's it.
MOTHER 1: Talking in the phone was good but I'm not sure if it will be the same when they come.
DAUGHTER: She's no more to me at that time than a drawing.
MOTHER 1: If I will be able to be patient to their character when they come. That's what I worry for.

Crying.

Scene 5: Storied Objects Room

This is a room constructed by domestic workers as a replication of their bedrooms, as a compilation of their experiences in Canadian homes. Within the room, there is a collection of artifacts. Concrete objects may be used to accentuate certain aspects of this abstract space. A guide introduces the fact that this is a domestic worker's room. The audience is given permission to enter the room, to move through it and touch and feel the objects. The metaphor of still life can be used to think about this room—with all of what stillness implies: a state of calm, a lull in the action—a static state filled with vibratory motion. Storied objects will include a photo album, an employer's calendar, a postcard of Pope John Paul II, pictures of children with accompanying letters, a diary with recipes to be prepared for employers, phone cards, a rosary, and Skyflake crackers.

GUIDE: This is a replica of a domestic worker's bedroom. It's a storied-objects room, meaning that every one of its objects has a story to tell. These objects were selected from conversations with domestic workers, who described objects that were significant in their lives.

THE EMPLOYER ROUTE

For these scenes the smaller audiences in the domestic-worker track are reassembled as an audience of roughly twenty-four persons. The audience is seated in bleacher-like seating and remains seated in the same position to view all three scenes, slightly readjusting their body to view the action located in different spaces. They are slightly more distanced from the actors but are still within roughly fifteen feet of each performance.

Scene 6: Stories of Need

This scene takes place in KAREN*'s house and involves two Canadian women in need of child care. This is a conversation around a kitchen table, although it is closer to interleaving interior monologues than it is a dialogue. It is a tightly choreographed scene. The scene begins in a naturalistic setting before actors begin to move through a series of repeating gestures that suggest the weight these women are under when it comes to securing child care. The text is initially delivered simultaneously before landing in a conversation between the two employers. It ends with a direct address to the audience. The intention is to stress the repetition of the same problems for women trapped in different but similar circumstances, to build empathy around the plight of Canadian women employed outside the home, and to call attention to the critical absence of child care in Canada. On screen behind the actors is a picture of a kitchen with two women sitting at an oval kitchen counter.*

GUIDE: We're going to meet two women who have tried to find Canadians to care for their children. Karen is a teacher living in Surrey, married with two young children. Denise works as a legal assistant and lives in Coquitlam with her husband and two children.

KAREN: I had no intention of hiring a live-in nanny. I wanted to find a Canadian woman who would come into my home to care for my child. I advertised in the local newspaper but I didn't get a lot of response to my first ad. I had a lot of people calling saying, "Well if you don't find anyone, I have a daycare in my home." But I didn't want that. I wanted someone to come in. I probably interviewed about ten women. I got some really old women and I got a few really young girls.

I decided on one who was mature, had grown children, in her fifties. She was very nice. I had her references checked. I have a friend who's an RCMP and so he checked. Did all my criminal-record checking. So it was great.

After only about two weeks I had to go away on business. After the first week, I phoned home and my husband said, "I think she smokes." And I'm like, "No, she told me she didn't." But my daughter was two and a half, and she said, "Oh, yeah, she smokes." Then John got home early one day and she was asleep on the couch and Christine was in the crib crying and Seana was running around in the backyard. When I came home

I phoned her and said, "You're not welcome back." You know, it's a job. So she was gone.

DENISE: We thought home daycare would be best. Because Nicholas was only six months old it would be better if it was just a small group, one or two children. So we met this one woman. She was an older woman, retired. German lady. And she seemed very nice. She talked about story time. Called the references. "Oh she's wonderful. It's been fantastic." That lasted four months. She wouldn't do what I asked.

Next up for us: our next-door neighbour decided to open her own daycare in her basement. So we said, okay, we'll bring him. It was fine for the first little bit but she turned out to be a chronic complainer. You got the feeling that she was just miserable. And because she was just getting started up, she bought second-hand equipment. The problem with the second-hand high chair was that it had wooden slots for the tray and one slot was missing so my son would come home at the end of the day covered in food. It was hard to talk about it with a neighbour because you don't want to . . . you want to keep the neighbourhood friendly.

More and more children showed up. Nicholas was the first one dropped off in the morning and there were times when I'd have to stand there and bang on the door for ten minutes for someone to wake up. It started to get uncomfortable but fortunately we moved and I had another baby so I was home for a while on maternity leave.

Yeah? So I called one of the young girls that I liked and she hadn't found anything yet. After one day she just said she didn't really want to do it.

I was scheduled to go back to work in November and so I put an ad in the newspaper in September. The first ad got a really poor turnout. I had one woman, she was probably about twenty. She had a three-month-old baby she wanted to bring along. I was like, no, no, you're not going to be able to handle a three-month-old, my six-month-old, plus a very energetic two-and-half-year-old. That's not going to work out.

Again, barely any response to my ad. I got a few people, hired a girl named Colette. I really wanted someone older. I said mature woman. But I hired this girl Colette because I couldn't find anyone else. She was nice, stayed for five months. What happened was her and her boyfriend split up and she moved home to White Rock and it was too far to drive.

I had an eighteen-year-old and a nineteen-year-old. The nineteen-year-old seemed very reasonable. I checked out references. I always did. And it seemed fine. She had her own car, and she drove here.

So fine, I mean what can I do?

So I ran another ad in the paper—

The first day she was late.

About forty-five minutes. She made me late for my first day back at work after six months. And then she was late a second time that first week. My stress level just started going through the roof. I think I had to miss a couple of days of work. She started to get sick a few times. And then after six months she gave her notice. She said she'd got a job cleaning instruments at a dental office.

I interviewed another couple again, same type of group, young girls, but I also had an older woman, forty-two, married to someone about my age, about twelve years younger. They just lived over here, and we had her for a year. She was really good.

She got sick quite a bit though. She ended up having an operation and so she was off two months just a few months after we hired her.

One lived down the street from us.

She had first aid.

So then, what did I do?

We'd got to the point where getting first aid was a miracle.

I found a girl called Samantha.

So we just went—

Again, barely any responses to my ad.

—if you can drive—

She was very nice.

—if you can speak English—

We had her for two weeks and then we were on holidays for two weeks.

—if you're normal—

But when we came home—

—and you don't look like you're doing drugs—

—there was this phone message saying—

—and you've good experience—

"I'm still in Winnipeg. Something's come up. I won't be home yet."

—that will do.

I was not in a good mood.

So I phoned her boyfriend and said, "I need her number in Winnipeg."

Mind you, everyone had experience.

"I have to talk to her."

Everyone had wonderful references.

He said, "Well, actually, her and I have split up." So I guess that's what happened. She never did phone me back. Not a note, nothing.

So we hired her. And the house was a complete pigsty by the end of the day. It was gross. The counters were sticky and stuff. I thought, "Okay, well, I'll say something in a couple of days." But within three days she quit.

So then I thought forget it, we're getting a live-in. I just can't handle this anymore. So I phoned a few agencies. I guess we always thought that it would be more money, but by the time I worked it out I think we are paying fifty or sixty dollars a month more and we're getting everything done. I kick myself now, but my husband really didn't want to do it. He was really reluctant.

Our child care got to the point where my husband and I were consistently late for work because she was late or wasn't here. And my husband's employers basically told him to make a decision—either his career with the company or get another job. We talked about it and said, "Enough is enough, I'm going to look after the children." We are going to move to a cheaper home. I've resolved myself to the fact that I'm giving up my career for now.

It's funny because my girlfriends say to me that my priorities have changed. My priorities would not have changed this much if I had not been going through this much stress. They've changed to this point because we have not been able to find anybody that worked out. And I don't even want to consider live-in at this point because I don't think it would be any better.

So we just had to look at a couple of resumés and we picked one and hopefully she works out. If she doesn't, the agency will replace her.

I can't remember why I was drawn to the nanny we chose. They're all very qualified. I think the other one we considered was quite a bit older and I just thought well I don't want to get into the situation where she becomes my mom! You know what I mean?

So I think this one that's coming is thirty. She has kids. I thought that was really strange. I thought, how could she leave? It's actually a baby. But as the nanny agent was saying, "It's for a better life," and so in a way she's doing it for the baby. Then you kind of think, well, what a sacrifice, really.

Scene 7: Employers' Stories Inside the LCP

This scene takes place within an employer's bedroom. A bed, chair, lamp, and television are set up. The intention here is to communicate the complexity of being an employer inside the home. The challenge of this scene is to convey the privilege of these employers' lives without parody.

Projected on the screen: "Richard and Stephanie are in their late thirties and live in Yaletown. She works in advertising; he works in management. They have a three-year-old son and a baby." The words are superimposed on a view from a False Creek condo.

RICHARD: When Stephen was six months old, we chose a Filipino nanny because we heard that they were very caring for the very young ones. So we basically only interviewed Filipino nannies.
STEPHANIE: We found out about Marlena from a friend of ours. How we worked it out was like this: we had two bedrooms upstairs and one room that we used as an office. So we sacrificed that. In that information booklet it told what a live-in caregiver is entitled to have. And it was a room with sleeping arrangements and a lock on the door. Although no one's ever locked the door.
RICHARD: And then we also gave her separate bathroom facilities. And she didn't need a separate phone, but we gave her one. We gave her a TV, a desk, an answering machine. It's different than working in Singapore or Hong Kong. Marlena told us stories of where the nannies were sleeping. It wasn't a pretty scene.
STEPHANIE: They're treated like second-class citizens in other countries!
RICHARD: At first she wanted to call us "Madam" and "Sir"! But we said, "Wooahhh, wait a minute." I think she was kind of taken aback by that! And we said to her, "That's not the Canadian way."

STEPHANIE: More than anything, we've become friends.
RICHARD: Yeah, we wanted to break the ice.

Projection.

STEPHANIE: But then she met this fellow from the US and became pregnant. Marlena got pregnant in like the first week of knowing him. They've been married a year and a half now, and every time they come up, they give us a call. And we still get invited to birthday parties and stuff.
RICHARD: We actually had a heart to heart with her because she was giving up her chance for Canadian citizenship and we just wanted to make her think of who she was marrying and why. She never planned a career or anything. Her goal in life was to work at McDonald's. And I have the feeling that there's gonna be a crossroad in her relationship with her husband. We might have to sponsor her again to be our nanny! Our son will be twelve and she'll be living with us again as a nanny!

Actually we loved Marlena, but when she left we decided in lieu of a Filipino nanny to go with a European nanny, because of the learning skills, the interaction. We were finding that Marlena was really good and loving and hugging and doing everything proper for him and feeding him. But the alphabet, the numbers, the colours, those things aren't happening. We would do tests from time to time. We say to her, "Today do nothing in the house, we want you to read to Stephen." And we put books in a certain position, and we come back at the end of the day and the books hadn't moved.
STEPHANIE: [You feel a little strange doing these tests, but—really—how else can you know what's going on during the day? You're not there. You can't see it. Your child is too young to tell you.]
RICHARD: So we finally made the decision to get a European nanny because we thought stimulation would come intellectually. I think that's the trade-off.
STEPHANIE: But European nannies are a lot more demanding and they're looking at you thinking, "Well, you live in a million-dollar house and you say you can't afford." You know, you can just see their minds working. So it's hard but the bottom line is, I mean we had to pretty much say, "Listen, Brigit, this

is how much I make and this is how much Richard makes. If we pay you any more than $1100 a month it's not worth me going to work." You have to say that to them. We had to do that with Marlena too.

RICHARD: I finally had to sit her down, and Stephanie was explaining our salaries and weighing it all out, and how we can, as a family, make, you know, six figures, and not have any money left at the end of the year. She cannot fathom that.

STEPHANIE: Well, I think she probably thinks that we're wealthy. In order to spruce it up a little bit, we've taken in a neighbour's child. We've done that for two years. They pay twenty-five dollars a day. We give Brigit ten, so she makes an extra $240 a month. We take fifteen.

RICHARD: It's a win-win situation.

Scene 8: Elder Care

This scene is designed to explore and communicate the growing need for affordable elder care in Canada, and the (sometimes) desperate situation Canadians face in securing quality care for ailing parents. It also focuses on the complexity of the relationship between caregivers, employers, and parents, the complexity of care within transnational Filipino families, the ambiguity of assessing work experience and exploitation in family and non-family situations, confusion about appropriate wages in contexts where the work is intermittent, and the insidious ways that the LCP constructs episodically undocumented workers. The scene is set in the home of NADINE*'s mother.*

An image of the actor with her mother is projected on the screen. As the scene progresses the images change as the mother and actor age.

NADINE: My mother had a stroke and she ended up in the hospital. We didn't know what the outcome would be. And so my sister and I started checking out different options.

We started by looking at assisted-care living. But the problem with that is that my mother doesn't like the thought of eating in the dining room, because she has Parkinson's. We asked, "Could she eat in her room?" And they said, "No, because she has Parkinson's she could choke." So she wasn't an appropriate candidate for these assisted-living places.

So then we went to the long-term care places and they were horrible. They were small little rooms, sometimes with a shared bathroom and all kinds of demented people around in the hallways asking which room they were in. And in the dining room this woman basically keeled over onto the table when we were there. Just like a tree, kind of fell sideways.

The woman who was setting the table just straightened her up. And I thought, oh my god this is horrible. I couldn't imagine my mother in one of these places.

Projection.

And my mother said when she was in the rehab hospital it felt like she was in prison. And she didn't like the beds with the bars going up the side. They put her in there so she wouldn't fall out. You know, quite frankly, maybe they were right. Because when she came home from three months in the rehab hospital, I woke up one morning and she was on the floor and she couldn't get up. She said she'd been there for five hours and she's freezing cold because the air conditioning was on and she didn't have a blanket on her. I just started to cry. It was awful. And after that happened she finally resigned herself to the fact that she did need someone all of the time.

We already had Augusta. She's a Portuguese woman who comes from eight to six, six days a week. But we needed more help. We needed someone to live in. My sister has a nice young Filipino tutor for her two kids. And she said that her cousin needed a job.

The cousin was invited to come from the Philippines to stay with her husband's family and take care of his grandparents. One of them had Alzheimer's. She took care of them twenty-four hours a day, seven days a week. For two years. And it seems they never gave her any relief at all. And they didn't give her any pay. So she'd basically never worked before in Canada except for taking care of her husband's grandparents.

And so I met Letty. She's thirty-two and she's married. Her husband is in the Philippines. And I said, "Would you like a job taking care of my mother? Augusta will still do all the cleaning and cooking and stuff but you could live here and be on call in the evenings when she needs you. Like you could go to sleep but we would have a monitor in case my mother needs you." And she said, "Sure." And so I said, "When we phoned an agency they said it was $1100 to $1500 a month. Since you have no experience I'm going to start by paying you $1300 a month for a two-month trial period." She told me that she had applied for citizenship and her papers are going through so she would rather I pay her under the table. She isn't allowed to work here until she gets her status. So I said, "Okay, we'll just do it like this."

Projection.

My mother doesn't understand why . . . she doesn't really see it as a job, taking her to the bathroom. She just thinks of it as like something you would do for anybody. If you just happened to live there, you would do it. She doesn't see it as wage-gaining work. It's like it doesn't compute to her that people have lives and they have other things to do. That this is actually labour. She thinks that her life is their life and that basically all they do is sit down and watch TV with her or wait until she has to go to the bathroom, which is like once every three hours.

We were feeling bad because Letty was working six nights a week and at first she was staying up all night. If you add it up, her hours are from six p.m. till eight a.m., when Augusta gets there. And that's fourteen hours, so we thought that was way too many hours. And we pay Augusta fifteen dollars an hour, so Letty's wages just don't compare. But then you think about—it's only three or four times a night that my mother needs you. So it's kind of a weird job. The flat rate was the only way we could really afford this. And I thought giving someone room and board could really help them out. But it's not helping Letty at all because she'd rather live with her family.

So it's kinda like this really awkward situation because I thought someone would be happy to have a place to live. Especially in central Vancouver. And all she does is go back to Coquitlam every day. Because she is so lonely. When she first came to my mother's house she was really really grieving. Really lonely.

I think Letty likes her job. It's her first job in Canada and we told her we'd give her a good reference. If she got her papers in order it would be a really good job for her. Her husband could come and move in with her.

I got her the Internet. I said, "Do you want a TV and cable?" And she said, "No I don't watch TV." And I said, "What do you want?" And she said, "I'd like Internet." And after she got that she seemed better. My sister says she spends all her time at night doing the webcam with her husband.

Projection.

I just want my mother to be as comfortable as possible and to be as happy as she can with her last days. So this is the only way we can do it. And it's my mother's money. She worked really hard all her life. Different jobs, tons of different jobs: waitressing and then hairdressing and then real estate. She saved all of her money and now she has this nice house. And she wants to stay there. She's lived there thirty years. And she knows all of her neighbours. She doesn't feel like going to one of these institutions. As far as I could see of these institutions they're horrible. I don't want my mother going there either. They'll leave her in a fucking diaper all day. My sister says that the hospital made her incontinent. She never had that problem before. They kept putting diapers on her. So now's she wearing a diaper every frigging day.

Scene 9: Truth and Consequences

All the members of the audience reconvene in a large open space to hear a final round of testimony. MICHELLE *is sitting at the end of a long, empty table with a cellphone placed in front of her. The* CITIZENSHIP AND IMMIGRATION CANADA

AGENT is standing at the opposite end of the table. The audience sits in circular tiered seating around the table. The interviewer is sitting in the audience. A microphone is on the table in front of MICHELLE. We no longer have guides to introduce us to the people on stage. The CITIZENSHIP AND IMMIGRATION CANADA AGENT's monologue is the one non-verbatim, constructed monologue in the play.

CITIZENSHIP AND IMMIGRATION CANADA AGENT: Hi everyone. My name is Ari Gunnarson and I am representing Citizenship and Immigration Canada, one of the agencies responsible for the Live-In Caregiver Program. I hope you've all enjoyed making your way through the archive. I am here to say a few words on behalf of the Canadian government. I know it's always easy to criticize the government, but before you judge us or the program, I'd like to present you with some basic facts.

The LCP is designed to help Canadian families. We have structured the program to provide the highest level of care to Canadian children at a cost that the average Canadian family can afford. Whether we're talking about the care of our elders or children, there's a great need in this country. And the LCP delivers. Before you call for removal of the live-in requirement, remember that this is what makes the program affordable for ordinary Canadians.

The federal government recognizes the difficulties of the LCP. As one measure of our concern, the federal government has funded all of the research that has been used to create this play, including research into the effects of family separation. But it's also important to recognize the benefits of the LCP to Filipinos, including their families in the Philippines. Consider, for example, how much money is remitted to the Philippines by women registered in the LCP.

The need for these remittances is great: in 2006 the Philippines government estimated that one out of three people in their country lives in poverty. Canada is the third largest source of remittances to the Philippines, after the United States and Saudi Arabia. About fifteen billion dollars are returned to the Philippines each year by migrant workers. This sum exceeds all other forms of development aid combined. The World Bank and many academic scholars now believe that the money sent home is a more effective means of stimulating the Philippines economy than more traditional forms of development aid.

That is not to say the LCP is perfect, but you need to recognize that it is the most generous program of its sort in the entire world. Why? Because it offers an opportunity for Third World women and their families to get Canadian citizenship. Lots of countries import domestic workers on a temporary basis but Canada is the *only* country in the world to offer citizenship after a short period of time.

Consider as well that lots of Filipinos want to take this opportunity: about twenty-two thousand people are currently registered in the program and lots more would come if they could. Shouldn't individual Filipinos have the opportunity to decide for themselves whether this is a good or bad program? As comfortable Canadians, who are you to make this decision for them?

I won't take any more of your time. Thank you once again for allowing me to explain some essential facts about the Live-In Caregiver Program and lay out some of its important benefits.

I've been given the opportunity to introduce Michelle. She's the daughter of a domestic worker who was reunited with her mother in Canada four years ago.

Michelle and Gerry (Researcher)

RESEARCHER: When did your mother leave the Philippines?

MICHELLE: My mother left when I was in grade five. So probably that's around 1998.

She went to . . . ? I think she was in Vancouver. I was eleven years old so I was old enough to know she was taking care of children. Two children to be exact.

The family that we had in the Philippines was kind of separated. So we're not really attached to relatives and stuff. So pretty much my dad and I have to live by ourselves. When my mom went to Canada, the separation was pretty hard on my dad. Unfortunately when my mom was in Canada my dad had a girlfriend.

I think that's the problem when your wife migrates or your husband migrates. You kind of look for somebody to support you and your family as well. Emotionally, my teachers were taking care of me.

My mom would take care of me in a way that she would send money and letters. But it's hard to connect when you're just sending letters, right. It takes a month before it gets to the Philippines.

RESEARCHER: Did you talk to your mom on the phone?

MICHELLE: I don't stay on the phone that much because after a few years being separated from my mom all I could talk to her about is my accomplishments. And then after that I don't know what to talk about anymore. And I end up just saying, "Ha? Ha ha. Oh yeah. Heh, heh, heh." I'm laughing but I don't know what I'm laughing about, right?

She talks a lot about other children, which I am not interested in hearing about. Since she's separated from me she doesn't know me that much. All the advice that she could give me whenever I tell her my problems is the usual things that a person could see watching teledrama.

RESEARCHER: Did your mom know about your dad's girlfriend?

MICHELLE: My mom knew about my dad, but she was patient enough to wait for all the papers to be processed and then they were going to get a divorce. But then she found out that if my dad couldn't come here, then my sister and I couldn't come here as well. So she had to be patient.

RESEARCHER: How long did it take you before you came to Canada?

MICHELLE: It was six years before I came to Canada. By that time I was seventeen and had graduated from high school and was planning to do accounting in the Philippines. But then I went here and I was back in high school. So it kind of got me confused.

Back in the Philippines school is awesome! Really! I love competition and in the Philippines the children that went with me in my private school—they like comparing their grades to my grades. So I had to go, go, go, go, go, go! It's very motivating because everyone is competing against each other, and it's seldom that you see a lazy person there. They have a goal towards university.

When I came here, it's culture shock. Because the kids here are quite different. I'm not really used to people complaining early in the morning about how tired they are!

I keep on thinking what would've happened if I just stayed in the Philippines. Probably I would be in first-year university already and with my friends. And maybe if I'm in the Philippines I wouldn't be this lonely. And I know how to live there. I wouldn't need my parents. When I moved here it's just like you're stuck in a matchbox. It's like a spider stuck in a matchbox and the only four corners you can go to are the four corners available to you. Having no connections with anybody, I just kept everything to myself.

I was arguing with my mom all the time: Like, "Why can't you just send me back to the Philippines so I can go to college already?" But she wouldn't, right? It got me very very depressed. The only heaven for me is work at McDonald's because I could just smile and ask, "Do you want fries with that?"

When I first went here I had no friends, right? The nearest people I could actually blend in with is the people from the fast-food restaurants. I got a job there because I went in and saw a lot of Filipinos. It was the easiest way I could have a sense of belonging. Because most of the Filipinos here, they work in the fast-food area.

But having those people that have been working in the fast-food area for like ten years already—being surrounded by them—you kind of begin to think the same way that they're thinking. So if they have smaller goals, you also have a smaller goal, which is to become a manager in McDonald's. I was thinking, well maybe this is the life in Canada. Really. You don't have to go to school. You just go to Walmart. Work there for a few years and then be a manager kind of thing. If I go to work, I'll have the money. I'll have freedom. So that was what was pushing me towards dropping out of school.

RESEARCHER: But you did finish high school.

MICHELLE: I thought to myself, I don't want to be just at the very bottom and just like the other Filipinos that are working in fast food or retail. So that's why I wanted to finish school. I worked in Tim Hortons for two years after school, but then I chose a medical-lab-assistant course. I chose it because it's short. It's a six-month program. Doesn't need a lot of money because the tuition fee is very low. And I liked the name, medical-lab assistant. Because I feel like a pro. Having that title instead of Store Manager in Tim Hortons. I like being an assistant better. I wanted the title. And now I love my job. Like, "We're going to be taking blood again! Where's my next patient?" It gave me direction to my life. It gave me more pride in myself.

Scene 10: Public Forum

After each performance, there is a talkback session, facilitated by an academic and a member of a community organization. This is an opportunity for audience members to discuss what they've gleaned through the archive, and to discuss and debate with experts with direct experience of the LCP: domestic workers, Canadian employers, advocates, and Filipino youth.

RAGE

Michele Riml

THE THRILL OF THE GUN: FEELING IN THE CONTEXT OF THEATRE FOR ADOLESCENTS

Nicholas Hanson

If you've flipped through the brochure of a Canadian regional theatre or summer company over the past decade, chances are high that one of the pages featured an advertisement for *Sexy Laundry*, Michele Riml's 2002 vibrant comedy about a long-married couple who spend a hotel weekend reigniting their romance. The play's Norm Foster-esque blend of hilarious antics with heartfelt sincerity has charmed sold-out audiences from Vancouver's Arts Club Theatre to Halifax's Neptune Theatre and more than a dozen cities in between—not to mention productions in Germany, Iceland, the United Kingdom, Poland, and Spain. Although *Sexy Laundry* is the most famous of Riml's plays, it is somewhat of a stylistic outlier compared to her more than a dozen other produced works, which often temper comedic insights with tense circumstances, incendiary conversations, and volatile issues. For instance, *Miss Teen*, the semi-autobiographical 1993 play that helped establish Riml's playwriting career, deals with a teenaged beauty pageant winner grappling with her father's cancer diagnosis; likewise, *Poster Boys* (2008) deftly traces the controversial intersections between advertising, sexuality, and faith. An ongoing relationship with Vancouver's Green Thumb Theatre resulted in a number of Theatre for Young Audiences (TYA) projects that examine contemporary issues. Riml's plays for elementary- and middle-school audiences include *The Invisible Girl* (2004, body image and popularity), *Tree Boy* (2007, environment and consumerism), and *The Skinny Lie* (2005, body image and deception); for high schools she wrote *Cool* (1995, peer pressure and popularity). Like Kristen Thomson's *I, Claudia* and Joan MacLeod's *The Shape of a Girl*, a pair of Riml's works attract crossover audiences of teenagers and adults: *Souvenirs*, a 2009 show about the intergenerational and intercultural conflicts between a sixteen-year-old girl and her immigrant grandfather, and *RAGE*, her 2004 play that investigates micro and macro perspectives on violence in schools. With intense situations, frustrated characters, and diametric viewpoints, *RAGE* typifies the emphasis on feeling that exists in contemporary Canadian TYA, especially for plays intended for adolescent demographics.

RAGE was commissioned and first produced by Green Thumb Theatre, and the play fits neatly within the company's artistic trajectory. Founded in 1975 with Dennis Foon as the inaugural artistic director, Green Thumb's early years featured programming similar to other TYA companies of the time: a mix of fantasy tales and folk stories. Green Thumb shifted gears in 1979 with their landmark production of *Hilary's Birthday* by Joe Wiesenfeld, which considered the impact of divorce on children, a topic controversial for school performances of that era. Over the next decade Foon sought to "put the teeth back in the teddy bear,"[1] as Green Thumb tackled a number of challenging subjects, often in Foon's own scripts, such as *Liars* (1986, alcoholism), *Skin* (1986, racism), and *Mirror Game* (1988, physical abuse). Patrick McDonald assumed the artistic director position in 1988; during his extended tenure, the company has gained an international profile with a number of their touring productions, particularly Morris Panych's *Co$t of Living*, a 1990 triumph that raised AIDS awareness, and Joan MacLeod's *The Shape of a Girl*, the 2001 solo show loosely based on the real-life murder of a fourteen-year-old girl. As noted in their mission statement, "Green Thumb Theatre creates and produces plays that explore social issues relevant to the lives of children, youth and

1 "History," *Green Thumb Theatre*, n.d, accessed 1 Sep. 2013. http://greenthumb.bc.ca/index.php/about-green-thumb/history/.

young adults";[2] a commitment to reaching that last cohort led the company to program mainstage productions aimed at audiences aged fifteen to twenty-four. Both *Souvenirs* and *RAGE* appeared in this series, as well as earlier works like George F. Walker's *Tough!* in 1993. Over the last generation, professional TYA activities in Canada have matured, especially in terms of their engagement with social issues; Green Thumb played an influential role in this development, along with companies like Concrete Theatre in Edmonton, Theatre Direct in Toronto, and Youtheatre in Montreal.

RAGE premiered in November 2004 at the Vancouver East Cultural Centre, in a Green Thumb production that Jerry Wasserman described as "thought provoking and viscerally powerful."[3] At the 2005 Jessie Richardson Theatre Awards (celebrating excellence in Vancouver's theatre community), *RAGE* was named Outstanding Production and Michele Riml received the Sydney Risk Award for Outstanding Original Play. Green Thumb's 2007 remount featured the original cast and played in Vancouver and Victoria; later that same year, Regina's Globe Theatre staged a production of their own. Théâtre la Catapulte's French-language version, translated by Sarah Migneron, has been performed in Ottawa, Toronto, and Sudbury.

RAGE's exploration of a topical issue like teen violence exemplifies how the type of subject matter favoured in contemporary Canadian TYA foregrounds feeling and emotions as essential elements. As an important point of context, "adults mediate the theatre-going practices of young people."[4] Teachers—not students—organize visits from touring productions or field trips to theatre venues, and even with shows that offer evening and weekend performances for adolescents (as was the case with the premiere of *RAGE*), parents and other adults often play a key role. Schools comprise the primary consumers for TYA

2 "About," *Green Thumb Theatre*, n.d., accessed 1 Sep. 2013. http://greenthumb.bc.ca/index.php/about-green-thumb/.

3 Jerry Wasserman, "RAGE," *Vancouverplays.com*, Nov. 2004, accessed 1 Sep. 2013. http://www.vancouverplays.com/theatre/reviews_theatre/review_rage_2004.shtml.

4 Nicholas Hanson, "Back to the Books: Evaluating the Economic Factors Behind Literature-based Theatre for Young Audiences Productions," *The Lion & Unicorn* 36.2 (2012): 193–208.

activities and they exert their will accordingly; as noted youth theatre scholar Roger Bedard bluntly describes, "School agendas dominate virtually every aspect of professional TYA companies, including: the subject matter, length, and style of the plays presented."[5] In Canada, the increased pressure to cover curricular expectations, especially at the secondary level, has compelled many schools to view theatre productions as frivolous and distracting; in response, TYA companies have developed shows with content that explicitly targets scholastic concepts. Theatre for adolescents often conjures perceptions of clichéd school assemblies with blunt messages like "just say no"; the emphasis of cognition over emotion reduces those "issue plays" to didactic lectures, at least from the perspective of students. Indeed, a play written about a topical concern might satisfy gatekeepers like teachers and principals, but holding the attention of students is another matter altogether, and therein lies the role of feeling. Green Thumb's mission statement declares their intention to "stimulate empathy,"[6] a goal that requires abstract ideas to be imbedded into characters that resemble real people who face complicated life situations. In the case of *RAGE*, oppositional beliefs about violence are personified in its two characters: Laura, the school guidance counsellor who decorates her office with a poster proclaiming, "There is no way to peace. Peace is the way," and Raymond, who adopts the moniker Rage because of his proclivity to "yell, kick stuff." Over the course of the play, Laura reveals her dissatisfaction with her career and her boyfriend, while Rage discloses his resentment of school bullies and his parents. The blurring of philosophical convictions with personal experiences not only catalyzes Laura and Rage's debate, but also prompts the audience to construct mental images of the anecdotes described by the characters. As a result of the brain activity required for that visualization process, spectators deepen their sense of empathy for both of the characters' situations. Thus TYA companies boost the marketability of their plays to school officials by featuring curricular topics like "teen violence," but they establish a rapport with adolescent audiences by facilitating emotional connections to the characters.

5 Roger L. Bedard, "Negotiating Marginalization: TYA and the Schools," *Youth Theatre Journal* 17.1 (2003): 90–101.

6 "About."

In addition to subject matter, the material conditions common to contemporary theatre for adolescents, reflected in a number of *RAGE*'s functional attributes, contribute to an emphasis on feeling. When productions are created to tour schools (or at least with the flexibility to do so after a mainstage run), they need to consider financial realities. In the current Canadian era, TYA productions often travel between venues in a single cargo van, which limits the space for physical objects and technical equipment, as well as the number of actors; moreover, the need to schedule performances within the structure of a school day has resulted in intermissionless plays with running times between forty-five and seventy-five minutes. With a two-person cast, one-act structure, modest set pieces, and minimal requirements for lighting or theatrical effects, *RAGE* typifies the impact of material conditions on TYA playwriting. By confining the characters in an enclosed space for a sustained conversation, Riml uses a device that appears throughout the theatre-for-adolescents canon, including Clem Martini's 1995 *Illegal Entry*, which chronicles a trio of would-be teenage thieves who lock themselves in a garage, and *In This World*, Hannah Moscovitch's 2009 play that places two sixteen-year-old girls on chairs in a small school office. These intrinsically confrontational scenarios maintain audience interest by relying on human tension instead of theatrical spectacle. The igniting of interpersonal powder kegs plays directly to the aesthetic preferences of adolescents; as playwright and Concrete Theatre artistic co-director Mieko Ouchi describes, "As young people transition from childhood into their teens, this often coincides with a rejection of non-realism, which is seen as childish, and a new association between 'good' acting and realism and emotional intensity."[7] Moreover, the depiction of passionate moments on stage stimulates emotional responses in the audience. From verbal sparring to physical confrontations, *RAGE* contains no shortage of thrilling exchanges that make the audience "feel connected to other selves in our world by virtue of our brain's replication of the neuronal basis (or biological precedent) of what we observe on other's faces."[8] As such,

7 Mieko Ouchi, Personal Interview, 11 Mar. 2011.

8 Erin Hurley, *Theatre & Feeling* (New York: Palgrave Macmillan, 2010), 35.

playwrights like Riml navigate the material conditions facing TYA by focusing on the human element of theatre, which augments the capacity for the audience's feeling response.

Though a number of youth-oriented plays deal with violence, *RAGE* differs in one important way: the onstage presence of a gun. In *The Stage Life of Props*, Andrew Sofer dedicates an entire chapter to guns, noting that the prop "traditionally demonstrates a character's control over temporal fate (even if that control is exerted only by bringing it to a full stop)."[9] Though adolescent audiences are more familiar with action movies than Anton Chekhov, they recognize his dictum that a loaded gun placed on stage must be fired. When Rage pulls a pistol from his jacket, he not only raises the stakes of the narrative, but also ruptures the illusion that zero-tolerance school policies can effectively create safe spaces. Further to that point, people may question Riml's use of a literal weapon to address the issue of teen violence; indeed, Colin Thomas's review of *RAGE* opines that the play focuses "too much about the thrill of the gun and not enough about the issues the gun represents."[10] Riml understands, though, that the thrill of the gun *is* the issue; youth violence is a savage, corporeal phenomenon, not a decorous, abstract one. The mere sight of a firearm—even a prop one on stage—stimulates affective responses like sweating and tightening muscles. By situating the play in a school office, Riml evokes the audience's contextual knowledge of Columbine, Newtown, and other tragedies, amplifying the autonomous reactions caused by the viewing of a "fake" gun in a "fake" school (and just imagine the affective potential of the gun in performances of *RAGE* that take place at actual school buildings). If, as many school officials believe, plays for adolescents should emphasize social issues, *RAGE*'s inclusion of a gun furthers their goal by using heightened emotional moments to sear memories of the production into the minds of the spectator, staying with them far longer than a pedantic lecture about the same topic.

9 Andrew Sofer, *The Stage Life of Props* (Ann Arbor: U of Michigan P, 2003), 171.

10 Colin Thoms, "RAGE," *Georgia Straight*, 2 Dec. 2004, accessed 1 Sep. 2013. http://www.straight.com/article/rage.

RAGE was first produced by Green Thumb Theatre in Vancouver, British Columbia, and presented by the Vancouver East Cultural Centre in 2005. The play featured the following cast and creative team:

Laura: Leslie Jones
Raymond (Rage): David Beazley

Director: Patrick McDonald
Lighting design: Jonathon Ryder
Production design: Craig Hall

This production was also presented as part of the PuSh International Performing Arts Festival. It went on to win the Jessie Richardson Theatre Award for best production (Green Thumb) and best new script (Michele Riml).

The play is approximately seventy minutes in length and performed without an intermission.

CHARACTERS

Laura
Rage

LAURA's office. A makeshift high-school counselling office. A desk, a couple of chairs, a phone, and a filing cabinet. Well organized. The walls are covered with a school calendar, a chalkboard, and two posters: a picture of Gandhi and a poster that reads "There is no way to peace. Peace is the way." LAURA *Whalen, thirty-eight, speaks on the phone. She packs up her desk and applies lipstick from her purse while she talks.*

LAURA: You're going to love it. It's my favourite. I have one thing I have to take care of and then I'm on my way. A kid I have to talk to. No, I won't be late. I'll be at the restaurant by six. I will eat. We'll have lots of time before the show . . . Hey, that's not fair. I already agreed: no serious talks. I said I wouldn't bring it up again. We'll just have a nice, quiet evening. Did you feed Ginger? I'm not reminding. I'm just asking. Sorry. Okay. I should go . . . yes. It's on. You did? Well the signal's hit and miss down here. What? No. Forget it, I can't. No, I feel silly . . . all right, all right . . .

LAURA *sings a few lines of "Do You Hear the People Sing" from Les Misérables before she's interrupted.*

What? I wasn't going to sing the whole . . . you asked me to. Never mind. It's not important. It's all right. Okay. Six. Let me go then.

LAURA *hangs up and gathers herself. She opens the door.* RAYMOND *Stitt, seventeen, enters. He carries a backpack.*

Come on in, Raymond. Sorry to keep you waiting. It's been one of those days. Let me just get your file here.

LAURA *grabs his file and beckons him in.*

Have a seat.

RAGE: I'd rather stand.

LAURA: Okay.

RAGE: And my name is Rage.

LAURA: Rage.

RAGE: Uh-huh.

LAURA: Is that what you call yourself?

RAGE: That's what my friends call me.

LAURA: Rage.

RAGE: Uh-huh.

LAURA: Why?

RAGE: 'Cause I go off sometimes.

LAURA: You go off?

RAGE: I go off. When I get pissed. I get mad. I yell, kick stuff, shit like that.

LAURA: How long have your friends called you Rage for?

RAGE: Forever. Were you singing in here?

LAURA: What? No. Oh you heard. No, I just . . . I was talking too . . . I'm going to see a musical tonight. *Les Misérables.*

RAGE: Victor Hugo.

LAURA: Yeah, with songs. I'm not sure he would have approved.

RAGE: So, am I out?

LAURA: What?

RAGE: Are they kicking me out?

LAURA: We're just here to talk.

RAGE: My grades have fallen.

LAURA: Yes, Raymond, you went from an A in History to a B+; you're every teacher's worst nightmare. I actually wanted to talk to you today about your oral history report . . .

RAGE: Yeah, I figured.

LAURA: I'm sure you did. So do you want to tell me what you were thinking?

RAGE: What's the point? Just tell me if I'm getting kicked out.

LAURA: Look I'm not going to lie to you. We're definitely concerned about a few things.

RAGE: What's there to be "concerned" about?

LAURA: Well, let's see. You kicked a hole in the wall of your History class, you brought a girl to tears, and to top it off you identify with one of the worst murderers of the twentieth century. And you think there's no reason for concern.

RAGE: Oh that.

LAURA: That.

RAGE: I didn't say I identified with him.

LAURA: Well, what did you say then? That's what I want to hear.

RAGE: I said I could see his side. And I articulated it. That's a good thing, isn't it? To see the other side. To put yourself in someone else's shoes. To know where they're coming from . . .

LAURA: So how did his shoes feel?

RAGE: *(fooling with her)* Familiar.

LAURA: Really? How?

RAGE: Like you really want to know.

LAURA: Like I really do.

RAGE: I don't know. Just doing the research and stuff I could see he was kind of persecuted before he became all-powerful.

LAURA: Okay. So was it the persecuted or the powerful that felt familiar?

RAGE: Familiar's not really the right word.

LAURA: It was your word.

She makes a note.

The school is concerned . . .

RAGE: Now the school is concerned.

LAURA: You really scared some of your fellow students.

RAGE: And they come whining to you?

LAURA: No. Mr. Lam could see . . .

RAGE: It was a fucking oral report. With handouts and diagrams. Ooh scary . . .

LAURA: Come on, Raymond, language— It was the content. And how you delivered that content. You know that.
RAGE: They didn't get it. They could have started with, "Excuse me, Raymond, we're having trouble understanding your point, please clarify."
LAURA: Could they? And what would you have done differently? Really?

RAGE shrugs.

So you would have continued on in the same vein? In a hateful and degrading oratory about the holocaust.
RAGE: Did Lam even give you my report to read?
LAURA: Mr. Lam gave me some of the highlights. It wasn't hard to get the picture.
RAGE: So no. The answer is no. "Mr. Lam did not give me the report to read. No, Raymond, I have not read the oral report about which we are now having a discussion."
LAURA: Calm down, Raymond. Have a seat.
RAGE: I have an opinion about the report. I have made a decision about you based on the report, but I have in fact not read the report.
LAURA: I think I got the gist of it.
RAGE: What does that mean?
LAURA: It means based on what Mr. Lam told me I think I have a pretty clear understanding of what went on, but . . .
RAGE: What about my side?
LAURA: Wait a second, that's what I was just about to say. I got Mr. Lam's interpretation. Now I'm interested in yours.
RAGE: Is that how you read a newspaper? Just the highlights.
LAURA: I don't actually read newspapers.
RAGE: Oh, that's reassuring.

RAGE moves to light a cigarette.

LAURA: Come on, Raymond. You know better.

RAGE: Do you smoke?

LAURA: No.

RAGE: Not ever?

LAURA: Raymond, if we're going to continue this discussion, you're going to have to sit down and talk to me. I'm here to hear your side of the story, remember?

RAGE puts his backpack on the floor and sits down at a table with chairs.

RAGE: They just totally dismissed my argument. Nobody even asked a question.

LAURA: And what did you want them to ask?

RAGE: Hitler was a powerful speaker. The way he spoke, delivered his ideas, was as important as what he was actually saying. I wanted to show them that. He was a preacher as much as a politician. He was dedicated to his beliefs and his delivery reflected that dedication. The pageantry, the ritual created a church for the people and he was God to them.

LAURA: And he was a sadistic madman.

RAGE: Millions of people followed him. Don't you want to know why? Don't you think that's an interesting discussion?

LAURA: But the way you went about it . . .

RAGE: The way I went about it wasn't expected because what is the point of doing what is expected! What is the point of standing up there and giving a bunch of dates and saying the Holocaust was bad and Hitler was bad and regurgitating Lam's history lessons so everyone can nod their heads and be right, and feel right and not even think for one second about where Hitler was coming from, and how it happened and who was listening to him . . . people listened to him, you know.

Pause.

I wanted them to ask why.

LAURA: And you think a diatribe on the destruction of the Jews, yelling obscenities in class, kicking . . .

RAGE: I was acting like Hitler.

LAURA: Are you sure? You're sure you just weren't out of control?

RAGE: This is pointless.

LAURA: Look, I'll tell you something: I think your commitment is really admirable, if a little misguided.

RAGE: So now they're gonna kick me out of school.

LAURA: I don't know. It all depends on what I say right here.

She taps her file.

RAGE: On what you say.

LAURA: I'm a very fair person, Raymond. Really. And I do want to hear what you have to say. That's why I think maybe we should slot some more time for tomorrow.

RAGE: You said you needed to see me today.

LAURA: Yes I did. And I'm sorry I kept you waiting. But I'm late now and I want to give you the time you deserve.

RAGE: I waited outside for fifteen minutes. While you were singing.

Pause.

LAURA: Okay. How have you gone off, Raymond?

RAGE: Like you don't have a list right there.

LAURA: I know about the wall. And the garbage can incident.

RAGE: Lame.

LAURA: It was destroyed. What were you trying to say there, Raymond?

RAGE: Nothing. It was a fucking garbage can . . . language, I know.

LAURA: School property.

RAGE: I did my time.

LAURA: *(checks file)* A three-day suspension.

RAGE: I was so far behind when I got back.

LAURA: So what else?

RAGE: What are you looking for? I don't torture animals or mutilate bugs if that's what you're looking for.
LAURA: Why would you even say that?
RAGE: Serial killer, major psycho profile. Alarm bells ringing.
LAURA: I don't think you're a psycho, as you put it. But it's my job to determine if you're a threat to other people, or to yourself.
RAGE: But you've already decided that.
LAURA: No, I haven't . . .
RAGE: You've got the whole Hitler story, my file. You said people think I'm a threat. Cut to the chase.
LAURA: Look, Raymond, I'm not sure what exactly you were doing. But I do get the sense that you were trying to do something . . . Obviously you're very bright. And I know you've thought about this a lot. But the school has to have a zero tolerance for violence. Especially now. You understand that, don't you?
RAGE: I kicked a wall. I didn't hit anyone.
LAURA: It's not just your violent action. Violence starts with the way we think about people. The way we talk about them. There's something about your identification with Hitler, the way you express yourself . . .
RAGE: *(mad)* Oh my God, I don't identify with Hitler! I was just making a point.
LAURA: You said his shoes felt familiar.
RAGE: . . . Because I was trying to see it from his side, right? To understand where he was coming from. A whole bunch of people identified with him. Isn't that interesting to you?
LAURA: Interesting? Maybe. Tragic? Yes.
RAGE: But not worth pursuing.
LAURA: I didn't say that. I think your choice of delivery is maybe more interesting. Or telling.
RAGE: "There is one principle that cannot fail to keep a man in everlasting ignorance. That principle is . . . "
LAURA: " . . . contempt prior to investigation." Herbert Spencer.
RAGE: You said that in that peace speech you made in assembly last year. After that girl was killed.

LAURA: You have a good memory.

RAGE: It was a good speech.

LAURA: Thank you.

RAGE: You said a lot of good stuff in that speech.

LAURA: I worked on it. It was important to me.

RAGE: That's what I was doing. Investigating. I figured if I could get in Hitler's shoes, act it out, kind of like almost be like him, I could get in his head too. If you can get in someone's head you have a better chance of understanding them.

LAURA: I think you're right about that.

RAGE: You do?

LAURA: Yeah, I do. But I don't know if you kicking walls or yelling in people's faces is the way to understanding. I do know that we should talk about this a little more. How about after math tomorrow?

RAGE: What, that's it?

RAYMOND gets up from his chair, taking his backpack.

LAURA: You have a free period, right?

RAGE: Just tell me now if I'm getting the boot.

LAURA: Raymond. I told you. I don't know. That will depend . . .

RAGE: *Les Mis* calls.

LAURA: Prior commitment.

RAGE: Are you going with someone?

LAURA: Yes.

RAGE: Husband?

LAURA: Partner. Raymond.

RAGE: Okay. Just one thing. That speech—your speech—do you really believe all that stuff? About being peace.

LAURA: I do.

RAGE: You don't believe in violence?

LAURA: No, I don't. I don't think it ultimately works. I mean how could someone—anyone—really *believe in* violence? It's like saying you believe in death.

RAGE: You could believe in its power. That it can change things.

LAURA: For the worse.

RAGE: Wars change things.

LAURA: Peace is what's really going to change things.

RAGE: So what? Everyone's gonna just stop fighting and be peaceful?

LAURA: Pretty radical idea, huh? No more fighting. Believing in non-violent solutions to all problems. What a concept.

RAGE: How is that even possible?

LAURA: It starts with ourselves. I don't have all the answers, but I know I can work on me. I can be part of the solution.

RAGE: *(looks to the poster of Gandhi)* "You must be the change you want to see in the world."

LAURA: You've been reading.

RAGE: I rented the DVD.

LAURA: I really do want to talk to you, Raymond; this is important.

RAGE: You know what Gandhi said about the Jews?

LAURA: When?

RAGE: In that letter he wrote. He basically said they should take what they were getting. They didn't put it in the movie. I googled him too.

LAURA: That's not what he meant at all.

RAGE: He said they should stay in Germany and take what they were getting.

LAURA: No, he called on the Jewish people to resist the Nazis with dignity and non-violence.

RAGE: And how were they supposed to do that?

LAURA: He believed that if enough people resisted non-violently they would call on the conscience of their oppressor and stop the oppression.

RAGE: Call on the conscience of a Nazi? What conscience?

LAURA: I believe he meant calling on the conscience of the German people.

RAGE: Did he even know what the Jews were going through? Did he have any idea?

LAURA: He'd seen his own people suffer. He knew about the power of non-violence. He'd suffered for it.

RAGE: So he didn't eat once in a while. Big deal. He wasn't roasted in an oven.

LAURA: I imagine Gandhi had no idea about the horror that was facing the Jewish people. It would be a terribly hard thing to imagine.
RAGE: Right, but he still had an opinion about what they should do . . .
LAURA: He didn't believe in war. It was one idea.
RAGE: It's easy to have ideas when you don't have to confront anything.
LAURA: He had a different way of confronting things. Taken out of context it seems callous, but if you look at his life—"Evil can be confronted through the power of love."
RAGE: So he was going to love Hitler off the planet. What about apathy?
LAURA: What do you mean?
RAGE: Can apathy be confronted through the power of love? Can people that just don't care one way or the other get off their asses and really help when confronted with love? I think evil does a better job at getting people moving. People don't really do anything unless their asses are on the line.
LAURA: I don't know . . .

She looks at the clock.

Raymond, I appreciate your passion, but this is a much larger conversation.
RAGE: You know what the politicians all said about that thing in Colorado? When those guys killed all those kids at Columbine? That it's happening too often. Like if it happened once in a while that would be okay.
LAURA: I agree with you.
RAGE: That if it happened once in a while it would be okay?

LAURA *puts on her coat.*

LAURA: No. That we're basically desensitized to violence, that we can tolerate a certain amount and we get queasy when the boundaries are pushed, but we stretch those boundaries all the time. That's why I think violent movies and games are dangerous. That, by the way, is why I don't read newspapers.
RAGE: Have you got kids?
LAURA: Not yet.

RAGE: I bet if you did you wouldn't let them go to any good movies.
LAURA: Not all movies are violent.
RAGE: You think you can protect kids from the world that way. They aren't going to know what hit them when they get out there. What about when some asshole kid starts picking on them because they've got acne or something?
LAURA: Why are you so angry?
RAGE: Well it isn't because of the movies. Movies don't make you do things. I never wanted to drink blood 'cause of *Dracula*. Way more people see violent movies and don't do violence.
LAURA: They may not "do" violence as you say, but I think they become more complicit to it. It just becomes the norm, the way things are. They participate by not making a choice.
RAGE: Is that why you went on about "being peace" when that girl was killed?
LAURA: It was such a terrible, senseless thing that happened. I didn't want it to just go by without trying to do something . . . if we could change . . .
RAGE: She's dead. You can't change that.
LAURA: But we can learn from it. Try in some way to honour her by committing to building a world where it's not so easy for all this anger and hatred to take us to these places. If we can't commit to peace in our own schools and homes and body, how can we expect the world to change?
RAGE: The world isn't going to change.
LAURA: *(points to her poster)* I believe it can. Through peace.
RAGE: So what do you do if someone attacks you?
LAURA: Physically?
RAGE: Yeah . . . attacks you.
LAURA: A verbal assault can be just as vicious as a physical blow.
RAGE: I'm talking about getting kicked in the head—a physical attack. Then what would you do?
LAURA: Well, hopefully I haven't created that in my life.
RAGE: What?
LAURA: Hopefully I'm not attracting it on some level.
RAGE: But it could happen.
LAURA: Of course it could happen.

RAGE: You have to defend yourself.
LAURA: You can defend yourself in different ways. There's an ancient principle of martial arts. That which you resist persists. When someone is about to strike a blow you merely move away and the force of his own aggression will take him to the ground.
RAGE: Oh my God, yeah, and then he gets ups and pounds you for making him look like an idiot.
LAURA: Well, it's just a premise, Raymond. Martial arts aren't my forte, so to speak. Look, this is all very interesting. I really would . . .

RAGE *blocks the door.*

I have to . . .
RAGE: Can you just give me an example. Of being peace?
LAURA: Raymond
RAGE: Please. I'm not joking. It's important.
LAURA: Being peace is having fire hoses turned on you and you just keep marching.

Pause.

RAGE: Have you ever had a fire hose turned on you?
LAURA: It's an example.
RAGE: Well, just so you know, when you have a fire hose turned on you, you can't even stand up, let alone march. The pressure of a fire hose can be one thousand pounds of water per second. If you hold a fire hose too close to a person you could actually rupture their internal organs with the impact . . .
LAURA: *(getting mad)* I said it was a metaphor, Raymond. Inspiration from the Civil Rights Movement.
RAGE: Okay. But can you give me something from this century. Closer to home. Something you've actually done as a pacifist.
LAURA: It's not one thing. It's a way of behaving. Of approaching things.
RAGE: But what have you done to make a difference?

LAURA: I try to make a difference every day. I take responsibility for creating my reality. I don't blame. I avoid conflict. And I practise . . . through yoga . . . through breathing. Imagine if every person in the world were committed to being peaceful. We'd have peace.
RAGE: Yoga.
LAURA: Hey, the yoga is just a means to an end. And it beats kicking holes in the wall.
RAGE: How would you know?

RAGE gives up. LAURA steps back from the door, puts her purse down.

LAURA: Okay. Okay. Wait. Sit down. Let me share something with you.

RAYMOND sits down.

You have to start with yourself, right?
RAGE: Whatever.
LAURA: Okay. Well, the other day I was in a coffee shop reading a book. And it was nice. Peaceful. And then I notice this older man sitting across from me. Staring. I look up and as soon as I meet his eyes, he starts talking. He says hello, I say hello. I try to get back to my book, but he just starts talking. He tells me that he's been in an accident and broken all his toes on both feet. That he has trouble moving around, how he had to cut the front out of his shoes . . . he goes on and on . . . about his son not visiting and then about his daughter-in-law not cooking or something . . . My coffee was getting cold. I just want him to be quiet. But he keeps talking about how his toes get cold, how he can't elevate them properly for blood flow, how much TV he was watching. It was so irritating. I could feel myself getting angry. Until I took a breath. Just reminded myself to be in the moment. I made a choice to be with this guy instead of worrying about my book and coffee. And the second I did, you know what I saw? He couldn't get out of the chair. The whole time he'd been talking to me, he'd been struggling to get out of the chair. He was rambling on to cover up the fact that he could not get out of the chair. He was

embarrassed. He had no balance. And I'd been too preoccupied to notice this poor man just needed help to get out of the chair.

RAGE: So?

LAURA: So I helped him out of the chair.

RAGE: That's it. Helping a guy with no toes.

LAURA: He had toes. They were broken.

RAGE: So that's it.

LAURA: It's a subtle thing, I know. Being present. Being kind. Noticing what's really going on.

RAGE: Fuck. That's depressing.

LAURA: Well, I told you it's something you practise.

RAGE: That's practising non-violence? You don't give anyone the finger when you're driving, do you?

LAURA: No, I don't.

RAGE: Do you ever tell anyone to shut up in a movie theatre?

LAURA: You don't have to say shut up to get someone to be quiet.

RAGE: You're a vegetarian, aren't you?

LAURA: Why?

RAGE: You're just that type. Non-violence towards chickens, right?

LAURA: It might be a good place for you to start. I eat fish.

RAGE: Fish have feelings too.

LAURA: No, actually, they don't, Raymond. Look . . .

RAGE: You have to get to *Les Mis*.

LAURA: I'm sorry.

RAGE: Me too.

LAURA: We will sort this out tomorrow.

RAGE: I may not be here tomorrow.

LAURA: Is that a threat?

RAGE: I might be sick tomorrow.

LAURA: Well, I guess that's your choice, isn't it?

RAGE: Everything's a choice with you, isn't it?

LAURA: We all make them.

RAGE: You ever been in a dangerous situation?

LAURA: Have you?

RAGE: Life is dangerous.

LAURA: You sound like you feel threatened, Raymond.

RAGE: That's when "being peace" gets hard. When it gets real.

LAURA: Is someone threatening you, Raymond?

RAGE: You're the one kicking me out of school.

LAURA: How are things at home?

RAGE: Here we go.

LAURA: What?

RAGE: Psychoanalysis 101. The mother did it.

LAURA: Maybe we could bring your mother in . . . to talk. Do you get along with your parents?

RAGE: Yep.

LAURA: Your parents are together.

RAGE: Glued.

LAURA: What does your dad do?

RAGE: He's a security guard for Hydro.

LAURA: And your mom?

RAGE: She works at home.

LAURA: She's a stay-at-home mom.

RAGE: Yep.

LAURA: That's something in this day and age.

RAGE: She's something, all right. It's a bit of a broom closet you've got here.

LAURA: It's just temporary. Until they get me an office. Do your parents get along?

RAGE: They go along.

LAURA: So they fight.

RAGE: My mother has never raised her voice in her life.

LAURA: That's admirable.

RAGE: She says everything very softly.

LAURA: She sounds nice.

RAGE: She's a cunt.

RAGE stares at LAURA.

LAURA: Raymond, that kind of language is wholly inappropriate and I won't tolerate it in here. It's offensive and demeaning to your mother and me. It's exactly what I'm talking about. Violence starts with the way we think and talk about people.

RAGE: Inappropriate means like when something doesn't fit, right?

LAURA: It does not fit at all.

RAGE: But you wanted to know about my mother?

LAURA: Yes, I do, but not if you're going to insult . . .

RAGE: It fits.

LAURA: What?

RAGE: The word. It fits.

LAURA: Okay, Raymond, that's enough. I can see there's a problem here. And I don't doubt that there's something going on with your mom and you. I can't get anywhere with you if you are going to communicate like this.

RAGE: Do you even want to hear what I have to say about anything?

LAURA: Yes I do. But not if you're going to use language like that or threaten me. There have to be rules of discussion.

RAGE sits, settling in.

RAGE: Rules of discussion. Rules of engagement. Military stuff is cool. Organized. There are rules. I don't want to "Yes sir, no sir" anyone myself. But I can respect it, you know. Like that thing in Colorado. It's too bad about the kids at that school but there's one thing you've got to admire about those shooters: they had a plan, right? Like 9/11. They set a goal. They had a mission and they were willing to die for it . . . like soldiers, right? I mean, you might not have been on their side of the war, but you can respect them for their follow-through. That they stood for it.

LAURA: You think they were fighting a war, walking in on innocent children and shooting them . . .

RAGE: "I submit to you that if a man does not have something worth dying for, he does not deserve to live." MLK.

LAURA: Martin Luther King was a pacifist. He wasn't talking about flying planes into buildings.
RAGE: Those Columbine guys were fed up. No one was listening to them. That was their point.
LAURA: I'm listening, Raymond.
RAGE: You want me to talk but if I say the wrong thing I get kicked out of school. If you don't agree with my feelings . . .
LAURA: There are no right and wrong feelings.
RAGE: Then why did you call me in here?
LAURA: To talk about choices and appropriate means of expression.
RAGE: So basically the rule is express your feelings, but not if the people in control don't like them. You're either with us or against us? I don't believe in censorship and I'm not a hypocrite. So who decides about these appropriate means of expression?
LAURA: Look, we all enter into a social contract.
RAGE: Well, I didn't sign up.
LAURA: Sure you did. You signed up when you came to school, when you hung your coat in your locker, when you got on the bus this morning. You sign up when you accept the benefits of our society.
RAGE: The benefits of our society. You know what makes me really mad? People who don't tell the truth. I hate that. You use all these words like justice and peace and benefits of our society, but they don't mean anything when some kid's pounding on you 'cause you looked at him funny, or you're getting kicked out of school for doing what's written on the blackboard . . . freely expressing yourself. You know there's a gun they make with a holder for an MP3 player on it? I read about it on the Net. It cracked me up, eh. The US Army uses it. We take killing very seriously, but hey, if you want to get down with Eminem while you blast the fuckers, here's a nifty little gizmo.

LAURA turns her back on RAYMOND, moving back to her desk.

LAURA: Look, we're way off track here.

RAGE pulls a gun from his jacket and points it at LAURA.

RAGE: I'd like to talk about choice for a minute.
LAURA: Is that real?
RAGE: It's a Colt 45. My dad uses it for target practice.
LAURA: Put it down. You can't have . . . this isn't a joke, Raymond. Put it down.
RAGE: Have a seat, Ms. Whalen.
LAURA: I . . .
RAGE: Sit down.

RAYMOND slams a chair down and LAURA sits in it, her eyes on the gun.

LAURA: What are you doing? Please, put it down.
RAGE: I will. I will put it down. I'll put it down right here. But here's the deal. One of us isn't going to leave this room today. You're going to make a choice.
LAURA: What choice?
RAGE: A choice for peace. A choice for violence. I don't know . . .
LAURA: What are you talking about?
RAGE: It's very simple. Me or you. It's your choice.
LAURA: It's my choice?
RAGE: You can shoot me and live. Or I can shoot you. One or the other.
LAURA: What? Why . . .
RAGE: Well, if you shoot me, you're not much of a pacifist, are you? And if you let me shoot you, then you really make your point, don't you? I mean you really stand for what you believe.

RAYMOND puts the gun on the table between them. He sits.

LAURA: Okay, you've made your point.
RAGE: I don't think so.
LAURA: I see what you're trying to do here and I don't appreciate it.
RAGE: *(laughing)* You don't appreciate it? It's probably not appropriate either. But here it is: you get to make a choice. A real choice. We both get to test our

beliefs. In your speech. After that girl was killed. You said we all have to be an example. We all have to stand up against violence. Zero tolerance. Zero participation. Create a new model. A new way of being with each other. Based on respect, understanding, tolerance. You warned us it would be hard.

LAURA: Raymond . . .

RAGE: You meant it, didn't you?

LAURA: You know I did.

RAGE: Then I guess I'll have to kill you.

LAURA: No!

RAGE: Okay, you kill me.

LAURA: I would never . . .

RAGE: We'll see.

LAURA: Raymond, I can't do this. This exercise. Whatever you're doing here. Trying . . . please, you're scaring me . . . I don't want to . . .

LAURA moves to get out of her chair. RAGE slams his hands on the table.

RAGE: Sit down. The only choice you get here is me or you. That's what it comes down to. That's your choice.

LAURA: There are people here.

RAGE: So?

LAURA: So they'll catch you.

RAGE: Yeah.

LAURA: You'll ruin your life.

RAGE: What life?

LAURA: Your life . . . your future.

RAGE: Don't have one. Don't want one.

LAURA: Of course you do. We all have dreams.

RAGE: No we don't. Some of us are just trying to make it through the day. If you shoot me right now, you could still make *Les Mis*.

LAURA: Raymond, I'm not . . .

RAGE: Pick up the gun.

LAURA: No.

RAGE: Pick it up.

LAURA: I don't want to.

RAGE: You're going to confront me with the power of love?

LAURA: You're not evil.

RAGE: How do you know? Touch it.

LAURA: What?

RAGE: The gun. Touch it.

LAURA: I don't . . .

RAGE: Touch it!

LAURA *reaches out hesitantly.*

Hey!

LAURA *jumps back.*

One thing. If you pick it up, you better be prepared to use it, okay?

LAURA: I'm not picking it up.

RAGE: 'Cause if you go for my knee or something, or if you miss, it'd be real easy for me to get the gun. And then we're done. Clear?

LAURA: You told me to touch it.

RAGE: Yeah, touch it.

LAURA *touches the gun.*

You've never even seen one before have you? You've never even seen a gun.

LAURA: Not up close.

RAGE: When you shoot me at this range, the bullet will enter my skull or heart, depending where you aim. Will kill me immediately. Which is the best way. But I recommend you use both hands because there might be some kickback. Pick it up. Here, I'll turn my back.

LAURA: Raymond, there's something very wrong. I know. And I can get you help.

As RAGE *talks he plays at turning his back and then turning quickly back to* LAURA.

RAGE: I realize that this is not in your job description. Shooting the psycho kid. Especially when you called me in to assess whether I'm a threat to anyone or not. Gee, it looks like I do fall in the threat category . . . come on, pick it up. You know that whole thing about Gandhi and the salt mines? I never got that. So many people got hurt there. They always talk about Gandhi and his peaceful process, but then look at all those guys that walked up and got their heads bashed in. Did Gandhi get his head bashed in? No.

With RAGE*'s back turned,* LAURA *makes a move towards the door.* RAGE *anticipates this and blocks the door—fast—grabbing her by the arm and throwing her to the floor. He piles a bunch of boxes up in front of the door.*

RAGE: That was pretty pathetic.
LAURA: You think that this is the way to change my beliefs, Raymond?
RAGE: *(yelling)* Rage. My name is Rage. And only if you don't believe in them.
LAURA: I can't do this.
RAGE: I just want you to be who you say you are.
LAURA: You can't be who you are with a gun in your face.
RAGE: Why not? There's always a gun somewhere. Maybe this is who you are.
LAURA: What did I do?
RAGE: You talked about that girl like it was all about you, not about her. Everybody clapped for you. They weren't even thinking about her. You must have felt pretty good about yourself.
LAURA: I felt terrible about that girl. Karen. About what happened to her. That's why I made the speech. I was trying to . . .
RAGE: Trying to what?
LAURA: To make a difference. To use it as an opportunity.
RAGE: An opportunity for whom?
LAURA: For all of us. To find some meaning in a terrible tragedy. To learn and grow. To try and do things differently.

RAGE: She's dead. That's the meaning.

LAURA: What would you have said?

RAGE: Find those guys. Rip their nuts off. Show them they can't do that. Make them pay for what they did.

LAURA: But it wasn't you. It was me. You're the one talking about freedom of expression.

RAGE: Ironic, eh.

LAURA: I'm sorry if you didn't like what I said.

RAGE: I didn't say that. I think your commitment is "admirable, if a little misguided."

LAURA: What do you want me to do?

RAGE: Stand up for what you believe.

LAURA: This isn't going to change anything.

RAGE: Yes it will. It will change you. You get to be Gandhi. See if it works.

LAURA: I don't want to be Gandhi.

RAGE: Well, "be peace" then.

LAURA: Look, if this is about kicking you out, I don't make those decisions.

RAGE: You said it's all in what you say.

LAURA: Yes, but then I have to talk to people. It's a committee.

RAGE: Of course it is. Like everything else. Decide in a group. If anything goes wrong, blame the group. No personal responsibility. So what good are you then?

LAURA: I can influence their decision.

RAGE: You can't do dick. Lam already said I'm history. Just like his class. He hates me.

LAURA: How do you know he hates you?

RAGE: I know.

LAURA: He's wrong. We agreed I'd talk to you.

RAGE: You just make people feel like their side is heard. And you're not even very good at it.

LAURA: I told Mr. Lam I wanted to see you before any measures were taken.

RAGE: So it is decided.

LAURA: No . . . he might have wanted that . . . but there's a procedure. You're smart. I can see that. I do want to hear about your ideas, but not like this.
RAGE: Sorry, not your choice.

The phone rings. LAURA jumps up.

Leave it.
LAURA: We can stop it right here.
RAGE: And what? You can explain to everyone what a sick and misguided boy I am? How I just need someone to listen . . . Look at this office. You don't have any pull with the big boys. You don't even matter. Being peace just means you're not going to create any problems for anybody.
LAURA: That isn't true.
RAGE: How many days a week do you work?
LAURA: Three.
RAGE: And you're what? The guidance counsellor slash drama teacher slash student advisor?
LAURA: There are cutbacks, but I'm working . . .
RAGE: And Lam is here full time and he's the vice principal.
LAURA: They'll listen to me, Raymond.
RAGE: Clearly.
LAURA: I can still help you, Raymond.

The phone stops ringing.

RAGE: You keep doing that. Rage. My name is Rage, okay?
LAURA: Do you think anyone's going to remember your name if you kill me? Raymond Stitt—murderer. Better known as Rage. You'll be on the news for a few days. You'll be the kid who killed at Crescent High. That's your claim to fame. Another bully. Another maniac.
RAGE: Not if you shoot first.
LAURA: I'm not going to shoot you.

RAGE: Then you'll be a martyr, right? A martyr for the cause of peace. Willing to die for your cause . . .
LAURA: You'll be dead or I'll be dead! It isn't going to make a difference. No one is even going to know what went on here.

RAGE pulls a tape recorder from his bag.

RAGE: Ah, technology. I was gonna do video but I figured you'd be a little self-conscious with the whole camera thing. Great sound bites, eh? I don't think you can get the real person on film like you can with tape. Less obtrusive. More real.

He rewinds and stops the recorder a couple of times, picking up sound bites of him and LAURA talking.

LAURA: This is not real.
RAGE: No? This isn't part of the reality you're creating? If this stuff gets on the Net someone could put it against some cool music. We could be a club song. I hope it gets into the States. They are way better with this kinda stuff. So if you're dead, I'll play the tape, okay? It's incentive. Everyone will know you stand for what you believe in.
LAURA: The only conclusion that anyone would ever draw is that you're crazy.
RAGE: You said I wasn't crazy.
LAURA: I don't think you are.
RAGE: See, you have to ask yourself: what would Gandhi do? Or Martin Luther King? Those are your heroes. That's who you read. I mean, were they saying non-violence in all things, oh, um, except when someone's pointing a gun at you? They all fucking died for what they believed. They only got a chance to be something because they faced something. That's why people remember them, right? No one is ever going to remember you or anything you say if you live for a hundred years. But if you die for it . . . Fuck, man. Remember that teacher, that high-school counsellor? She preached non-violence, love in all situations, and she died for it. Like MLK.

LAURA: I'm not that per . . .
RAGE: You could have a poster with a quote on it.

The phone rings again.

Fuck! Pick it up. But don't say anything. Just fucking talk normal.

LAURA *picks up the phone.*

LAURA: Hello? Hi. Sorry. Yeah, I'm still here. You did. I'm just talking . . . I just finished talking to a student. I'm going to get my things together and I'll be on my way. What? Yes. I picked it up from the cleaner's. It's in my car.

RAGE *motions for her to hurry up.*

No. I can't. I really can't. Okay. I'll see you at the theatre. At the Vogue.

LAURA *hangs up.*

RAGE: What do you mean you can't? You really can't what?
LAURA: Sing. He wanted me to sing again. From *Les Mis*.
RAGE: And you're going to marry this guy?
LAURA: Yeah. I hope so.
RAGE: He's a loser.
LAURA: How would you know?
RAGE: He fucking makes you sing on the phone. He likes *Les Mis*.
LAURA: He's never seen it. I like it. He's going for me.
RAGE: You're forcing him.
LAURA: I bought the tickets. They were a present.
RAGE: Don't you think it's kind of weird that they sing about the French Revolution and you cry while they all die.
LAURA: It's beautiful.
RAGE: It's violent.

LAURA: It's theatre.
RAGE: You said the Vogue.
LAURA: What?
RAGE: The Vogue. You said the Vogue. *Les Mis* isn't at the Vogue.
LAURA: Yes it is.

RAYMOND loses it. He kicks over the trash can and gets into LAURA's face. LAURA crouches down by the desk, trying to hide from him as he throws things around the room, sweeps books and pens from the table. Raging.

RAGE: No it's fucking not! Don't lie to me, you fucking bitch. You said you wouldn't lie to me. You're trying to send him a message. It's at the Queen Elizabeth. I saw the sign— You're not taking me seriously.
LAURA: Yes. I am. Raymond?
RAGE: This is how it is. You shoot me. Or I shoot you. I'm not fucking kidding about this. One of us is going to die. You want to do it now—you can go to your fucking show at the fucking Queen Elizabeth. But don't fuck around with me! What are you doing?

LAURA shakes her head.

Don't do that.

LAURA keeps her eyes closed and seems to be praying under her breath.

LAURA: *(inaudible)* Our Father who art in heaven, hallowed be thy name. Thy kingdom come, thy will be done, on earth as it is in heaven. Give us . . .

RAGE kicks the desk right by LAURA's head.

RAGE: Open your eyes. Stop that!
LAURA: What, or you'll shoot me?

LAURA gives up on the praying. She sits on the floor, leaning against the wall. RAGE pulls himself together, listens to hear if anyone is coming. He sits on the floor close to LAURA. Silence.

RAGE: You believe in God, too?
LAURA: I don't know. Do you?
RAGE: No.
LAURA: Clearly.
RAGE: What?

LAURA shakes her head.

I used to. When I was a kid. Think of God as this guy in the sky kind of deal. I thought like he was watching all of us like TV. Like each person is a channel. And when he's watching your channels he can make stuff happen in your life. Like if he doesn't like the way the story's going, he can change it. Then I figured there're so many channels to watch. He can't pay attention. He probably never even got to my channel.

He notices LAURA staring at him.

What?
LAURA: Nothing.
RAGE: Just say it.
LAURA: You're still a kid.
RAGE: Huh?
LAURA: You said when I was a kid.
RAGE: A little kid.
LAURA: Right.
RAGE: Obviously I don't think that anymore.
LAURA: That's too bad.
RAGE: Why?

LAURA: Because I think it's better to have something to believe in than nothing at all.
RAGE: So you do believe in God.
LAURA: I don't know. I think so.
RAGE: You think so?
LAURA: Is this about God?
RAGE: Believe me, this is not about God. But it is about what you believe. "Non-violence is not a garment to be put on and off at will. Its seat is in the heart, and it must be inseparable from our very being." You do believe that stuff, right? All that stuff you said.
LAURA: I didn't say that. Gandhi said that.
RAGE: You said it in your speech. You quoted him. You believe it, right?
LAURA: I want to.
RAGE: Then how would you resolve this situation, Ms. Whalen? What's your non-violent solution?
LAURA: I guess I would start by asking you to stop pointing that gun at me.
RAGE: Okay.
LAURA: And I would suggest that we talk.
RAGE: Talk. Okay then, so talk.
LAURA: Obviously you're really angry with me. I've done something to offend you. And I'm sorry . . . I'd like to understand you better . . .
RAGE: You didn't want to understand me better twenty minutes ago.
LAURA: I was distracted. I'm sorry. Why don't we say you've made your point. And talk now.
RAGE: Okay, talk.
LAURA: What friends call you Rage?
RAGE: Huh?
LAURA: You said your friends call you Rage.
RAGE: Diesel and Snoop.
LAURA: Diesel and Snoop.
RAGE: Eric Cummings and Harrif Dahl.
LAURA: How'd they get Diesel and Snoop, when you got Rage?

RAGE: Diesel farts. Gas—petroleum. Fuel—diesel. Harrif goes through people's stuff all the time. Snoop.

LAURA: And you go off.

RAGE: Yeah.

LAURA: Do your other friends call you Rage?

RAGE: I don't have other friends. You don't have a lot of friends either, eh?

LAURA: I have friends. So what do all the other kids call you? They make fun of you, don't they?

RAGE: Shit Stitt.

LAURA: What?

RAGE: Shit Stitt or Gaymond Shit or if all else fails just fag.

LAURA: Are you gay?

RAGE: Does it matter?

LAURA: No, but people tend to pick on people who are different.

RAGE: Yeah, well, fag seems to cover just about everything. Creative, eh?

LAURA: I used to get Einstein.

RAGE: Einstein?

LAURA: 'Cause I was smart.

RAGE: Smart's not different.

LAURA: It is to some people. My father used to say, "Being smart is the least attractive quality in a woman." Nice, eh?

RAGE: Enlightened.

LAURA: So these names, do they call them to your face?

RAGE: Not anymore. They don't have to. Violence starts with the way we think about people, right?

LAURA: Right.

RAGE: What do your friends call you now?

LAURA: They call me by my name. Laura.

RAGE: And your "partner"?

LAURA: He calls me Laura.

RAGE: No little pet names. Honey Bunny, Lovie Dove . . .

LAURA: No.

RAGE: He ever call you anything else? Anything mean?

LAURA: No. Never in a serious way.

RAGE: In what way? He playfully calls you bitch?

LAURA: No, he doesn't playfully call me those things. If he ever did use a term like that it would be in anger and he didn't mean it.

RAGE: What did you do?

LAURA: I didn't do anything.

RAGE: So he just said pass the potatoes, fuckhead? What did you do? Just tell me what he said.

LAURA: He just called me a name.

RAGE: What name?

LAURA: He called me a controlling bitch.

RAGE: Why? What did you do?

LAURA shakes her head. RAGE lifts up the chair he's leaning against and slams it down hard.

What did you do?

LAURA: I hid his golf clubs. It was stupid. I hid his golf clubs because we have an agreement about picking up the house. And I didn't think he was keeping up his end of the bargain. He missed a golf thing.

RAGE: He must have been pissed.

LAURA: We worked it out.

RAGE takes a soda from his bag.

RAGE: You want one?

LAURA shakes her head no.

If you kick the machine near the guy's can you get three for the price of one. But you gotta do it when the money's falling. So your father was an asshole, eh?

LAURA: He just had strong ideas about things.

RAGE: Like what?

LAURA: Me.

RAGE: So did you measure up?

Pause.

LAURA: I didn't picture myself in a basement.

RAGE: Why don't you quit? Fuck, you are a chicken, you know. You're a coward hiding behind your great big peace sign. See, we don't create our own reality. Reality creates us. Avoiding confrontation isn't being peace.

LAURA *gets up from the corner.*

Where are you going?

LAURA: *(resigned)* To my chair. You've got the gun, remember. Is that okay with you?

RAGE *pulls out another can.*

RAGE: Whatever. I got Sprite too.

LAURA: No thank you.

RAGE: My mom thinks this stuff is poison. She musta told me the story about the nail rotting in the can of Coke like a million times.

LAURA: You get a real kick out of it, don't you?

RAGE: What?

LAURA: Scaring people. The gun. Banging things. The Hitler thing?

RAGE: The Hitler thing was real.

LAURA: You know what I know about people who like to scare people? They're really the ones that are scared.

RAGE: Here we go.

LAURA: You're a smart guy. You could make your point without a gun. Without screaming at your classmates. I think you're scared, Raymond.

RAGE: Of what?

LAURA: Scared that no one will listen to you. That you don't really have anything to say? I don't know. You just seem scared to me.
RAGE: If I was scared I wouldn't be here. I have the courage to follow through. I'm not some fucking shuffler.
LAURA: Shuffler.
RAGE: Losers. People going nowhere. Who just get up every day and go to work at their crummy jobs and can't change anything and come home and watch fucking *American Idol* and go to sleep and get up and do it all over again.
LAURA: Maybe getting up is hard. Maybe the people that just get up and show up to their crummy jobs, that take the good and the bad, that make sense of it, find meaning where they can, hope for something better, maybe the shufflers are the ones with courage. Real courage. Did you ever think that maybe you're the one without any courage?
RAGE: Well, you're pretty brave giving me a lecture on courage when I hold the gun.
LAURA: Well, you seem to need a gun to say what you need to say.
RAGE: You started listening, didn't you? All people care about is who has the gun, and is it pointed at them. See, long as it's not pointed at them they can go about their business, acting like everything's all peaceful, or talking about how we live in a violent world and doing nothing about it, meanwhile some guy's getting killed.
LAURA: Some guy?

Pause.

What happened to you?
RAGE: Nothing.
LAURA: Who hurt you?
RAGE: Nobody hurts me.
LAURA: Anymore.

Pause.

So this is it, Raymond?

RAGE: My name is Rage.

LAURA: So you've said. But I figure if you're going to kill me I can at least call you what I want.

RAGE: I hate Raymond.

LAURA: You sure do.

RAGE: Hah.

LAURA: I'm just sorry you see yourself as such a victim.

RAGE: I'm not a victim. I'm choosing this.

LAURA: You're reacting to something I said or did. Victims are reactionary. What made you shut down?

RAGE: I'm not the one who's shut down.

LAURA: Your mom pushes your dad around. That's it? What does your dad do?

RAGE: He doesn't do anything. MIA. Missing in action. My mom starts talking and he goes to his room. That great space in his head. He zones.

LAURA: He doesn't stand up to her?

RAGE: We had this guy he works with over for dinner. We never have people for dinner. He was talking to this guy, Jim, they were joking and stuff. He leaned over his plate. Slurped up his spaghetti. She hates that. He had this smile on his face 'cause like he was having fun with this guy—his friend—from work. He didn't see her get up. Like she was just walking into the kitchen, you know. And when she walked by him, she just tipped the plate into his lap and kept walking. And he . . . he tried to laugh it off, right, like it was a joke or something. He just kind of picked it up and put it back on the table and kind of laughed and looked at his friend. And his friend didn't say nothing. Just kinda did this shrug thing. And we finished dinner. The guy just left. My dad walked him to the door. He had this big spaghetti stain on his pants. Then he went into the den and turned on the TV. And I . . . I cleared the table. That's my job. Clearing the table.

Pause.

LAURA: And you? How does she treat you?

RAGE: She loves me.

LAURA: Well that must be hard.

RAGE: Like I said. I don't care. About her or him or anyone.

LAURA: But I think you do care about people.

RAGE: No I don't.

LAURA: What about Diesel and Snoop?

RAGE: Losers.

LAURA: You don't care about them? How you're going to hurt them?

RAGE: They'll get over it.

LAURA: But you're close to them?

RAGE: Close is stretching the definition of our relationship.

LAURA: You hang out with them.

RAGE: Not anymore.

LAURA: Why?

RAGE: They bailed after the whole Hitler thing.

LAURA: They were intimidated.

RAGE: Whatever. They don't have the brainpower to think it through. They're sheep. But worse. 'Cause all the other sheep don't want anything to do with them, so they're like wannabe sheep. Pathetic.

LAURA: And they dropped you.

RAGE: So?

LAURA: So how does that make you feel?

RAGE: Freedom from stupidity is very liberating.

LAURA: I don't know, when even the losers don't want to hang out with you, it must hurt.

RAGE: Hey, I don't have any illusions about my place on the high-school food chain. I just know I don't like junk food.

LAURA: Can I hold the gun?

RAGE: What?

LAURA: I want to hold the gun now.

RAGE: Why?

LAURA: Well if I'm going to shoot you, I have to hold the gun. Right?

RAGE: If you try to get out . . .

LAURA: You've explained all that already.

RAGE hands her the gun. He steps back across the room, preparing himself to be shot. LAURA holds it, her hands shaking, and then points the gun at RAGE, who closes his eyes. They stand like this for a moment.

You talked to me. You like talking to me. It's not easy to shoot someone you've talked to.

She lowers the gun and then puts it on the desk.

I don't think either one of us is going to die today.

RAGE leaps across the room, pushing LAURA into her chair and yelling into her face. Furious.

RAGE: You're fucking stupid, lady. I didn't say it was going to be easy. You think we're all connected now. Because we had a little chat. Because I opened up. You think it's all about talking, don't you? It's all words. This shit—"Peace in action," "Be the change you want to see in the world." More talk. All these great words floating around out there. Everywhere. Anything you want to hear. There's so many of them it doesn't matter anymore. Talking is bullshit. My mother talks all the time. Teachers talk all the time. When I was in grade five I didn't talk and got the shit kicked out of me. Then I talked, and talking got the shit kicked out of me in grade six, seven, and eight.

RAGE paces with the gun, agitated. LAURA tries to collect herself. Beat.

LAURA: Could I have a cigarette?
RAGE: What?
LAURA: May I have a cigarette, please?

RAGE takes his pack out and offers a cigarette to LAURA.

RAGE: I knew you smoked.
LAURA: Thank you.
RAGE: Welcome.
LAURA: Light?

RAGE puts the gun down and lights LAURA's cigarette.

RAGE lights himself a cigarette. LAURA rolls her chair to the side. She leans back and blows the smoke up into the air. They stare at each other.

RAGE: What?
LAURA: Nothing.
RAGE: Say something.
LAURA: Why me?
RAGE: What?
LAURA: Why not Mr. Lam or Principal Getty?
RAGE: Because they're too easy. They *really* don't care. They just wrote me off. At least you're like a worthy opponent. With Lam—I'd be like here's the choice and he'd be like, "Fine, give me the gun"!
LAURA: And how did you know I wouldn't?
RAGE: It would bug you more. You're the pacifist, right.
LAURA: What if I'm not. What if I'm not sure what I believe . . . This all falls apart. You're not proving anything. You're just scaring your guidance counsellor. Maybe I'm not a worthy opponent.
RAGE: At least you think about stuff.
LAURA: But that's a good thing, right?
RAGE: Yeah. But you think about stuff and talk about stuff that's all powerful and meaningful and doesn't change a thing.
LAURA: How do you know that?
RAGE: Because nothing's changed.
LAURA: I changed you.
RAGE: The fuck you did.
LAURA: You said you don't care about anyone. Right?

RAGE shrugs.

You care about Karen. You heard my speech and that made you angry. Angry enough to express yourself. Angry enough to do this. Why would you go to this length if you didn't care?

RAGE: So even if I did care, what does that change?

LAURA: It changes you. You said it before.

RAGE: I'm not changed. I'm the same as always. Trust me.

LAURA: So tell me who you are.

RAGE: I know I'm not pretending to be someone I'm not.

LAURA: That really gets you, people pretending to be what they're not.

RAGE: It's hypocritical.

LAURA: But you don't care about anyone, so how do you ever get close enough to know they're pretending.

RAGE: I know you're pretending.

LAURA: About what?

RAGE: About everything. About being all peaceful and happy.

LAURA: I am happy. Why wouldn't I be happy?

RAGE: 'Cause you work in a shit job in a shit office. 'Cause you're like way over thirty and not married. 'Cause you're still here at six o'clock.

LAURA: You don't have to be married to be happy.

Pause.

RAGE: I did try something after you made that speech. I wasn't fucking pissed right away, you know. You know how you said that thing about just try one thing differently.

LAURA: If we all made one step . . .

RAGE: Yeah, we'd be that much closer. Whatever. I sat in the caf for lunch. Every day for a week. With everyone else. Usually I eat in the smoke hole. So I sat in the caf.

LAURA: And . . .

RAGE: And nothing. I ate lunch.

LAURA: Did someone say something . . . mean?

RAGE: Nobody said anything. At all.

LAURA: So it was lonely.

RAGE: It was nothing. It didn't make a difference.

LAURA: It was courageous on your part, Raymond. It's hard to do things differently. But at least you know you're willing to try.

RAGE: When you say something, big, like how things could change for kids if we just talked to each other. Tried to see each other differently. When you say it with all that feeling, people get excited. They get excited 'cause there's hope, right.

LAURA: There is hope.

RAGE: Yeah, but hope sucks. 'Cause while you're hoping and it stays the same, it feels worse, 'cause now you're thinking maybe it could be different. You're thinking about how it could be better. Before you were just trying to get through the day, right?

LAURA: Yes.

RAGE: I thought about it a lot, eh, like about the whole world and shit. Like if you really could change people just by being an example of something good. 'Cause people are mad, right? 'Cause things aren't working out for a lot of people in this world. And, you know, they're tired of just going along with it. And that's what they're saying. And I think, maybe Gandhi listened. It's hard to listen.

LAURA: Raym . . . Rage . . . I'm sorry.

RAGE: What?

LAURA gets up and crosses to sit with RAGE.

LAURA: I'm sorry for what's happened to you. I made that speech . . . but I never thought about what you might take away . . . how confusing. It's very complicated. I was talking and I didn't think. I don't think sometimes.

RAGE: It's okay. It's what people do. Talk and have good ideas about how to make the world better, and then go home to your boyfriend or to a musical or something. You don't really have to make a difference. 'Cause it doesn't make a difference to you.

LAURA: But I do want to make a difference. I don't want school to be hell for you. Fucking Jonathon Lam. I tried to tell him, you know, that if you were acting this way, then something was going on. And there is something going on, Rage. You're hurt and you're broken and you need help.
RAGE: And Lam, what did he say?
LAURA: He said he wants you out of here.
RAGE: He's right.
LAURA: No he's not.
RAGE: There are people who are just the losers, you know. It doesn't change for us. I'm like that girl. Karen. You gotta look it in the face. Accept it. I'm cool with it.

LAURA puts her hand on RAGE's arm.

LAURA: It's not like that. You're not a loser or a winner. You're just a person. Like me. Trying to have a life. Trying to . . .

The smoke detector goes off. LAURA makes a break for the door. She makes it out. But RAGE hauls her back in. He hauls LAURA onto the desk with him. He tries to rip the alarm out of the ceiling.

RAGE: What the?
LAURA: Help!
RAGE: What are you doing!
LAURA: Help me!
RAGE: Get back . . .
LAURA: Help, someone, help me!

RAGE throws her onto the ground.

RAGE: Shut up! How do you turn it off?
LAURA: I don't know.

He straddles her, yelling.

RAGE: Tell me how to turn it off.

RAGE knocks the smoke detector off the ceiling with the butt of the gun. LAURA screams as he turns on her with the gun.

You knew it was there.
LAURA: I forgot it was there. Please.

RAGE holds the gun by the door, listening to see if someone is coming down the hallway.

RAGE: Get behind the desk.
LAURA: What are you doing . . .
RAGE: Someone's going to come. Get behind the desk.

LAURA gets behind the desk. Her purse is sitting not far from where she is. A cellphone is visible in the front pocket. RAGE turns off the lights and locks the door.

LAURA: What are you going to do?
RAGE: Shut up.

RAGE stands to the side of the door listening for someone. LAURA huddles behind the desk, listening. She sees the cellphone. She tries to reach for it while RAGE is at the door, but she can't see him.

You set me up. You did that on purpose.
LAURA: . . . I'm sorry.
RAGE: Don't talk. Who's still here at six? Who's in the building?
LAURA: I don't know. Not very many people. The janitor.
RAGE: There are kids on the track.
LAURA: They wouldn't hear it. I'm sure no one heard . . .

RAGE: You better hope not because if they did they're dead.

LAURA grabs the phone and pushes some buttons as RAGE stands by the door.

LAURA: *(into the phone)* They won't come down here. It's like you said. I'm in the basement. No one comes down here unless the furnace is out of whack. I'm right beside the furnace and it's always freezing in here. Crazy, huh? You'd think they could get . . .
RAGE: Shit. Shit. I hear someone. There's someone coming!

As RAGE comes around the desk LAURA shoves the phone in her purse, which she chucks under the desk. RAGE gets down beside her.

Don't say a word.

LAURA shakes her head.

I mean it. It won't be you. It'll be them.

LAURA nods her understanding. The two of them crouch side by side behind the desk, listening. The sound of footsteps becomes clear. Someone pauses outside the door. The doorknob turns, jiggles. The sound of keys being pulled out and fumbled with. Pause. LAURA and RAGE stare at one another. Holding their breath. The sound of keys being put away. The doorknob jiggles one more time. The sound of footsteps moving away. RAGE lifts his finger, warning LAURA to stay quiet until the person is really gone.

Shit.
LAURA: He didn't have a key. He didn't have a key.

LAURA puts her hand on RAGE's arm.

He didn't have a key. I have a key. He didn't have a . . .

RAGE: I get it. A key. Chill.

LAURA: He sould have. It must have been Mr. Parry. He should have a key, but he didn't. He couldn't get in because . . .

RAGE: Fuck, would you relax for a second.

LAURA is crying and gibbering now.

LAURA: He heard. He must of. He came down to check, but he couldn't get in. He's okay. I'm okay. Right? We're okay . . .

RAGE: Are you like having a breakdown or something?

LAURA: I'm pregnant.

RAGE: What?

LAURA: I'm pregnant.

RAGE shakes his head, not comprehending LAURA's shift in subject.

I'm having a baby. A baby. That's the first time I've said it like that. I'm having a baby. I always say I'm pregnant . . . And Jack, well . . .

RAGE: Get up.

LAURA: He doesn't want it. I mean, it's like you said, we're not even married.

RAGE: Get up. Come on!

RAGE pulls LAURA to her feet.

LAURA: I'm only three months. Rage. I want to have this baby. I want this baby.

RAGE: Well you know what you have to do then.

LAURA: *(freaking)* I can't. I can't. You can't make me. I can't. I can't!

RAGE holds her up against the wall.

RAGE: Shut up! Relax. Relax. Get back in the fucking moment and be peace now!

LAURA is bent over with a panic attack.

LAURA: I . . . I . . .
RAGE: Fuck. Breathe.
LAURA: I . . . I . . . can't . . .
RAGE: Jesus Christ.
LAURA: I . . . I . . . okay, okay . . .
RAGE: Okay. Sit down . . .
LAURA: No.
RAGE: Sit down.
LAURA: No, I can't. I won't.

LAURA tries to hold on to him. RAGE pushes her into the chair. He looks up at the hole where the smoke detector was. He paces with the gun.

RAGE: So he got you pregnant. But he doesn't want to get married. What did you do trap him? Thought he would marry you if you had his baby. Still doesn't want you, eh? You're kind of old to have a baby, aren't you? Don't they have more birth defects if you wait too long?
LAURA: I'm thirty-eight.
RAGE: Thirty-eight. Fuck. If this is what thirty-eight looks like you may want to shoot yourself too. I mean, part-time job in a broom closet. Guy who won't marry you. Pregnant. Driving a Toyota Tercel. A blue Toyota Tercel. Living in an apartment. Yoga at Fitness World on Fridays. You're a loser.
LAURA: You've been following me.
RAGE: You don't go anywhere.
LAURA: If I play that tape. You're not going to come off very well.
RAGE: If I die. You won't even give them the tape. You'll tell them the story. In your own words. It'll be like you say. Right? See, that's why you are not happy. "Happiness is when what you think, what you say, and what you do are in harmony." You lie about everything.
LAURA: I don't lie about everything.

RAGE: Okay, you want to drag this out. Let's play a game. You like games. I'll even go first.

RAGE takes all but one bullet from the gun and points it at his head.

See, you could get lucky here. Do you want me to pull the trigger?
LAURA: Stop it.
RAGE: All you have to do is tell the truth. Just say that you want me to pull the trigger.
LAURA: I don't.
RAGE: Oh, so I should point it at you? Now do you want me to pull the trigger?
LAURA: No.
RAGE: Well make a choice, this is an easy one.
LAURA: Please don't point the gun at me.
RAGE: Okay. You answer a question and I won't.
LAURA: What is it?
RAGE: Do you love him? Jack?
LAURA: I don't know.
RAGE: Does he love you?
LAURA: No.
RAGE: Good. Your turn.

RAGE puts the gun to his head.

LAURA: What?
RAGE: Ask me a question.
LAURA: When did you go from being bullied to being such a bully?
RAGE: When I got taller. My turn. Did you really try to stop Lam from kicking me out?

He turns the gun back to her.

LAURA: I . . . no. He told me they'd made a decision.

RAGE: So it was never up to you.

LAURA: No, it wasn't.

RAGE: So you lied?

LAURA: Yes.

RAGE: So you are a liar.

LAURA: Yes.

RAGE: Fair enough. Ask me.

LAURA: Are you going to kill me?

RAGE: Are you going to kill me?

LAURA: Stop it.

RAGE points the gun back and forth at himself then at LAURA.

RAGE: What, this? Me. Or you. Eeny, meeny, miny, mo . . . You or me. You or me.

LAURA jumps out of her chair, pushing RAGE. RAGE holds onto the gun as LAURA rages.

LAURA: You! Point it at you. I don't want that thing in my face. Get it out of my face, you fucking little psychopathic freak! Why are you doing this? I haven't done anything to you. I don't deserve this. You think this is it? High school. You think this is what it's always going to be like? You think you know something? You're seventeen. You don't know anything. You've probably never even been laid. Hey, Rage, have you ever been laid? Ever had a girlfriend? Ever had a real friend? Or do you just cry about your sissy daddy and your mean mommy. Ooh, spilled spaghetti. You're traumatized for life. Yes, you are going to be kicked out of school because you're a loser. You scare people. You are a loser. You're a loser, Rage. You're a fucking loser! Is that what you want to hear!

LAURA throws a chair across the room.

RAGE: "Try turning to your neighbour and smile when you'd normally walk by. Talk to that boy or girl who sits alone in the cafeteria. Try to see them differently." You know what my mom says about trying? It's a rocking chair. Keeps you moving, but you never get anywhere.

RAGE puts the bullets back into the gun.

I'm not afraid to die, you know.
LAURA: I believe you.

Silence.

RAGE: I gotta follow through. You know I gotta stand for this. Otherwise I'm just like you. Just talking. Sorry.

Pause.

Do you really like it so much?
LAURA: What?
RAGE: Life.
LAURA: Of course I do.
RAGE: I guess you're lucky.

He tries to hand LAURA the gun. LAURA pushes the gun away.

LAURA: I'm not . . . I can't. I won't do it.
RAGE: Okay. Close your eyes.
LAURA: What?

RAGE points the gun at her. LAURA does not close her eyes.

Not all the time. I don't like it all the time. It's up and down. It's not always the way I want it.

RAGE: If it was the way you wanted it? What would it be like? What would you like? Tell me.

He holds the gun on LAURA.

LAURA: What would I like? Does it matter? Who cares what I would like. I would like to get out of bed and feel happy, not tired and drained and afraid of what's coming next, what's not working out . . . I would like to stop pretending. Stop trying so goddamn hard to make things work. I want to just . . . to feel peaceful . . . to just be . . . to . . . I want to see my baby's face. To be alive. To live. I want to live. Please. I want to live.

RAGE *crosses to* LAURA. *She steps back, afraid he's going to shoot her now. He pushes the gun in her hand, holding her hands over the gun for a moment, almost gentle in its contact. He cocks the trigger for her and raises the gun in her hands to his chest. He steps back in place across the room.* LAURA *holds the gun on him as he speaks. Halfway through his speech the sound of sirens comes up.*

RAGE: You know when you're surfing the Net you can talk to people. There's people there that will talk to you about anything . . . they don't know who you are . . . you can't feel 'em. They could be anybody saying anything. They're just these words typing out on your screen . . . more words. I'm like talking to them, having this intense conversation about guns or basketball or whatever and I'm laughing at a joke and I hear myself laughing and it's weird 'cause I'm alone and I'm laughing. I don't wanna be alone and laughing in a little room in front of a computer anymore. I just don't.

The sirens come to a stop. LAURA *lowers the gun, relieved.* RAGE *looks up to the window and the flashing lights of the police car.*

How do you think they knew?

LAURA: Sometimes the signal works and sometimes it doesn't. You never know if the person you're talking to can hear you.

RAGE stands for a moment and then lets out a deep, primitive howl of anger and despair before rushing LAURA.

RAGE: AHHH!

LAURA raises the gun instinctively and fires at him. RAGE falls violently to the floor. LAURA lets out a deep moan and falls to her knees beside him.

LAURA: No.

Lights fade down slowly as LAURA sobs over RAGE's body.

End.

THE GLASS BOX

Theatre Terrific

devised by

Kyla Harris, Watson Moy,

and Susanna Uchatius

THE "PANACHE" OF SOPHIA LOREN: THE AFFECTIVE POTENTIAL OF THE DISABLED BODY IN THEATRE TERRIFIC'S *THE GLASS BOX*

Allison Leadley

The Glass Box, which was first performed as a work-in-progress at the 2008 Magnetic North Theatre Festival before appearing on Vancouver and Victoria stages in January and February of 2009, reflects the mandate of Vancouver-based company Theatre Terrific to "support . . . artists of all abilities,"[1] as well as the company's current artistic director Susanna Uchatius's ongoing commitment to "universal human stories."[2] This is not only reflected through the play's focus on sexuality, sexual desire, and being sexually desired, but also through the play's frank treatment of human sexualities across a spectrum of desires, abilities, and experiences. As the company's website states, "*The Glass Box* blends and refracts the experiences of three disparate, sexually active people: a 55-year old, straight, able-bodied woman, on the verge of a latent but powerful sexual awakening, a 23 year-old woman in a wheelchair, in full ownership of her bisexuality, and a 38-year old Down Syndrome man who has a fully satisfying, albeit solo, sex life."[3] Moreover, the production's minimalist

---

1 "About," *Theatre Terrific*, n.d., accessed 2 Dec. 2013. http://www.theatreterrific.ca/.

2 Kirsty Johnston, *Stage Turns: Canadian Disability Theatre* (Montreal: McGill-Queen's UP, 2012), 82.

3 "The Glass Box," *Theatre Terrific*, n.d., accessed 2 Dec. 2013. http://www.theatreterrific.ca/production/the-glass-box.

aesthetics and the play's non-linear structure typify the company's preferred avant-garde aesthetic, which *Vancouver Theatre Guide* describes as a "form of expression . . . unlike that of the traditional entitled theatre community."[4] Thus the play moves through various states of temporality and consciousness, recreating memory and fantasy and conflating the various states of self while fusing monologue, song, autobiography, celebrity "tell-all," and quiz show.

Inspired by a conversation on disability, pleasure, and sexuality that occurred between Kyla Harris and Uchatius after completing an acting workshop together,[5] the play calls upon the cast's real-life experiences, anecdotes, and observations surrounding their individualized sexual histories, as well as Harris's personal experience as a patient within the UK's National Health Service.[6] Through the framework of the celebrity game show, Kyla Harris, Watson Moy, and Susanna Uchatius—embodying their personalized notion of the ideal sexual icon: Cleopatra, Brad Pitt, and Sophia Loren, respectively—answer a series of questions related to sexuality that include, but are not limited to, inquiries about their past sexual encounters, their desires for future sexual experiences, and their expectations of romantic partnerships. Throughout the duration of the play, Harris, as Cleopatra, tabulates their respective scores in a large, white three-ring binder that contains both the "standardized criteria" on which they base their scoring system (with points for personal grooming, bodily functions, musical taste, disposition, loyalty, and expected lifespan) as well as "the rules for rehabilitation after trauma" (these include instructions to "enjoy the process," maintain "realistic expectations," and prepare the body before sex).

The play gestures towards a voyeuristic impulse that encapsulates both our supposed collective cultural fascination with "celebrities' lifestyles through

---

4 "Theatre Terrific, Professional Theatre," *Vancouver Theatre Guide*, n.d., accessed 2 Dec. 2013. http://www.gvpta.ca/vancouver-theatre-guide/ensemble/theatre-terrific/.

5 "Piece Poses Provocative Questions," *Canada.com*, 29 Jan. 2009, accessed 2 Dec. 2013. http://www.canada.com/story_print.html?id=a4ee71d6-c34f-4838-bcc5-5af9d78df8a7&sponsor=.

6 "Kyla Harris—The Artworks and Journal of Kyla Harris," *kylaharris.net*, 2014, accessed 1 Feb. 2014. http://kylaharris.net/.

'kiss and tell stories' "[7] and what Kirsty Johnston notes in her analysis of the play as the persistent and intrusive question that has plagued Harris as a disabled woman: "can you have sex?"[8] The assumptions that the disabled subject is either asexual, impotent, or both is, as scholar Michael Rembis notes, inextricably linked to the medical model of disability that locates the material body of the subject as the site of pathology, impairment, and disability. As he writes, "The inability to perform gender and sexuality in a way that meets dominant social expectations is seen as an *intrinsic* limitation."[9]

Historically, the exceptional body of the disabled subject has been presented as the object for visual consumption of the able-bodied viewer through the tradition of scopophilic practices that include the public medical lecture or the highly affecting practice of the freak show (which was deliberately designed to solicit fear, surprise, and wonder within the viewer).[10] While these practices are outdated and largely abolished, they have had far-reaching and lasting implications in shaping modern notions of "normal" and "abnormal" or "healthy" and "disabled" and in reinforcing this supposed physical and cultural superiority of the so-called "healthy" able body (and, by extension, the implicit inferiority of the disabled body).[11] Harris's cry for the spectator to "Look at [her]!" and her claims that her very physical presence "remind[s] people that they are going to die" evoke these feelings of abject terror and point towards the affective power within this visual exchange. Harris's acute awareness of the feelings of pity, fear, or surprise that her presence awakens within the spectator gestures towards the lasting social and political implications of

7 Sean Redmond, Introduction to The Star and Celebrity Confessional, a special issue of *Social Semiotics* 18.2, as quoted in Mike Featherstone, "Body, Image and Affect in Consumer Culture," *Body and Society* 16.1 (2010): 199.

8 Johnston, 148.

9 Michael A. Rembis, "Beyond the Binary: Rethinking the Social Model of Disabled Sexuality," *Sexuality and Disability* 28.1 (2010): 51, emphasis added.

10 Thomas Fahy, *Freak Shows and the Modern American Imagination: Constructing the Damaged Body from Willa Cather to Truman Capote* (New York: Palgrave Macmillan, 2006).

11 Rosemarie Garland Thomson, *Extraordinary Bodies: Figuring Physical Disability in American Culture and Literature* (New York: Columbia UP, 1997).

such cultural practices as the freak show. But the play also serves as a broader critique of the privilege of the gaze within contemporary clinical practices. In his article on the live display of othered bodies, scholar Raymond Corbey describes the visual exchange of the gaze between or, rather, directed towards bodies as acts of "optical empiricism" in which "to see was to know."[12] Within Johnston's analysis of *The Glass Box* as a critique of the so-called "clinical practice of disability,"[13] she suggests through her reading of theorists, such as Leonard Cassuto, that contemporary medicine is rooted in these same quantifying impulses that seek to "standardize and quantify"[14] the material body. The divisive nature of the gaze between or, again, directed from the able-bodied viewer towards the disabled subject, or from the doctor towards the patient, is symbolized by the eponymous glass box; created through thin lines of bright, white light that form the outline of a cube, the glass box both defines and contains the actors, clearly demarcating the bodies of the performers from that of the viewer.

The ever-present three-ring binder that Cleopatra/Harris uses as her scoring guide also acts as a visual signifier to point to the significance of the clinical model in shaping notions of disablement. It is salient that the binder is one of the few physical stage props that is not mimed within the play and, in the climactic confrontation between Cleopatra/Harris and Loren/Uchatius, the binder must be forcibly extracted from Harris's possession—a poignant moment that points to the seemingly inextricable relationship between the clinical model and disabled subjectivity. Harris's emotional monologue at the play's climax however, points to the insufficiency of this model. As Harris states, "[R]eading the binder, if you read the binder, you'd realize I'm normal and I don't *feel* normal."[15] Here, Harris's conceptualization of normal—and abnormal—gestures to a more nuanced notion of disabled embodiment that

12 Raymond Corbey, "Ethnographic Showcases, 1870–1930," *Cultural Anthropology* 8.3 (1993): 338.

13 Johnston, 150.

14 Ibid.

15 Emphasis added.

exceeds the tidy quantifiable binaries between "normal" and "abnormal," or "able" and "disabled."

Unlike the typical narratives or assumptions that surround disability and sexuality that cast the disabled subject to be "incompetent, impotent, undesirable, or asexual,"[16] *The Glass Box* also points to a more nuanced thinking about disability and sexuality. As Harris notes of the typical associations of sexuality and disability: "It is so taboo. Not many people put the two together. Because in the media, anything that portrays people with disabilities, it's usually in a hospital setting. Or with pity. Or something dramatic and traumatic."[17] In contrast, *The Glass Box* portrays narratives of disability and sexuality that incorporate and include narratives of desire, desirability, and romance that are played out both alongside and through the highly visible and "hyper sexual"[18] persona of the celebrity. This affective power of the celebrity icon is what Mike Featherstone identifies as "presence." As he writes, "[It is] not just a certain style, but . . . something more ineffable, something which you need to experience to understand. It is something which works in a different register—*an intensity.* It is an unstructured non-conscious experience transmitted between bodies."[19] When Uchatius describes Loren's so-called "panache" or when Moy identifies Pitt's "goodness" they evoke these so-called ineffable qualities that excite the viewer's imagination. In simultaneously inscribing and enacting the affective power of the celebrity icon, they are able to inscribe and enact their own fantasies and desires through and against the imagination, desire, and fantasy conjured by the celebrity figure.

Furthermore, in enacting the affective potential of the celebrity figure as a means of articulating disabled sexuality, the aforementioned supposed incompatibility of disability and sexuality, or the negation of disabled sexuality from within popular culture and media that both Remis and Harris allude to, is not only challenged but the typical affective exchange between normative

16 Rembis, 51.

17 See "Piece Poses Provocative Questions."

18 Johnston, 149.

19 Featherstone, 199.

and non-normative bodies typified by cultural frameworks (such as the freak show or medical clinic) is also recontextualized. Rather than the terror or surprise that the freak show sought to instill via the exceptional body, or the feelings of charity and pity that Harris suggests the disabled subject conjures in popular representations of disability, the disabled experience is reframed through the pleasure, desire, fantasy, and fascination of the celebrity presence. As Elizabeth Christie and Geraldine Bloustein note of the political, social, and pedagogical potential of affect for members of the disabled community, affect "becomes the process through which alternative ways of perceiving and engaging with the other can be brought into being, physiologically engaging the viewer's or spectator's senses."[20] As the authors explain of sites of media—including cinema, photography, music, and dance and, as I wish to add, theatre—these forms are "powerful and effective vehicles, especially when, for example, challenging medical discourses of disability, because they have the potential to reimagine disabled bodies."[21]

Thus, via the appropriation of the celebrity persona, the affective potential of the disabled body is reimagined and reconfigured. By extension, this in turn reframes and recontextualizes the audience's later encounters with the so-called personas of Loren, Pitt, and Cleopatra. While *The Glass Box* situates affect as a site of what Christie and Bloustein define as "intervention," it is significant to note that the play resists such tidy conclusions. Returning to the notion of the avant-garde aesthetic and alternative dramaturgy that defines Theatre Terrific's productions, the play remains ambiguous. "Happy Days Are Here Again" plays over the speakers, signalling what Pitt identifies as "the end"; but whether he is referring to the game show, the production, or both is unclear. The final moments of the play deliberately undermine the upbeat tempo and cheery lyrics of the soundtrack. Neither of the women fully exit the confines of the glass box (as Pitt/Moy does) and the physical presence of the material body is emphasized through the stage directions that direct the pair to "danc[e] awkwardly"—abandoning the seductive sway and

20 Elizabeth Christie and Geraldine Bloustein, "I-cyborg: Disability, Affect and Public Pedagogy," *Discourse: Studies in the Cultural Politics of Education* 31.4 (2010): 492.

21 Ibid., 493.

sexual abandon with which Uchatius characterized Loren's movements. When Cleopatra questions whether the "messy and glamorously gnarled pieces" are "juicier," the women respond with neither affirmation, confirmation, nor denial but instead the promise of "Maybe?"

The Glass Box was devised by Kyla Harris, Watson Moy, and Susanna Uchatius, and first produced by Theatre Terrific at the Playwrights Theatre Centre Studio in Vancouver, BC, from April 22 to 25, 2009, with the following cast and creative team:

Cleo: Kyla Harris
Brad: Watson Moy
Sophia: Susanna Uchatius

Director: Joanna Garfinkel
Dramaturg: Joanna Garfinkel
Set and lighting design: Naomi Sider
Lighting design: Parjad Sharifi
Stage manger: Nicole Lamb
Graphic design: Kyla Harris
Photography: Mairin Deery
Program design: Elena Chalatnik

Special thanks to Jan Derbyshire, who directed an early version of the script.

CHARACTERS

Brad
Cleo
Sophia

Prologue

The sound of water.

SOPHIA *is looking through the glass at the new-people world outside. She presses against the glass. She finds one set of eyes. She waits. She looks. She finds a face that will stay with her. She smiles at him. She fluffs her hair. She looks at the rest of the audience and then comes back to him. She moves slowly. She silently mouths hello. She looks for that nice face again. She finds him. She smoothes her dress. She looks back at the spectators. She stands still. She shakes herself and turns a little. She watches. She laughs. She begins to sing quietly. The first verse of "Bing! Bang! Bong!" from the film* Houseboat. *She cocks her head and winks. She pulls up and stands up very still. She waits. She slowly turns her back to the audience. She stands still. She hums the tune. She looks out one wall, the next, and the next. She comes back to the audience, finds her corner, stands very still.*

SOPHIA *looks at the audience, puts her finger to her lips.*

SOPHIA: Shhhhhh.

She smiles. She begins to sing and sway, dancing around the box.

She keeps singing, bumps into a wall, and pushes away. She pulls up proudly and walks back to her spot. She looks over the whole audience. She stops and rests on the face she once held.

I'm here. Do you like my glasses? I design them myself.

She adjusts her glasses and blows a kiss. She smiles, waits, stands, sighs, and tilts her head.

The sound of water.

Scene 1

SOPHIA *takes a small apple from her pocket. She wipes it on her dress, lifts it to her mouth, and takes a bite. She eats. Stops. Eats. Bites. Stops. Bites. Watches. She eats every single bit of the apple until there is only the core left. She holds this in her hand. She looks at the audience. She looks down at her cleavage, shrugs, and puts the core down her dress, very properly. She nods. She sighs. She stands and smiles.*

SOPHIA *stumbles around (the dark glasses are like a blindfold on the now-dim stage). She finds the edge, where the audience must be.*

SOPHIA: Oh! Scusa. Sono felice che lo trovato. *[I'm so happy I found you.]*

Pause.

I'm so glad I found you. Here we are. You and me.

Pause.

It's not easy to find the things one needs. Sometimes it takes a very long time . . . And I can't see where I'm going. It's very difficult. But I found you and here you are.

Pause.

You and me. What do you want to do?

Pause.

Che? *[What?]* I don't think we should. You silly man. Lei e un bambino! *[You little boy!]*

She laughs.

They are very . . . ahhhhh . . . how you say . . . outspoken. They like much attention. I know you will understand . . . They are good friends with my hips. This goes this way and these go that way.

The chime sounds.

Well . . . let us begin.

The rolled-up carpet begins to move.

Welcome to tonight's show!

Muffled sounds from the rolled-up carpet.

Ta da! *Bella* Sophia is here.

The carpet moves.

CLEO: It is I!

The carpet thrashes. SOPHIA begins to sing and dance.

The carpet begins to unroll.

You and I will have much fun . . . trying and tasting . . .
Caesar?

Pause.

Hm.

The carpet unrolls to reveal CLEO. SOPHIA *stops and peeks over the rim of her dark glasses.*

. . . And what have we here?
It is I, your mistress. Come, eunuch—
SOPHIA: Eunuch?
CLEO: —fan me. I must cool my lust before my love arrives.

CLEO *notices* BRAD, *who has been hiding.*

Ah, but my love is here! Brave Caesar, the Queen of the Nile is at your feet.
BRAD: No, I'm a movie star.
SOPHIA: *(looking at* BRAD*)* Of course, yes, yes.
CLEO: Cleopatra of the Nile, Ruler of Egypt and Second in Rome. But I can tell we're going to be great friends, so you may call me Cleo.

She extends her hand, expecting a kiss. BRAD *and* SOPHIA *look at each other dubiously and kiss her hand.*

Good evening, ladies, gentlemen, and every gender in between, welcome to tonight's show . . .

Canned applause.

(pointedly) Our first guest tonight has starred in over fifty films, including *A River Runs Through It*, and has been named the sexiest man alive by *Vanity Fair* four years in a row. Please welcome . . . Brad Pitt!

Canned applause.

BRAD: Hello. I am Brad Pitt. I look nice in my movies and I'm good.
CLEO: Our next guest this evening is a contemporary sex icon and film star that started out at the age of sixteen in Pozzuoli, Italy. Tonight we are here to talk about her cookbook titled *Pasta and Me, A Love Affair*. Please give a warm welcome to Sophia Loren!

Canned applause.

SOPHIA: Si. Good evening, Brad and . . . Cleo. *Buongiorno* to you!

She smiles and uses both hands to kiss to the audience.

CLEO: Today we will be talking to you about your achievements and what it means to you to be a sexual icon. *(A chime sounds.)* When you hear the chime, you must take a card and ask each other a question, and I will record the answer in points.

The chime sounds and all characters look up to where the sound has come from. CLEO *opens a binder and takes out a card that she hands to* BRAD.

Brad, why don't you start with asking Sophia a question?
BRAD: Okay. Yes. When can I talk about my movie and fishing?
CLEO: Later, Brad.

BRAD *takes the card from* CLEO *and reads it out to* SOPHIA.

BRAD: Do you consider yourself attractive?

SOPHIA: Mamma mia. I consider myself lucky. I have been fortunate and unfortunate. But my looks . . . lucky. What you see, darling, I owe to spaghetti.

Canned laughter. Canned whistle.

BRAD: Spaghetti?
SOPHIA: Yes. I eat simple; I live simple. Maybe that is what is best?
CLEO: It's not that simple. Life has not been simple.

Pause.

For any of us.
SOPHIA: Yes, I hear you have had a hard time.
CLEO: I had to use my wits.
SOPHIA: Are you saying I used my . . .

Canned laughter.

CLEO: No, darling, we are of different times. We use what we have to.
BRAD: I don't use anything. I like fishing.
CLEO: Sophia . . . what do you do best?
SOPHIA: Best? I think I do comfort best.
CLEO: How?
SOPHIA: I seek to give comfort to my husband, my children, my friends, my fans.
CLEO: Are you fulfilled?
SOPHIA: Yes! I am filled. I am full to the edges. Is that not so, Brad?
BRAD: Yes.
CLEO: What about brave?
SOPHIA: I am lucky. I was born both wise and poor. I did not choose bravery, I chose survival, and I used whatever tools I had.

Canned applause.

BRAD: Yes. So do I.

CLEO: Perhaps a few different ones though.

Canned laughter.

SOPHIA: I will ask you the same, Brad. Do you consider yourself attractive or desirable?

BRAD: I'm one of those people you hate because of genetics. It is the truth.

Canned laughter and a whistle.

SOPHIA *takes another card. She reads it to herself and at first looks puzzled, then looks up at the audience.*

SOPHIA: Oh no, I couldn't . . .

CLEO: It's part of the show, darling . . .

SOPHIA: What is your sexual preference? Men, women, or both?

BRAD: *(laughs)* Women. Only women. I've been in love with many women. Most of them I have worked with, or ones I've seen on TV.

SOPHIA: *(to herself)* Si, si. Marcello Mastroianni, Peter Sellers, Cary Grant, my beloved Carlo.

BRAD: I've had many crushes. My first crush, Tracey Gold from *Growing Pains*. She is beautiful. I used to sing to her.

Canned "awwwww."

BRAD *takes out a comb from his tackle box, combs his hair, stands, and sings "Butterfly" by Andy Williams.*

This is great. I want to ask you another question!

Is sex an important part of your life?

SOPHIA: Oy, what kind of show is this? I am here to talk about my love affair with pasta. I am not just about sex.

CLEO: I love food. Antony and I have had so many banquets; you want to talk about pasta?
SOPHIA: Always. *(looks over at BRAD)* Perhaps Mr. Pitt likes pasta too?
BRAD: Oh yeah. Tortellini, spaghetti, lasagna . . .
SOPHIA: What about the sauce? Is the sauce important or is the pasta more important?
BRAD: Yeah. Both.
CLEO: Sauce. I love the sauce.

Whistle.

SOPHIA: See, we all love pasta.
CLEO: We all love pasta. I want to know about what really turns you on.
SOPHIA: *(to CLEO and BRAD)* I am here to talk about my cookbook! For my audience I will have a conversation about pasta! *Basta* with the sex.
CLEO: You're not famous for your cookbook.
SOPHIA: Ah, *si*, but it is the cooking that makes the Sophia.
CLEO: Well, ladies, gentleman, and every gender in between, you've heard from two of this century's sexual icons. More to come on mastication, masturbation, and marriage.

Canned applause.

Scene 2

The show's chime rings.

SOPHIA: Ah! Time for a *sonnellino.*
CLEO: Not so quickly. Here.

CLEO hands SOPHIA a card.

You're going to play Antony. *(to* BRAD*)* Darling, will you take care of me and be my maidservant?

BRAD: Oh yeah. Okay.

CLEO: I assure you it has to do with fishing.

SOPHIA: He is not a maidservant, he is a man.

CLEO: What does that matter? The gender dichotomy bores me. Let's play.

SOPHIA: Ba bene. But . . . how would anyone think I was a man?

CLEO laughs as BRAD hands SOPHIA and CLEO fishing rods.

CLEO: You're pretending to be Sophia Loren, aren't you?

CLEO motions for BRAD to put an olive-branch wreath on SOPHIA's head. He does so.

The light changes. The sound of running water. Antony (SOPHIA) and CLEO are sitting high up on a bench with their legs dangling over the edge.

SOPHIA: *(as Antony)* Why don't the fish bite?

CLEO: Maybe it's your position?

Antony moves closer to CLEO.

SOPHIA: *(as Antony)* They know me. I've fished here before.

CLEO: I know. Don't be disappointed.

SOPHIA: *(as Antony)* I can catch.

CLEO: I know you can, but you aren't able right now.

SOPHIA: *(as Antony)* Am I not a good fisherman?

CLEO kisses Antony.

CLEO: The fish must be sleeping.

SOPHIA: *(as Antony)* Fish don't sleep.

CLEO: No, they rest.

CLEO moves Antony's head to her lap and strokes his hair. Antony rests. Pause. Antony abruptly sits up.

Try again. These are your waters. These are our waters.
SOPHIA: *(as Antony)* Fish! Bite!
Do you always catch the fish you want?
CLEO: I have caught you in this game, haven't I?
SOPHIA: *(as Antony)* Love isn't a game.
CLEO: Life is a game.
SOPHIA: I have tried and they rest.
CLEO: Love.

CLEO puts Antony's head in her hands.

You can conquer Rome. You can catch a fish. Try again.

CLEO whispers to the maidservant. The maidservant, unbeknownst to Antony, attaches a fish to Antony's hook. Antony feels a tug on his line, pulls up the fishing rod, and drags up the fish.

ALL: A fish!

They bow seriously. Applause. The light changes and the sound of water stops.

Scene 3

BRAD is looking through his tackle box. CLEO and SOPHIA look over at him.

CLEO: What are you doing?
BRAD: I'm looking for my lucky lure.
CLEO: Why is it lucky?
BRAD: It catches fish.
CLEO: What kind of fish?
BRAD: Big ones.
CLEO: What do you do with big fish, Brad?
BRAD: Eat them.

SOPHIA walks over and squats down to help him look for his lure.

SOPHIA: I bet you're a good fisherman.
BRAD: I am.
SOPHIA: What does your lucky lure look like?

She laughs and sings as she pokes through the lures.

La, la, la . . . lucky lure . . . looks like . . .
Like this . . .
And this . . .
CLEO: I think you caught a big fish, Brad. What are you going to do with it?
BRAD: I don't know.

CLEO gestures and the chime rings.

CLEO: Question time.

SOPHIA stops dancing.

(holding the cards out to SOPHIA) Your turn.
SOPHIA: Why do you always get to decide who asks and when?
CLEO: The queen's prerogative.
SOPHIA: I think you like to fish more than Brad does.
CLEO: Go fish.

Canned laughter. SOPHIA takes a card and reads it to BRAD.

SOPHIA: What does it mean to have a love life, Brad?

BRAD thinks for a while.

BRAD: You get to know this person really well.
SOPHIA: How do you get to know this person really well?
BRAD: We hold hands.
SOPHIA: That's nice. What else do you do?
BRAD: We hug, we kiss . . . we get a chance to hold each other. If you feel sad, they're always there. You have a friend to spend time with. You will always be there for her. That's all I can think of.
SOPHIA: That sounds nice.
CLEO: How quaint. What about sex?
BRAD: That's part of the husband/wife thing.
CLEO: Do you think you have to be married to have sex?
BRAD: No.
CLEO: When do you have sex then?
BRAD: Well, when the time comes.
CLEO: Sophia five, Brad ten.

BRAD thinks for a while. He bends over and puts all his lures back into the tackle box. SOPHIA and CLEO watch and wait. SOPHIA finally speaks.

SOPHIA: I can tell you have something else to say.

Pause.

What is it?

BRAD: Falling in love is like falling for each other.

Canned "Awwwww!"

CLEO: Look, sex and love are not—

SOPHIA: *(indicating the key rings on her ears)* I like this. It's nice.

Scene 4

SOPHIA smiles and begins to dance and sing again. This time, she sings the entirety of "Bing! Bang! Bong!," dancing throughout.

Canned applause when she finishes.

CLEO motions and the chime rings.

CLEO: When did you first hear about the bing bang bong?

SOPHIA: I was raised a good Catholic. The nuns taught me about the sex.

BRAD: I was born sex. I didn't have to learn it.

The sound of a school bell.

CLEO: Vell, class. Ve vill today learn about ze sex.

CLEO turns into a nun in posture. SOPHIA and BRAD kneel, childlike. CLEO unrolls an imaginary picture of a disconnected pregnant belly.

Zis is ze voom at ze height of pregnancy.

SOPHIA: *(to BRAD)* Voom? What is a voom? It looks like an elbow. A pregnant arm?!!! I didn't know you could have a baby through your arm!

BRAD: The nuns know best.

CLEO: Uns here ve have ze female genitalia. Uns here ve have ze male parts.

SOPHIA: But how do they work?

BRAD: The penis goes in the vagina.

CLEO: Ve must always draw zem apart.

SOPHIA: I don't understand?

CLEO: Ven you are married to God and commit yourself to him, you have to have za faith. Faith gives you knowledge.

The sound of a school bell. CLEO drops the nun posture and rolls up the imaginary scroll.

SOPHIA and BRAD maturely sit.

SOPHIA: *(turns to BRAD)* How did you learn?

BRAD: Like you learn how to fish.

SOPHIA: Can you teach me how to fish?

BRAD: First, you find the right tools for fishing.

CLEO: A hook.

BRAD: Then you check the waters.

SOPHIA: I can only fathom! I didn't date much.

BRAD: Then you need a guide to show you the right fishing spots.

CLEO: And then you linger.

BRAD: Show your partner how to jerk the rod.

SOPHIA: *(shivers)* Oh Brad!

SOPHIA and CLEO look at each other.

BRAD: Make sure you hold tight when you pick up the fish.

SOPHIA: *(holds BRAD)* Like this?

BRAD and SOPHIA nuzzle.

CLEO: No. That was the easy part.

Pause.

It's what came after that was confusing.

SOPHIA and BRAD separate.

SOPHIA: What did all those strange bits have to do with me?
BRAD: I think it's about commitment.
SOPHIA: No, I think it was about making some sense out of the stuff in my underwear. It was about how my stuff was different than the stuff in the boys' underwear. Somehow these things were supposed to fit together. Somehow. Somewhere. With somebody.
CLEO: No one gave you a map. How could you find your way there?
SOPHIA: And when I asked I was told not to even think about going there . . . with anyone!
CLEO: Plastic anatomy and no instructions. Experience gave you answers.
SOPHIA: The first time I shaved my armpits, my mother called me a prostitute.
CLEO: So when did you first "experience"?

Scene 5

Everything is quiet in the box. BRAD is practising with his fly rod. He whips it back and forth, making it snap. CLEO is reclining, stretching her head and neck side to side.

SOPHIA: I learnt at a young age how to use what I've got now.
CLEO: *You* learnt that?

SOPHIA: Yes. At the circus.

Canned laughter.

Really. I saw my first stripper at the circus. My sister and I were eleven or twelve. There was one tent on the midway . . . forbidden. Adults only. We snuck around the back. Someone had made a clean little L-shaped rip with a knife in the perfect place. We took turns peeking in. All I could see were the backs of men; sweaty, smoky smells, music and men shouting. For one quick flash I saw a blue tassel . . . a flashy redheaded lady swinging a blue tassel on her breast.
CLEO: What did you do?
SOPHIA: We went home and practised.
CLEO: With what?
SOPHIA: Flashlights in the bedroom.

SOPHIA puts her finger to her lips and looks at BRAD.

Shhhhhh. You have to go to sleep.
BRAD: Okay. Will you wake me later?
SOPHIA: Yes. I promise we will. Now go to sleep.

BRAD takes off his vest, neatly folds it into a pillow, lies down, and pretends to sleep.

The lights go out. We hear CLEO and SOPHIA giggling and fumbling. One flashlight is turned on.

CLEO: Did you see her do that thing with her breasts and that made those tassels spin all the way around?
SOPHIA: How did she do that?
CLEO: I don't know, but I bet she could marry any man she wants.
SOPHIA: She had nothing on; that's a sin.
CLEO: Grow up. It's what you have to do to get a man.

SOPHIA: Really?

CLEO: We better practise or else we'll never get married. A man doesn't want to marry a woman who doesn't know how to take her clothes off. I could show you.

SOPHIA: Is it what you have to do to get any man?

CLEO: Any man.

Silence.

SOPHIA: We could try.

CLEO: Not without taking our clothes off. Do you want to go first?

SOPHIA: No.

CLEO: Okay. You hold the light. I'll pretend I'm the lady on stage.

SOPHIA: Okay.

SOPHIA shines a flashlight on CLEO.

CLEO: You also have to be all the men watching and yell things at me.

SOPHIA: I can't yell, our brother will hear us.

CLEO: Just whisper the stuff then, but make it dirty.

SOPHIA: Like what?

CLEO: Like . . . "Yeah, baby, yeah."

SOPHIA: Turn away from Satan, you prostitute.

Silence.

CLEO: Did you really think she was a prostitute?

SOPHIA: Yes.

CLEO: She was a stripper.

SOPHIA: What's the difference?

CLEO: A stripper takes her own clothes off and a prostitute takes everyone else's clothes off.

Canned laughter into chime.

Scene 6

BRAD coughs, yawns, wakes up. Lights up.

SOPHIA: Did you have a good sleep?
BRAD: Oh yeah.
CLEO: Did you have any dreams?
SOPHIA: Dreams . . . the subconscious paying a visit. I have a good imagination.
CLEO: I bet you do.
SOPHIA: Imagination. 1963, Academy Award for Best Foreign Film, *Yesterday, Today and Tomorrow*. Nothing makes a woman more beautiful than the belief she is beautiful.

Want me to show you?

BRAD: Okay.

SOPHIA looks out at the audience.

SOPHIA: Okay.
CLEO: A successful strip will get you six points.
SOPHIA: A man does not marry a woman who doesn't know how to take her clothes off.
CLEO: We're ready.

BRAD puts his fishing rod down and clears his throat.

Are you ready, Brad?
BRAD: Yes. I'm ready.

SOPHIA looks at the audience.

SOPHIA: You don't touch. Capici?

SOPHIA smiles and looks up.

Capici?

The lights dim. We hear the sound of the record starting on a turntable. The music is "Abat Jour," the song Sophia Loren strips to in the film Yesterday, Today and Tomorrow.

SOPHIA slowly unbuttons her dress and lets it fall to the floor. Her slip is short and she is wearing garters and stockings. She sits herself on a chair and takes her shoes off, one at a time.

She hesitates. The music gets a little louder. She undoes one garter and raises her leg and slowly pulls off one stocking. She stretches it and shoots it across the space. SOPHIA laughs and does the same with the second one. SOPHIA gets up and begins to sway and dance. SOPHIA turns and lets her hands slide down her back and bum. She turns again and smiles, and then stands still. The music keeps playing.

CLEO: That's it?
SOPHIA: Yes.

CLEO drums on the table or a piece of furniture nearby.

CLEO: Take it all off. More.
SOPHIA: I can't.
CLEO: *(to BRAD)* What do you think?
BRAD: I don't know.
SOPHIA: You know this is just pretend. Like a movie.
CLEO: You only did half the job.
SOPHIA: I'm finished. Fifty percent is all you need.

Pause.

When does *this* end?
CLEO: When we finish.

Scene 7

CLEO: On with more intimate life details with Brad Pitt and Sophia Loren.

CLEO points to the cards.

SOPHIA: May I?
BRAD: Yes, you may.
SOPHIA: My dear, do you ever want to get married?
BRAD: Maybe. Maybe I might.
SOPHIA: Did you ever have a date?
BRAD: Oh yes.
SOPHIA: What did you do on your first date?
BRAD: We went to a movie. We went out for dinner at McDonald's and we talk a lot.
CLEO: Anything sexual?
BRAD: We touched hands and we had our first kiss.
SOPHIA: Oh, nice.

Pause.

Do you want to talk about sex, maybe?
BRAD: It's kind of interesting.
SOPHIA: Why is it interesting?
BRAD: It came out of the blue. The first time I saw this—I saw it in a picture.
SOPHIA: You saw this picture—
BRAD: It made me think—it was new. It was shocking.
SOPHIA: And then what?
BRAD: I accidentally saw it on the Internet. I'm not supposed to see it.

SOPHIA: Is sex a bad thing?

BRAD: Not really.

SOPHIA: What's good about sex?

BRAD: I don't know.

SOPHIA: What's it like to fall in love?

BRAD: Like it feels good to be around each other.

SOPHIA: Does it always feel good?

BRAD: Yes. Most of the time.

SOPHIA: Like diving into a deep, warm pool

CLEO: Water can lie. It can be shallow.

SOPHIA: Why so pessimistic?

CLEO: When you dove in, where did you land?

SOPHIA: Married. To a nice Catholic dentist.

CLEO: How was the water?

SOPHIA: Comfortable.

CLEO: What kind of fish?

SOPHIA: Oral sturgeon.

Canned laughter.

CLEO: And you?

BRAD: Nothing. I don't have a girlfriend.

CLEO: Maybe you need to change your lure.

BRAD: That's a good idea.

BRAD goes to his tackle box. SOPHIA retaliates.

SOPHIA: And how about you, mistress of many?

CLEO: It's all relative, isn't it?

CLEO & SOPHIA: You be careful . . . I know too much . . .

SOPHIA: About what?

CLEO: About your accident.

SOPHIA: Everyone's had an accident in love. What was yours?

CLEO: Antony. Antony and I loved like wine.

SOPHIA: Wine?

CLEO: I drank a case of him.

SOPHIA: That can blind you.

CLEO: It did. I lost our child.

SOPHIA: I'm sorry.

Pause.

That must have been hard. What did Antony do?

CLEO: He kept fishing at every port.

SOPHIA: Did he catch many?

CLEO: Oh yeah.

SOPHIA: Ouch. What did you do?

CLEO: Sank to the bottom. And you?

SOPHIA: I eventually floated to the top. Belly up.

CLEO: You, the sex icon? The only time I thought you'd be belly up was—

SOPHIA: The only person I allowed myself to be belly up with was my husband!

CLEO: Someone you desired made you an offer.

SOPHIA: I was married!

CLEO: Yeah . . . but you chose to refuse.

SOPHIA: I had other people to look after. My children.

CLEO: So you sacrificed yourself?

SOPHIA: *(hesitantly)* No, I took care of myself.

CLEO: Right.

Pause.

Get my chair. And bring me the board.

CLEO is brought her wheelchair. She transfers herself independently, using the board. SOPHIA is forbidden from looking.

Scene 8

CLEO: Why don't you pick another card?

BRAD: Do you masturbate?

SOPHIA: Excuse me?

BRAD: Do you masturbate?

SOPHIA: Yes. I know the word. No, no I know that. What I don't understand is why we're doing this.

BRAD shrugs.

CLEO: Sexual assessment. I have been collecting facts from your answers from the beginning and . . .

She shows the binder.

I have the criteria to evaluate your sexual worth.

SOPHIA: My worth?

CLEO: Yes. I am going to determine what your sex life was previous to "the accident."

SOPHIA: My accident?

CLEO: Yes. You had an accident and I need to determine what your sexual life might have been if you'd never had "an accident."

SOPHIA: Why?

CLEO: To calculate the worth of the sexual experiences one will never have, or, in your case, the sexual opportunity you never took.

SOPHIA: I don't want to talk about that. No one wants to know those kinds of things. Who would want to know about that? I don't want to talk about—

CLEO: You don't have to talk about it; you're already in a display case.

SOPHIA: Why would anyone want to know about my . . . my missed opportunity.

CLEO: I see what you could have been and what you could have had.

SOPHIA: There's nothing for you to see.

CLEO: Why are you still hiding?

SOPHIA: I . . . I don't know.

CLEO: Number one: A man named Rick offered you a weekend of loving extramarital sex.

SOPHIA: That's dirty pool.

CLEO: Number two: You turned it down—

SOPHIA: You don't have the right to do that in front of everyone.

CLEO: That's life. I dove in shallow water at fifteen. I didn't have the luxury of choice. You had sexual opportunity and you gave it up.

SOPHIA: I was married.

CLEO: Number three: He died in a helicopter crash the next day. Number four—

SOPHIA: Please. Don't.

CLEO: You think if you had said yes, it wouldn't have happened. Number five: Your marriage smashed, fractured, and died.

Pause.

Based on that reaction, I'll give you a seven.

SOPHIA: Seven?

CLEO: Seven. Let's get on with the evaluation.

Scene 9

SOPHIA: I need to move. Could we just move a bit? I need to move.

SOPHIA looks up. Stamps her foot. Some sort of gesture.

CLEO and BRAD also look up.

The Tiger Lillies song "Freakshow" comes on.

Oh, thank you, thank you.

They all dance.

CLEO: *(over the song lyrics, improvising the timing)* Good grooming and maintenance . . . two points.
Bodily functions unaffected . . . fifteen points.
Good taste in music . . . one point.
Charming and flexible late in life . . . three points.
Loyalty to a mate . . . two points.
Expected to live beyond male counterpart . . . six points.

The song ends and they all stop dancing.

There are rules for rehabilitation after trauma and you need to learn them.
SOPHIA: You think so, do you?
CLEO: Yeah. *(confiding in her)* You're going through rehabilitation. You suffered a trauma and you didn't acknowledge it. It's all right. You don't have to soften it. In fact, it's better if you don't.

Bring me my binder. I will give you some rules. Fuck off if you don't want them.

Scene 10

SOPHIA: I never dated very much.
CLEO: Number one. Enjoy the process. Date for the sake of dating. Not everyone is at the same level of understanding of their bodies and minds. Date out of curiosity and without expectations.
SOPHIA: I was a scrawny pin. The only bumps on my body were my knees. Everything else was bone. I had a nickname in school: Boney Maroney. All the other girls wore bras and I was in undershirts till high school.

CLEO: Number two. Be realistic. During rehab, choose people you have a connection with regardless of physical or mental differences. Don't aim low, but be realistic.

SOPHIA: Years later, after a divorce, I was on my own and back at university. Things were going well, but I was getting lonely. I wanted some companionship. I thought maybe someone to go to the movies with, talk about books, you know, sort of a good friend guy.

CLEO: Number three. Don't be too available. Busy yourself with daily practises such as stacking cups in OT or pulleys in the gym. Knowing that you are not waiting around is attractive and mysterious. Everyone likes a bit of a challenge.

SOPHIA: I was taking an English class and desperately needed a copy of Sylvia Plath's *The Bell Jar*. I couldn't find one anywhere. Friends told me about a professor who had donated thousands of books to the university. They suggested I give him a call.

CLEO: Number four. Reveal yourself slowly, especially if you are feeling insecure. Insecurity is a natural phase of the rehabilitation process and it is easy to let yourself confide in anyone about bowels, bedsores, short-term memory, etc., but at this early stage of relationship, not everyone wants to hear these intimate details.

SOPHIA: I'd never called a man before. I mean, you know, to ask them for something. It seems so . . . so blunt. But I needed that damn book . . . and the company would be kind of nice . . . maybe. So I poured a glass of wine and practised what to say.

CLEO: Number five. Be prepared. To be spontaneous with sex you need to take some initial steps. If you are planning on having sexual intercourse and urinate through catheterization, catheterize before and after. Being physically prepared will allow you to enjoy your experience and be at ease.

SOPHIA: After the second glass of wine, I picked up the phone. I dialled. Ring, ring, ring. "I am not home at this time, please leave a message after the beep and I will get back to you as soon as possible." Think fast. Hello . . . Thisissusanna andIneedthebook*TheBellJar*. Couldyoupleasegivemeacallat5643321. Thankyou. Bye . . . Shit.

Pause.

Three days later he called. He apologized for not being able to answer my call. He did not have *The Bell Jar*, but could he come over this Friday.

CLEO: I give you a point five for that.

SOPHIA: Point five?! I got a date by myself. That's initiative.

CLEO: But you needed an excuse. *The Bell Jar*? Oh please. Point five it is.

SOPHIA: But it worked. He was interested . . . attracted to me. He called.

CLEO: You're confused. His attraction to you has no bearing on your own self-worth.

Pause.

SOPHIA: This is what I get from the queen of seduction who rolled out of the carpet . . . ta-da . . . to smite mighty Ceasar.

CLEO: I knew myself and loved myself before Caesar or any man.

SOPHIA: You've only had to think of yourself.

CLEO: You've had the luxury of choice.

SOPHIA: Not with my responsibilities.

CLEO: Stop being the martyr.

SOPHIA: People depend on me.

CLEO: Have you ever thought of yourself as beautiful, independent of someone else?

SOPHIA: I've never really thought about it. I remember being twelve or thirteen, standing on a street corner. I was on my way home from ballet class. A couple were standing behind me waiting for the light to change. They were speaking in German and didn't know that I could understand. The man was saying to the woman: "Sie wird eine hubshe." She is going to be a beauty.

CLEO: That's just someone else quantifying your worth.

SOPHIA: I am not a narcissist. Beautiful? To be honest, I sometimes prefer the ugly bits. They're juicier.

CLEO: You didn't answer the question.

SOPHIA: Look at you, playing it safe, blasting off deflective questions, afraid to show any weakness, shored up in your "queenliness."
CLEO: Ooooh . . . I'm trying to help you.
SOPHIA: No you're not. You're hiding. You just point and smear guck around. Who the hell do you think you are?
CLEO: Someone who understands and has been through it.
SOPHIA: You've had a horrific accident. You think that grants you divine insight? Your accident does not grant you wisdom. It's just a shitty, ugly thing.
CLEO: That you have no idea about.
SOPHIA: What matters, your royal highness, is what you've learned from that whole shitty, ugly thing and what you do with what you've learned.
CLEO: I've learned things you couldn't even think of.
SOPHIA: I don't count points on people. Scrap the royal self-righteousness. You were dealt a rotten hand. Join the club. Na . . . Mach da Bap zu!
CLEO: That's hiding in language, too!
SOPHIA: You're talking to decades of hard-learned lessons. Read my wrinkled lips: Shut your mouth!
CLEO: Okay.

Pause.

You want people to see you like Sophia Loren because you want to be seen as sexy.

Scene 11

SOPHIA: Sophia does it all with such panache and no shame. I wish I could do that.
CLEO: And that is?
SOPHIA: Be sexy and not feel guilty. I want to be one loaded-full-to-the-top lady. I know how to do that . . . but I'm afraid. I don't want it misunderstood . . . or

stepped on. I mean, it feels good to walk into a room and men turn . . . but I'm not . . . hungry . . . or "hunting." Can't I like that?

Pause.

You know what I love best about Sophia Loren? There's a scene from a movie . . . I don't know which one it is . . . I just saw a clip. But there is Sophia walking down a city street with such abandon. She swings her hips and her breasts are there like two . . . two happy babies. She's simply dressed . . . a skirt, blouse . . . short hair . . . no makeup, flat shoes. She strides down that street . . . beautiful and sexy, and I think, if anything got in her way she would flick it off like a dry bread crumb. And yet, if you stopped her to talk, I know that she would be warm, ready to laugh, and full of love.

Pause.

I want . . . all of that . . . with respect . . . Why can't I have that? I have a very good brain in this body. I wish I could stand here . . . naked . . . and talk about Joseph Campbell . . . the wondrous horror of living . . . follow your bliss . . . and have no one blink an eye. Respect.

Do you know . . . I dance in private? It would blow your mind to see how I can dance . . . and if I did that in public . . . what would happen? I know exactly what would happen.

CLEO: Tell me.

SOPHIA: Don't play stupid.

CLEO: Stop hiding.

SOPHIA: Give me one reason not to hide.

Silence.

(to BRAD) One reason.

BRAD: You're beautiful.

SOPHIA: I wish.

Pause.

(to CLEO) Now, it's my turn to ask you a question.

BRAD *moves to hand her the cards.*

CLEO: Yeah. Uh-huh.

Pause.

SOPHIA: What is with that ridiculous binder?
CLEO: I told you, we need to do a sexual assessment.
SOPHIA: I'm not going to talk to that.
CLEO: Talk to me then; I'm just following the rules.
SOPHIA: Try using your own rules.
CLEO: The rules are my own but criteria needs to be standardized.
SOPHIA: Standardized? *(SOPHIA laughs.)* That's impossible.
CLEO: I'm doing this for your benefit.
SOPHIA: *(facetiously)* Oh mighty Queen of the Nile . . . did it benefit you?
CLEO: This isn't about me; I'm talking about you.

Pause.

Fuck.
SOPHIA: Oh my, I don't think so. You are holding on to a folder of judgments that someone else made of you and you have to let it go.
CLEO: My sexuality was assessed and given a value. It was mandatory and I had no choice.
SOPHIA: You're not just that binder.
CLEO: I'm not in the mood.
SOPHIA: And I have been?

CLEO: *(lightly)* Let's talk about something else.

Pause. CLEO *puts on a smile.*

Tell me about your family. How did they—

Sneak attack. They brawl over the binder. SOPHIA *gets it, but is tackled and* CLEO *rolls over it.*

SOPHIA: So that's it.
CLEO: Play Antony again.
SOPHIA: No, it's too late. This show is already way off the tracks.
CLEO: I thought you do comfort best.
SOPHIA: Sure, for those who want it.
CLEO: Please play Antony. *(to* BRAD*)* You have to play too.
BRAD: Can you call me Watson?
CLEO: Sure. Watson.
SOPHIA: All right. Set the scene.
CLEO: It's after the war and Cleopatra and Antony have been defeated. They're in the mausoleum and are preparing to commit suicide with a group of their followers called the "Order of the Inseparable in Death."
SOPHIA: All right . . . Antony I am.

SOPHIA *assumes a rigid, upright noble stance. She nods to the audience.* CLEO *assumes a noble stance also and nods to the audience.* SOPHIA *and* CLEO *both look at* BRAD.

SOPHIA *indicates where he must sit, facing them with his back to the audience.*

(as Antony) Thank you. All of you who are here to celebrate our demise.
CLEO: You who have made life joyful; you whom Antony and I have feasted with, made love with, and now will die with. To the war!
BRAD: "To the war!"

SOPHIA: *(as Antony)* To your afterlife!
BRAD: "To your afterlife!"
CLEO: My afterlife?
SOPHIA: *(as Antony)* To your eternal youth!
CLEO: My youth?
SOPHIA: *(as Antony)* To happiness and never-ending love.
CLEO: What is this? A fucking fairy tale?
SOPHIA: You said this is just a game.
CLEO: Yeah, but not tonight.
SOPHIA: What are you saying?
CLEO: Look at me! I remind people that they are going to die.

Pause. SOPHIA looks at CLEO and gestures for her to give up the binder. Pause. CLEO gives it up. SOPHIA reads from the binder.

SOPHIA: Sexuality Assessment 926422, regarding the sexual and fertility consequences following a traumatic spinal-cord injury. Bodily functions pertaining to sexuality and fertility are not impaired. Social functions and interactions significantly reduced, which will affect future sexual self-esteem . . . What the hell is this?
CLEO: It's what someone was paid to do . . . to tell me who I am and what I'm worth.
SOPHIA: Are you telling me that one, or Cleopatra . . . the great seductress . . . a woman of power and profound thought, would let this garbage . . . this trivial, dripping crap . . . define who she is? Are you letting the words of some little teeny tiny neck-tied bean counter dictate your state of being? How dare you belittle yourself like that! How dare you!
CLEO: You're doing it yourself. You're doing it right now.
SOPHIA: No I'm not. I wouldn't even try to tell you what you're worth. You have to do that yourself.
CLEO: I'm worth it. I know I'm worth something. It's just so much easier to see what I'm not. It's easy for me to not place anything on what I've done or who I think I am. That's one of the reasons I'm so attracted to Cleopatra; she became

known for what her sexuality could get her, how it enhanced her reign over Egypt. I want to feel the kind of extraordinary pride and strength of self that I imagine her to have had. I want to feel the strength of who I am and I want people to see that . . . but reading the binder, if you read the binder, you'd realize I'm normal and I don't feel normal, so I don't want to be seen as normal. I don't want people to see me the way I see myself; I don't want people to know just how normal I am, because if I was, how would I be able to conquer my own Rome?
SOPHIA: Kyla, conquer yourself.
CLEO: I'm sorry. I'm so sorry.

SOPHIA signals to BRAD and together they undress CLEO.

How much do you regret not going to Rick?
SOPHIA: Ten out of ten.
CLEO: Yeah. Regrets are always ten.
SOPHIA: Eleven.
CLEO: You couldn't have saved him.
SOPHIA: Maybe not. I don't know.
How do you feel out of your binder?
CLEO: It's still fresh. I'm just settling into myself.
SOPHIA: I'd say it's a pretty nice self to settle into.
CLEO: That's an idea that I'm going to have to get used to.
SOPHIA: *(to BRAD)* Do you still fish?
BRAD: I haven't in a while, but I'll start again.
CLEO: Fishing reminds you of your dad, doesn't it?
BRAD: Yeah.

"Happy Days Are Here Again" starts to play.

Oh. It's the end.

After some of his best moves, BRAD waves to the women and steps out of the box and into the audience.

I see them and they see me like I see me.
SOPHIA: Really? I wonder, what do they see?
CLEO: The messy and glamorously gnarled pieces—aren't they juicier?

SOPHIA takes the old apple core from her cleavage.

CLEO & SOPHIA: Maybe?

The box disappears but CLEO and SOPHIA remain, dancing awkwardly, as the stage dims to black.

THE SALON AUTOMATON

A PLAY FOR ONE FLESH-AND-BLOOD ACTRESS AND THREE AUTOMATONS

Nathalie Claude

translated by Nathalie Claude in close collaboration with Moynan King

ACTING, AUTOMATION, AND EXISTENTIAL ANXIETY IN *THE SALON AUTOMATON*

Moynan King

The Salon Automaton begins with a long slow lighting fade accompanied by an audio track that sounds like a historical version of *muzak:* simple, melodic, repetitive, and decidedly mechanical in its production. About halfway through the fade one can clearly make out the silhouettes of four seated characters and a set that is framed in the shape of a birdcage in cross section. Gradually, over the very long fade, some details emerge from the dark and we are confronted with the scene of an intimate salon. The salon has a lived-in feel, mildly decrepit and a bit dusty, but elegant and charming in a style that combines hints of Art Nouveau with an Edwardian manor house. There are four characters in a semicircle on chairs around a coffee table, which serves as the scene's centrepiece. The characters are seated and completely still, strikingly still, eerily still. Their stillness is beyond a freeze; they are rapt in a restful yet lively suspension. The bulk of the set is now fully lit, and the characters sit like a portrait, suspended in time, evoking the distilled quality of suspense itself. The tableau remains static, immobile, until the central character, the Hostess, speaks. When she speaks only her lips and eyes move, the rest of her body remains rigid, in solidarity with her three guests. She welcomes her guests and invokes the muses. When her invocation is complete we hear the sound of a mechanical clock: tick tock, tick tock. The eyes of the Hostess move in time with the sound. Tick tock. She lifts her hand with a clear and singular articulation of the wrist. Tick tock. The Hostess's eyes dart in the direction of stage left, at her two female companions seated there, then stage right, where the lone male character sits immobile, focused front.

The Hostess is Nathalie Claude, the creator and performer of this "play for one flesh-and-blood actress and three automatons." Claude has created a theatrical world for herself and her three android co-stars that is distinctly Edwardian in its aesthetic yet resoundingly Enlightenment in its philosophical and scientific premise. René Descartes's *Treatise of Man* proposed a definition of man as statue or machine inhabited by a thinking ghost—introducing the concept of interactive dualism and laying the philosophical basis for the greatest question of the Enlightenment: what is meant by human? The Enlightenment was also, not incidentally, the golden age of the automaton. The advent of mimetic machines, such as Jacques de Vaucanson's "high-society spectacle in which an android played the flute and a mechanical duck was seen to digest its food,"[1] comes on the heels of Cartesian dualism and aligns the invention of such "toys" with the philosophic considerations of their time. (A fact that resonates well with Donna Haraway's suggestion that "the boundary is permeable between instrument and concept. Historical systems of social relation and historical anatomies of possible bodies, including objects of knowledge . . . mutually constitute each other.")[2] The style and content of Claude's work are essentially concerned with the human condition in a timeless way that gathers historical and contemporary philosophies of human beings together. Her relationship to the automatons—as her cultured guests—ultimately brings into focus the fact that our own human existence is moving towards an increased automation and, like the key-wound mechanisms of the clockwork automaton, towards an inevitable halt. The Hostess's drama is consciously enacted and re-enacted week after week, every Friday night. All four characters overtly theatricalize the body—and inspire theoretical rumination on the art of acting and the trouble with mimesis, in general. In fact, the automaton may be seen as an extension of the actor whose actions,

1 Gaby Wood, *Living Dolls: A Magical History of the Quest for Mechanical Life* (London: Alfred A. Knopf, 2003), 15.

2 Donna Haraway, *The Haraway Reader* (New York: Routledge, 2004), 23.

through familiarity (memorization) and repetition (rehearsal), become automated, become second nature, and result in a new and spontaneous vitality.[3] The paradox of spontaneity emerging from mechanistic repetition, whether rehearsed (as in the case of the actor) or programmed (as in the case of the automatons), invokes the force suggested by the Cartesian ghost in the machine (a potential energy in all matter), and is made manifest in this production where the fully mechanized, electronic energy of Claude's twenty-first century automatons are expected to keep pace with the organic energy of the charismatic actor that is Claude herself. And they do, they really do!

The opening sequence of Claude's play accentuates the dramatic tension between motion and stillness—between life and death—through the gradual revelation of the distinction between Claude and her machines, and the demonstration of the various "degrees of liberty"[4] of each of the automatons. In *The Salon Automaton* the first human expression that we hear from the automatons is the sound of breath. This emission of breath invokes the ancient concept of pneuma, the human spirit as embodied in the breath through which imagination and emotion can be transferred from one individual to another. The Hostess invites her automated companions to breathe with her, summoning them to action, and enjoining them to begin their performance by warming their voices and tuning themselves to each other "in perfect communion." Claude's early training in the European tradition of *mime corporel* and her work with physically based companies such as Omnibus and Carbone 14 contribute to her unique prowess as a performer and her highly gestural and focused acting style—her face and body comprise a language unto themselves. Claude's command of the stage and expertise in its conventions render

---

3 Joseph Roach, *The Player's Passion: Studies in the Science of Acting* (Ann Arbor: U of Michigan P, 1993), 16.

4 "Degrees of liberty" is the term Claude uses in the text to refer to the automatons' capabilities; what they are able to do. All three have a detailed set of motor "skills" involving the face, neck, and arms. In addition each automaton has a "special skill": the Drinking Patroness drinks champagne, the Dandy Poet can gesticulate grandly with both of his arms, and the Cabaret Artist has increased gesticulation in her right hand and wrist and each of her fingers can move individually.

her performative passions infectious to an audience. She is, as Erin Hurley has written, "a hugely charismatic performer with a gift for seriously, emotionally, imaginatively and intellectually engaging spoof."[5] Nathalie Claude is a funny and compelling artist who fully inhabits her characters, drawing spectators into the spatially and temporally determined fantasies that form the basis of her work as a creator/performer. As a creator/performer her reputation is built on her solo work and this, *The Salon Automaton*, emerges directly out of that work, constituting the third instalment in a series known as *The Madness Trilogy*. The first two instalments, *Lapine-Moi/Rabbit-I* (2005) and *Cerveau fêlé 101/Broken Brain 101* (2006), rely, like *The Salon Automaton*, on an overtly theatrical performance and staging style along with the distinct maintenance of a fourth wall; they are worlds unto themselves, inhabited by original and meticulously detailed characterization and design elements. (Original and—I just have to add—brilliant sound scores by Isabelle Lussier are a fundamental element in each of the three instalments, for example). But *The Salon Automaton* marks a stylistic departure within the trilogy in a number of ways. *Lapine-Moi/Rabbit-I* and *Cerveau fêlé 101/Broken Brain 101* are considerably shorter works (twenty and thirty minutes long respectively) and are each completely bilingual; they are written in both English and French, alternating between the two languages with such fluid clarity as to render translation for a unilingual (English or French) audience unnecessary. But the thing that separates *The Salon Automaton* from its predecessors, positioning it firmly on the outskirts of the solo tradition, is the presence of three lifelike automated characters who populate the world of the salon and who, as I suggested above, wholly engage the sympathies of the spectator on a deep emotional and intellectual level. Through recorded human voices, gestural mimicry, and their intimate relationship with the Hostess these robots embody the theoretical premise of the James–Lange theory of emotion, which holds that physiological manifestation is the essence of emotional response; that is to say, emotions are not only communicated through a physiological response but also that emotion may not even be said to exist without it.

5 Erin Hurley, "Companioned Solos: Nathalie Claude's Trilogie de la folie," *Canadian Theatre Review* 149 (2012): 23.

Therefore, the impact of a passion expressed by an actor (or an automaton), if accurately executed, will illicit exactly the same response from an interlocutor or spectator as the expression of a genuine emotional experience because the "mind's perception of the physiological manifestation is the emotion."[6]

Claude's automated companions are in fact contemporary electronic mechanisms replicating historical clockwork automatons. They are, in short, performing the role of automatons performing the role of guests at the Hostess's salon. The original clockwork automatons, popular as marketing tools (think of its contemporary offspring, the Eaton's Christmas window displays) and spectacle (smoking monkeys or toy acrobats were popular versions), predate audio recording technology. Rather than mechanically generated sound, Claude's automatons have recorded vocal tracks performed by actors. Likewise their motor mechanisms are not the windup clockwork variety, but rather the product of advanced electronics and detailed programming. The control software was custom designed for the show by Simon Laroche who, Claude asserts, "kind of created the characters with me, because in rehearsal he proposed a lot." As the robots evolved along with the script, the text influenced the gestural programming of the characters so, for example, "Simon would make a gesture combining the neck and the eye as the Patroness said: 'Wellllll.' " It was a unique rehearsal process because "everything had to be decided in advance, every gesture, every mood." There were, Claude notes, "two puppet masters, in a way."[7]

Laroche's custom program "resembles a lighting-control software with recorded cues, and timing and delay transitions in between."[8] The show has more than 1,500 cues for the movements and voices of the automatons alone (not including the traditional lighting and sound cues for the production).

---

6 Roach, 84.

7 Nathalie Claude, Personal Interview with Moynan King, 12 Aug. 2013. All subsequent quotations from Nathalie are taken from the same interview.

8 Simon Laroche, Personal Interview with Moynan King, 5 Aug. 2013. All subsequent quotations from Simon are taken from the same interview.

> And in addition to these there were specially programmed cues (such as the automatic blinking of the eyes, or mouth-movement sequences, for example). During the show, cues were being recalled for playback and would automatically follow one another until an indication in a cue would tell the software to wait for further human input. (Laroche)

This interplay of technology and "human input" are key to the theatrical magic of this unique play, and something to bear in mind as you read. In a recent discussion with Claude I asked her what it was like to perform with automated humanoid actors. "They are very reliable," she said with glee, and continued:

> They are rigorous, like clockwork. I am used to working with very precise actors who know their craft, and the intonation of the automatons was very real and very true but the intonation was exactly the same every night. There was no surprise; the only surprise was if something went wrong—if there was a delay, or something froze on the technical end. At the same time I really managed to get lost during the performance, and sometimes I truly forgot they were robots. I thought they were fabulous actors!

Claude's theatrical manifestation of the search for the perfect companion has its roots in the literary tradition of Prometheus, Frankenstein, and Pygmalion. At the base she had decided everything; she had control of everything. And her character, the Hostess, is in turn revealed to have created her companions herself. "So," Claude reminded me, "if anything happened I had the knowledge and the improvisation skills to deal with it. Let's say the Dandy Poet burst into flames—I could have continued the show." Claude's confidence and radical narcissism are transferred onto the Hostess, who is "on top, no matter what. The Hostess was the hostess of the whole ceremony." This ceremony is characterized, at its foundation, as a disavowal of the isolation and desperate loneliness of a character plagued with a contagious illness. This disavowal is one that breaches the boundaries of sanity (remember this is the final instalment of Claude's *Madness Trilogy*), and insanity is the historical hallmark fate of the character who keeps company with mechanical or otherwise fabricated beings. While Claude expresses complete satisfaction with her mechanical collaborators on stage, the same cannot be said of the desolate Hostess, whose frustration with her companions' limitations results in behaviour that is ultimately unhinged. And as the Hostess spirals into the depths of her own madness the sympathies of the audience become singularly invested in the automatons. The existential crisis of the lonely, sick Hostess is expressed as the existential crisis of the automatons, as they panic, wondering, in a moment of Cartesian reversal, "I do not think, therefore do I not exist?"

In production, *The Salon Automaton* ends as it begins, with a long slow lighting fade. The mechanical tick tock of the windup clock has been replaced with the electromagnetic sound of a theremin, whose eerie tone is uncannily corporeal and humanoid. The dramatic tension between motion and stillness, between life and death, are once again brought into sharp relief. The mortal stillness of the Hostess is paradoxically contrasted with the emotional physiology of the slowing movements of the automatons, whose voices meld in expressing infinite awe at the wonder of "your humanity, your humanity, your humanity . . . "

A NOTE ON THE AUTOMATONS AND THEIR "DEGREES OF LIBERTY"

Each of the automatons are rooted to their chairs. They can move their heads from side to side and up and down and execute diagonal tilts of the neck, as well as open and close their eyes and mouths, allowing for extensive facial expression.

In addition, each automaton has a special skill suited to their individual character type. The Dandy Poet, the wordsmith and wit, has the ability to gesticulate widely with his arms, which is excellent for accentuating his (occasionally grand) declamatory style. The Drinking Patroness, suitably, can drink champagne from a glass that is forever poised in her downstage hand. The glass, when filled with liquid, seems to magically drain as she lifts it to her lips. The Cabaret Artist, the most sensual of the three, can move her right arm up and down, and each of the fingers of her right hand are able to gesture individually.

The mechanical programming and realization of these eerily life-like creatures is the genius of set designer Raymond Marius Boucher and robotics designer/electronic art performer Simon Laroche.

The Salon Automaton is the third part of *The Madness Trilogy*, a set of solo plays created by Nathalie Claude. The first two plays, *Rabbit-I* and *Broken Brain 101*, were created at the Edgy Women Festival in Montreal and presented in Toronto, New York, Berlin, and Ljubljana, Slovenia.

The Salon Automaton was first produced in French by Momentum and Usine C from October 7 to 25, 2008, at Usine C, Montreal, with the following voice cast and creative team:

The Hostess of the Salon: Nathalie Claude
The Cabaret Artist: Céline Bonnier
The Drinking Patroness: Marie-France Lambert
The Dandy Poet: Patrice Coquereau

Director: Nathalie Claude
Assistant director and stage manager: Colette Drouin
Set design and props: Raymond Marius Boucher
Automatons programming: Simon Laroche
Sound design and original music: Isabelle Lussier
Costumes: Judy Jonker
Lighting design: Claude Cournoyer
Makeup and hair styling: Angelo Barsetti

The English version—made possible through a creator/performer residency at Buddies in Bad Times Theatre, where Nathalie Claude worked in close collaboration with Moynan King—was first produced in Toronto at Buddies, from December 1 to 12, 2009. It featured the following voice cast and the same creative team as the French production:

The Hostess of the Salon: Nathalie Claude
The Cabaret Artist: Moynan King
The Drinking Patroness: Leni Parker
The Dandy Poet: Clinton Walker

CHARACTERS

The Hostess of the Salon: a flesh-and-blood actress
The Cabaret Artist: an automaton
The Drinking Patroness: an automaton
The Dandy Poet: an automaton

Scene 1: Welcome!

HOSTESS: Bienvenu, bienvenu, and WELCOME, one and all! You, madame, the Drinking Patroness, welcome! And you, mademoiselle, the Cabaret Artist, welcome! And you, monsieur, the Dandy Poet, welcome! Welcome to my humble salon for another stimulating evening, which, I predict, will be an exceptional one.

Already I sense a rather marvellous atmosphere floating around in the room, invoking a powerful tranquility, that is indeed intoxicating.

I perceive—as vividly as the owl scrutinizing its prey in the darkness of the night—I perceive the amazing potential of this unique moment, which I am about to happily share with you all, my precious guests.

OUI! I feel a strong energy, mounting all around, activating the senses! The hearing is aligned and receptive, the sight streamlined and effective, the smell inclined and perceptive, the touch refined and suggestive, and the taste defined and selective!

Vous le sentez n'est-ce pas, mes amis?

Tonight, as we do each and every Friday night, we will discuss everything, because I insist that everything has a reason to be discussed.

Ladies and gentleman! Yes, monsieur, ladies first. In fact tonight, the feminine, by its obvious number, will win gracefully over the masculine. Do not think too much about it, sir, it is simply a question of mathematics and common etiquette.

Tonight we will not delve too deeply into any one question and risk extensive boredom. Instead we will suggest gently, discuss rapidly, and converse with agility! Speaking only to the point of inspiration, and halting before any petty confrontation!

And now, I call upon the muses, imagined, alive, and dreamt! And in particular you, Calliope! Muse of all muses, queen of supreme eloquence, grace us with your divine wisdom, and loosen these shy tongues that wait patiently for a glimpse of any worthy inspiration with which to express themselves!

A very long pause punctuated by the tick tock of a wind-up clock.

But, but, but, here I am talking, talking, talking a blue streak, and I have not even given you any sensible amount of time to settle in and make yourselves comfortable, forcing you to patiently listen on and on to my chattering and babbling without head nor tail, beginning nor end, and not offering you even a pause for breath. Breath, the life source that unites us all, so naturally, so humanly . . . So, to officially begin this very special evening, my friends: RESPIRONS! LET US BREATHE! All united in perfect communion. LET US BREATHE!

The AUTOMATONS open their mouths wide and emit the sound of breath.

We then hear the sound of an orchestra tuning in preparation for a concert mixed with the sounds of the automatons vocalizing and warming up their mouths, lips, and throats, like actors preparing their voices for a show.

HOSTESS: The, the, the, the—
THE THREE AUTOMATONS: The, the, the, the—
HOSTESS: Salon!
THE THREE AUTOMATONS: Salon!
HOSTESS: Automaton!
THE THREE AUTOMATONS: Automaton!
HOSTESS: The Salon Automaton!
POET: The Salon-Automaton!
ARTIST: The Salon-Automaton!
PATRONESS: The Salon-Automaton!

The sound of an organ from a Catholic mass underscores the following as the HOSTESS speak-sings like a priest delivering the Eucharist.

HOSTESS: Let us exchange, and share our deepest thoughts, our brightest ideas.
I give you the power of speech.
Embrace this power and share it with the world.
This is the true beauty of my salon, imagined for you.
Let an explosion of words flow from you, revealing, you and me, and us, and all of creation altogether.
And now discuss anything, and talk about everything.
Truly I say to you, this is the reason for our weekly alliance, created for you, my faithful disciples, my apostles, my dear friends.
You will do this in remembrance of the love you have for me?
Won't you? Won't you?

The THREE AUTOMATONS *answer in the singing style of devotional response.*

THE THREE AUTOMATONS: Yes, blesséd hostess, we will do this out of love for you.

Suddenly they all change their tone from reverent call-and-response to exuberant conversation.

Yes, yes! Yes!
PATRONESS: Yes, oh yes!
ARTIST: Good, very good, yes!
POET: Yes, and yes and, yes!
PATRONESS: And I would say yes!
ARTIST: And let me add: Yes, yes, yes!
POET: YES!
ARTIST: YES!
PATRONESS: YES!
ARTIST: And, if I may also say: BRAVO!
PATRONESS: Oh, yes, BRAVO!
POET: All together then: Bravo!
ARTIST: An inspiring . . .

POET: And very inspired . . .
PATRONESS: Introduction. Yes!
THE THREE AUTOMATONS: Yes! Yes! Yes!

They all turn their heads, for the first time, towards the HOSTESS. *The* HOSTESS *sits.*

Scene 2: Champagne!

HOSTESS: AHHHHHH, mes amis, mes amis, my friends! What a lively demonstration of your overflowing enthusiasm! You are all clearly of a splendid disposition to make this evening an incredible triumph! Thank you, thank you, thank you, I deeply appreciate it. I truly do. You know how important the success of my salon is to me. Secretly I dream of hosting the greatest salon. Its audacity, refinement, and celebrity will spread throughout all circles of society, giving it the dazzling reputation of THE salon were one should be. THE salon, the ONLY salon. MY salon. My humble salon. The only salon that ever was and became the salon where one would be able to say, like you tonight, my dear friends, I was there at that salon; I was there!
POET: I was there—me, the dandy poet—I was there!
ARTIST: I was there too, monsieur; me, the cabaret artist; I was there!
PATRONESS: I was there too, mesdames, as well as you, monsieur; me, the drinking patroness; I was there!
HOSTESS: Because, really, the absent ones always miss out on something.
THE THREE AUTOMATONS: The absent ones always miss out on something.

The AUTOMATONS *emit mechanical and repetitive music through their mouths.*

HOSTESS: My friends, let us embark! Let us step into the core of the conversation. Shall we? Shall we begin gently, with the most banal of questions: How are you? You, monsieur the poet, our volcanic intellectual? And you, mademoiselle the artist, our shining star? And you, madame the patroness, our golden-hearted benefactress? How are you? Comment allez-vous?

PATRONESS: Very well, thank you. I feel well; I am well. I am rather quite well. Very, very well. And since it is my turn to speak, I would like to . . .

POET: Everything is going quite well. Life is beautiful. My life is beautiful, but at times also cruel. All in all, however, quite beautiful and well. A beautiful cruelty, life. Life is so beautifully cruel.

ARTIST: Cruel, yes, tirelessly cruel. But fine, yes, it is all fine. It will all be fine, even though this cruel life has many shades of darkness: dark as tar, dark as ebony, dark as ink. Darkness is an absolute, my friends.

POET: The dark side of life is necessary, mademoiselle; it creates a shocking contrast with your pink cheeks, and by its very existence reveals all the colourful shades of the universe.

ARTIST: Monsieur, our perfumed dandy, I know my colours. The darkness is my sister, my lover, my destiny. I am not complaining, I am simply making a point. Nuance.

PATRONESS: All this darkness, this cruelty, that which I like to call: the descent. And it's opposite, the luminous contrary: the ascent! And since it is my turn to speak, I would . . .

POET: Descend to re-ascend!

ARTIST: Go up, but always fatally, end up going down . . .

HOSTESS: To descend, abandon hope, be completely discouraged, without faith . . . but then suddenly to believe again, rise up, resist, fight, stand up, and win! Let me see. Let us compare this with the movement inside a clock, or a watch that stops its mechanism at its spring's end. We take the clock key and wind the key inside the clock and MIRACLE, everything starts working again. Life's tick tock, tick tock, tick tock has triumphed! And so it goes, the fragile pendulum, living inside of us all. So it goes, until the next disappointment, the next fear, the next terror, the next challenge, the next struggle, until the next CRUEL, BITTER GIFT OF LIFE ITSELF.

But, anyhow, life is a beautiful thing, and it just feels so good to be alive! Merci la vie. Merci la vie. Merci. Merci. Merci.

A long pause. We hear the sound of a loud, ominous heartbeat.

After a moment the AUTOMATONS *interject and break the sombre mood.*

THE THREE AUTOMATONS: Ha, ha, ha! Merci la vie! Ha, ha, ha!
HOSTESS: But tonight, my friends, all I really care about is your brilliant and delicate minds.
POET: Now that you mention it, my dear hostess, before I set foot into your welcoming home I emptied my mind of all distraction, confusion, and ignorance. For you tonight, madame, my mind is a blank page—tabula rasa.
HOSTESS: Oh, monsieur, you worry me. A blank page, tabula rasa? You are taking quite a risk, presenting yourself here, in my salon avec l'esprit comme page blanche. Remember, we are only admitted here because we have all our wits about us!
POET: I did not forget it, madame. I simply washed it of all impurities!
ARTIST: Ha. Ha. Ha. Impurities? Don't you mean, monsieur, a thorough house-cleaning?

The HOSTESS *and* PATRONESS *laugh.*

I myself am here in total purity. True, I am complex, replete with sin, and imperfect, but alas, devoid of vanity. You see me here as I am and my mind did not require a trip to the laundry!
POET: But mademoiselle, we would expect no less of you. You in all your simplicity, you in all your triviality. Who knows, perhaps later you will titillate us with one of your diverting little pantomimes?
PATRONESS: Oh, yes! One of your little pantomimes, mademoiselle, that would be so amusing! And since it is my turn to speak, I would . . .
ARTIST: As you know, monsieur, it doesn't take much to fire up my zeal. A simple shift of the hip, a dancing hand, a precise gaze, and the net is cast. My public, having fallen into a swoon, is eating out of my hand. My simplicity is surprisingly efficient. I won't waste my breath on you, monsieur le poète, but if you provoke me further, I will gladly take you on!

HOSTESS: Now, now, my dear guests, do not forget the rule. No quarrelling in my salon. We are all simply expressing our point of view. But monsieur, I do hope that at some point tonight you will indulge us in some sprightly repartee, perhaps a raging poem against a seductive pantomime?
POET: But of course, madame. Anything you want. I am your devoted servant. And mademoiselle, you know that our little rivalry is actually the spice of the salon. Please do not take offence. This is who I am; it's the way I was made, pedantic, petulant, and shockingly intelligent!

The sound of a whinnying horse and a trot come out of the mouth of the poet.

PATRONESS: Dear hostess.
HOSTESS: Yes, my dear friend?
PATRONESS: Ah, good, FINALLY, someone is paying attention to me. I was beginning to wonder if I had become invisible to the human eye. May I speak?
HOSTESS: But absolutely, madame the patroness. Please, please grace us with your words of wisdom.
PATRONESS: So, then, let me say a few words. You all know how I delight in the sparks of our diverse minds. And you all know how much I enjoy quenching my thirst at the fountain of your dazzling talents. I am your most faithful admirer, your friend of the ARTS! An aesthete, really, being myself an artist of the song, an artist of the stage, an artist of the word, a writer, if you will, at times, but only for the pleasure it brings as a modest dilettante. Oh, and did you know that I have even tried my hand at pantomime? Can you imagine? *(She laughs.)* But in all humility, I could not be mentioned in the same breath as you, mademoiselle.

I have occasionally indulged in painting, as a distraction. My style is peculiar and original but the fact that I seem to insist on using, on the same canvas, buttercup yellow and fire-truck red often spoils the result. I am at this very moment in the process of having this bizarre reflex analyzed by my genius psychoanalyst, Doctoress Spielrein, who is particularly interested in this aberration. Do you know her, the doctoress Spielrein? She is fabulous!

And as you already know, I am still completely passionate about anthropology.

And for the past three months, oh, and this is so typically me: "*Why do more, when you are already doing too much*?" So, as I was saying, for the past three months I have been taking anatomy classes: how to dissect a cadaver: Thrilling!!!! I have been learning all about the heart, the lungs, and the stomach! And I have met the most sublime woman, Constance de Garland; she is so passionate about anatomy that she has devised a very discreet, but very expensive, way to transport, in the trunk of her new car, a fresh cadaver every time she goes to her country house! She is never bored! A resolutely MODERN WOMAN, indeed!

Oh, and did I tell you about my archaeological expedition to Egypt, the land of Nefertiti, last December? Quite exotic. We were promised a mummy, and we only found insignificant vases. Disappointing. Extremely disappointing. I still dream about MY MUMMY, my own personal MUMMY, that I should have discovered all on my own. MY VERY OWN EGYPTIAN MUMMY! Very, very disappointing. I still have a lump in my throat when I think about it . . . Oh yes, throat! My throat! My subject has finally come back to me! My throat is craving golden bubbles. I dream of shared wisdom, visions, and discussions, but before anything else, Madame Hostess, my throat is thirsty for fine champagne! Champagne?

HOSTESS: Ohhhh, quelle sotte je fais, quelle vilaine hôtesse! What a dreadful hostess I am! But YES, of course, I completely forgot! Forgive me, my friend. And, oh, look, you already had your glass in your hand, patiently waiting to be honoured. Ahhhhh, champagne!!!!!!!

POET: No, madame, you are not a dreadful hostess! You skilfully allow your guests to become thirsty, obliging them to be patient, so they may enjoy the thrill of delayed gratification. Teaching them the musicality of heightened appreciation, culminating in a final crescendo when that first sip finally comes in contact with their parched lips.

ARTIST: How you play us, madame; we are but instruments in your hands.

HOSTESS: This is the sport of the salon! To bring together human beings that I deeply love, human beings that I know very, very well. To bring them together and make their souls vibrate as one. I am talking about you, my friends.

The AUTOMATONS *hesitate before answering.*

ARTIST: Mmhhhhh, yes, us—humans—that you deeply love, yes!
POET: Mhhhhhhhhhhhm. The sport of the salon, madame, sport played between . . . humans.
PATRONESS: Mhhhhhhhhh, vibrate, between humans, as one, madame.
ARTIST: Vibrate!
POET: Play!
PATRONESS: Drink!
HOSTESS: Yes! And now let us raise a glass. Champagne! Champagne! Ohhhhhh, champagne! Excuse me, please, if you will.

The HOSTESS *starts to leave but stops before exiting through the upstage curtains. The* AUTOMATONS *are completely immobile. She speaks in an aside to herself.*

They are perfectly happy. Yes, my guests seem to be perfectly happy. This brings me such joy. They are contented by the simple fact that we are sharing this very moment together. So perfectly simple, so simply perfect. Our intellects are in perfect pitch, totally synchronized. Our brains are like magnets, irresistibly attracted one to the other. Everything is perfect. This evening is perfect. The ambiance is perfect. My outfit is perfect. The lighting is perfect. The scent is perfect. Everybody is smiling happily. Happy to be here, with me. I am the hostess of this salon, and I am living a moment of pure perfection. I could die right here, right now, and I would be perfectly happy!

The THREE AUTOMATONS *close their eyes. The* HOSTESS *exits upstage. There is a musical interlude wherein a sweet, old-fashioned tune comes from the mouths of the* AUTOMATONS.

Shortly, the hostess returns with a tray of glasses and a bottle of champagne, dancing to the music. She carefully places glasses in the hands of the ARTIST *and the* POET *and pours them all a glass of champagne. The music stops.*

To the salon!

The AUTOMATONS *open their eyes and resume humanoid attitudes.*

PATRONESS: To the salon!

The PATRONESS *raises her glass, having had a permanent champagne flute in her hands from the beginning of the show.*

ARTIST: To the salon!

The ARTIST *raises her glass but it falls from her mechanical hand and smashes on the floor.*

POET: To the salon!

The POET *raises his glass and it falls from his mechanical hand, smashing on the floor.*

Scene 3: Broken Fragment

The PATRONESS *takes a long drink from her champagne while the others contemplate the pile of broken glass on the floor.*

HOSTESS: Oh, la maladresse! La maladresse! I am terribly sorry, terribly sorry. Let me clean that up. Don't worry, my friends, it's just a little accident, that's all. I'll be right back.

The HOSTESS, *discouraged, exits upstage to fetch a broom and cloth.*

ARTIST: Oh no, no, no, "la maladresse, maladresse," the meaning, the meaning "maladresse," what is THE meaning?

The ARTIST *strains to comprehend this new word, searching her mechanical brain for the definition. The* HOSTESS *returns and begins to clear the mess.*

POET: Madame, it is I who feel responsible. Sometimes my own movements are so strange to me. I am a pensive man, so pensive that sometimes I forget I even have a body.

The HOSTESS *sweeps the broken glass into existing piles of glass at the edge of the room and under the table.*

HOSTESS: It is I, monsieur, who feels clumsy at times and out of my body, but really, it's no problem . . . I will take care of everything.
ARTIST: Oh yes! I found it, maladresse is *awkwardness*! You realize that awkwardness is often about hiding a truth. My truth? I prefer the existential high of the beloved "green fairy" to the superficial bubbles of the "bourgeoisie"!
PATRONESS: Well, we all have our rank and place! You see, here, I am the one and only true lover of the golden bubbles, AS IF I was born with a champagne glass—in my hand!!!!!!

She laughs nervously and, taking a long swig, drains her glass of champagne.

HOSTESS: *(with two new glasses in hand)* There, there, an unfortunate incident, already forgotten! We won't discuss it anymore! Champagne?
PATRONESS: Why not?

The HOSTESS *fills her glass.*

HOSTESS: *(to the* POET*)* Champagne?
POET: NO! Thank you . . . for now. I am just furious at the prospect that I might have stained my suit. My beautiful suit made of French linen and Scottish velvet, with its intricate brocade, hand-sewn! What a mess!
HOSTESS: *(to the* ARTIST*)* Champagne?

ARTIST: Thank you, no, none for now. If, however, during the evening I find myself dying of thirst I will take a sip from your glass, dear patroness? You won't mind, will you?

The HOSTESS pours herself a glass and sips.

PATRONESS: My glass is your glass, and everything I have is yours as well. Your destiny is linked to mine and you know it. Move me, amuse me, trouble me, shock me . . . as you wish, BUT, make me forget myself. That is my only demand.
HOSTESS: Well, to you and I, dear patroness, a toast!
HOSTESS & THE THREE AUTOMATONS: Santé!

The PATRONESS, miraculously, raises a second glass, draining it of its contents. She makes sounds of delightful satisfaction while the POET and the ARTIST mime the act of drinking champagne along with her. They accompany their mime with the sounds of drinking and swallowing: gulp, gulp, ahhh, etc. . . .

Scene 4: Cucumbers and Amusements

HOSTESS: Ohhhh, all these little distractions have made me completely forget that I had specially prepared for you, as I always do, my cucumber sandwiches that you like so much! If the stomach is famished, the mind won't flourish!
ARTIST: *(sarcastically)* Of course, your famous cucumber sandwiches! *(hushed)* That look like a wet handkerchief served on a plate!
POET: *(equally unenthusiastic)* But what a delicacy they are!
PATRONESS: *(and also sarcastically)* The definitive delicacy of your salon, madame!
HOSTESS: I'll go fetch them! If you will excuse me once more. She who is absent always misses something!!

The AUTOMATONS all laugh.

If I miss out on any delicious gossip I expect a full report when I get back. Promise?

THE THREE AUTOMATONS: Promise!

The HOSTESS exits to a room upstage, which, only partially lit, we can now vaguely see. Once she is gone the THREE AUTOMATONS close their eyes and mouths. We hear, once again, the sweet tune of the interlude music while the HOSTESS busies herself in the offstage room.

The HOSTESS returns with a tray of sandwiches.

HOSTESS: Voilà! My cucumber delectation for your appreciation! Did I miss anything?
Some speculation, some declamation, or perhaps even some revelation?

She goes to each of the AUTOMATONS, placing a napkin on their laps.

PATRONESS: No, no, no, nothing really, banalities . . .
ARTIST: Futilities . . .

The POET's mechanical brain seems to race as he blurts out the following:

POET: Futility: the quality of having no useful results; uselessness. Lack of importance or purpose; frivolousness. A futile act. In vain, pointless, ineffectual, unsuccessful. Also: frivolous, foolish, senseless, facetious, superficial, feather-brained.

Really, nothing, madame, you have not missed a thing.

HOSTESS: Well, I am delighted to hear that, monsieur le poète, but sometimes you do express yourself quite literally, as if you were a dictionary! It is a fabulous diversion!

POET: I AM a *dictionary*. I was born that way. There is a universal dictionary, and a general encyclopedia, programmed skilfully into me!

The other two AUTOMATONS *express discomfort with the* POET*'s proclamation.*

HOSTESS: *(surprised)* Programmed? He said programmed; I don't understand . . . programmed? What do you mean when you say programmed? Maybe what you wanted to say was . . .

She continues to mutter under her breath.

PATRONESS & ARTIST: *(through their teeth)* NOOOOOOOO, no, no, not programmed, not PROGRAMMED . . . NOOOOOO . . .
PATRONESS: *(trying to save the day)* I think . . . what you really want to say is that you are CULTIVATED. Yes, WELL-EDUCATED, yes, and because of that you feel at times like a dictionary, and we might even say, in some ways, that you ARE a dictionary!
ARTIST: And monsieur, if you ARE a dictionary, well then, I am . . . I AM an electrical lamp!! And if I say CLICK, oh, can you see the light shining through my nose? A practical, and very theatrical, "métamorphose"!
PATRONESS: And . . . I AM a bottomless jug! It's true, I'm telling you! You can fill me up, and fill me up again! There is no end— The Drinking Patroness can take it! I have drunk, and will drink, ten times more than you might think!

The AUTOMATONS *laugh exaggeratedly.*

HOSTESS: And me, I am a sad cucumber sandwich in waiting *(hiding behind the plate of sandwiches)* that nobody has even considered tasting; my heart is in deep, deep suffering!
ARTIST: Oh, yes, we completely forgot! The cucumber sandwiches! Mmm! Mmm! Mmm!
PATRONESS: Sweet delicacies. Oh, you do know how to spoil us, madame!

POET: Ahhhh, poetry! The lightness of the cream, the tenderness of the cucumber, the smoothness of the bread . . .
HOSTESS: Eat! Eat, my companions! Mademoiselle, eat, please?

The AUTOMATONS *are each offered a sandwich, which they refuse because of their "degrees of liberty."*

ARTIST: Oh, um, I'd prefer to wait a bit . . .
HOSTESS: Well then, madame, please, eat, eat?
PATRONESS: Oh when I finish this . . . *(referring to her champagne)*
HOSTESS: Very well. So, monsieur, if you please, eat, eat?
POET: I am not very hungry tonight, madame, only my eyes will feast on them.
HOSTESS: Really? Really? *(disappointed)*
THE THREE AUTOMATONS: *(final)* REALLY.
HOSTESS: Very well then. They are so tasty.

She eats alone, but the AUTOMATONS *join her with sounds of eating and appreciation.*

THE THREE AUTOMATONS: MmmHHH, mmmm, mmm, mmhhhhmmm, ahhh . . .
HOSTESS: So, my friends, since you have no appetite tonight, what would you say to some *intellectual* appetizers? Or, if you prefer, some witty wordplay to chew on?
ARTIST: Yes! A game to distract me from the present, which can be so unpleasant!
PATRONESS: Yes, tasteful amusements: charades, anagrams, and champagne!
POET: I am armed and ready for a match of verbal fencing! What merriment do you suggest, madame?
HOSTESS: Let's play "I Can Give You a Phrase With"!

A kitsch TV game-show jingle plays each time the title of the game "I Can Give You a Phrase With" is said.

ARTIST: YES! "I Can Give You a Phrase With"! *(jingle)*
POET: "I Can Give You a Phrase With"? *(jingle)*
PATRONESS: Yes, "I Can Give You a Phrase With"! *(jingle)*
HOSTESS: . . . With the word, the word . . . ? Cucumber! Cu-cum-ber!
POET: Oh yes, I know that game! "I Can Give You a Phrase With"! *(jingle)* . . . Cucumber . . . Oh!

In your flower garden, wisteria, roses, daisies, then, strangely, by caprice or female eccentricity, every summer, I have seen, standing proudly in the sunniest section, a queer anomaly: two or three CUCUMBERS, madame—a disturbing image, a jarring vision that I will simply call vulgarity.

HOSTESS: Good, BRAVO! Bravo, monsieur! A very long phrase, but nicely put. Now, mademoiselle?
ARTIST: *(thinking)* Mhmmm, mmmh . . . I have already eaten my CUCUMBER today, and there really isn't much more to say.
POET: Banal, but charming.
PATRONESS: I would rather say that she hit the nail on the head! So, my turn! *(thinking)* Mhmmmm . . .

The CUCUMBER is a vegetable known to soothe tired eyes, indeed, but we should not forget the delicacy of its flesh in salads, or cold soups, so we could say happily: the CUCUMBER has "multiple personality"!

HOSTESS: Et c'est la vérité! My turn, my turn now! "I Can Give You a Phrase With"! *(jingle)* Cucumber, cucumber . . .

She picks up a sandwich and stands.

The English CUCUMBER was caught napping when the baguette's French crust became its fatal wrapping!

She pops the sandwich in her mouth.

POET: Delectable! And she ate it all in one mouthful!
ARTIST: Bravo, madame!
PATRONESS: Bravo, one and all!

THE THREE AUTOMATONS: Ha, ha, ha, ha!!!!
HOSTESS: Bravo to us all!

The HOSTESS *calmly removes the napkins, one by one.*

Slow, creepy, piano music plays.

The HOSTESS *slowly removes her coat, preparing for the more intimate and intense part of the evening to come.*

Scene 5: Mortality

HOSTESS: And now, my friends, shall we try to find a new word to lighten up the tone? What do you say? "I Can Give You a Phrase With" . . . *(jingle)* mmmmmmmmh . . . let's dig, let's all dig down deeper into ourselves, dig down deeper to the joyful abyss, my friends. Everyone into the abysmal depths!

Oh! I have a fresh new concept that might inspire us all! Let me read you an excerpt of what I wrote this morning when I woke up, hum? Où est-il, où est-il? Oh, there, there it is, found it!

She has been pretending to look for it when, all along, she knew exactly where it was and had planned this performance. She puts on reading glasses and proceeds to read from a piece of notepaper.

"When the November rain drizzles down the window, and makes her feel lonely, so lonely, ever so lonely / or when the sun is shining brightly, but she feels absolutely nothing staring at all this beauty / or when she feels powerless and totally desperate regarding life's meaning and the reasons for being, she knows exactly what to do: she firmly hits her fingers with a hammer, paf! paf! paf!

Ouch!!!!

And suddenly, quite wonderfully, she finds her way back. The pain returns her to her senses, shows her the path to follow, and gives her the courage to continue until tomorrow."

She tears the paper into pieces

You understand my reflection, my intention? I am toying with the idea that physical pain can be an excellent antidote to the tortures of the soul, a precious ally. Interesting, no? We should try it. Don't you think?

She turns towards them.

Hey? Hmmm? HMMM?
THE THREE AUTOMATONS: *(uncertain of how to react, then trying to be encouraging)* Yes, interesting, madame. Interesting. We should try it. We WILL TRY IT! A hammer on the fingers! Good plan!
ARTIST: Ah . . . vicious, physical pain. Sometimes, after my shows, when I have performed in many cabarets in the same evening—pantomimes and silly dances all night long—my joints ache terribly, the pain in my joints: elbows, knees, wrists, and in particular my fingers, oh my fingers . . . physical pain . . . I know it all too well . . .

The HOSTESS crushes the broken champagne glasses on the floor with her foot.

POET: *(teeth gnashing, nervous)* My teeth hurt sometimes. *(sound of gnashing teeth)* There is a physical pain in my teeth. *(gnashing sound)* Mostly during very intense writing sessions. I get a vile pain in my teeth. *(gnashing sound)* I know what physical pain is; oh, I know!

The HOSTESS crushes broken glass that is under the table.

PATRONESS: *(nervous)* And I, sometimes, I experience physical pain in my eyes; my eyes hurt sometimes. When I am at the theatre, or the music hall, looking through my opera glasses, my eyes hurt me so badly sometimes . . . I get a pain in my eyes that is suddenly there, and then suddenly is gone. I know what pain is!

The HOSTESS *reaches under the coffee table and takes a piece of broken glass in her hand.*

She puts the piece of glass in her mouth and begins to bite down on it as she returns to her chair.

HOSTESS: *(while chewing the broken glass)* We are poor mortals and our body is the vessel in which we will sail for all of our existence. This body, this envelope, makes us suffer, love, cry, and rejoice all at once. But sometimes it is too much to bear, and we suddenly long to be rid of it—long to be rid of it before its fatal expiry date!

She chokes on the glass in her mouth and coughs.

Pardonnez-moi. Excusez-moi . . . Je dois . . . je vais . . .

She exits upstage, coughing and trying to swallow the remaining glass in her mouth. We see her silhouette through the curtain. She takes a hammer, lays her hand on a table, and hits her fingers with it, hard. She screams in pain when the hammer falls. The AUTOMATONS *scream as she hammers her hand. She returns with a bloody bandage on her hand, carrying the hammer. She is ecstatic.*

INVIGORATING!! I feel better; oh, I feel so much better. I feel so good, so goooooodddddd! Anyone else care to try?

She proffers the hammer.

THE THREE AUTOMATONS: NO, thank you!
HOSTESS: Are you sure?

THE THREE AUTOMATONS: Absolutely!
HOSTESS: Your loss! Ohhhhh, here I am, jumping from rooster to donkey, or, if you prefer, hopping from one subject to another, but I have it! Yes, I have found it! A powerful and frightening word! Let's play once more "I Can Give You a Phrase With" *(jingle)* with the word, le mot: MORTALITY!

The AUTOMATONS *bray loudly like a donkey, which is followed by a long silence.*

ARTIST: Really, madame, that is your choice? I am not afraid of dark themes, but I don't want to be the one to obscure the joy of your lovely salon.
HOSTESS: But it is done. My choice is made: MORTALITY.
PATRONESS: Yes, MORTALITY. Really?
HOSTESS: I am only going to tell you one more time. I insist. MORTALITY.
POET: Well then, I obey. But, you have been warned. MORTALITY!

"For those who question continually their own MORTALITY, the more time passes, the more they think about the cemetery; so to end it all beautifully, without being forgotten dreadfully, I offer you two wise thoughts: start writing your memoir instead, or quickly shoot yourself in the head!"
HOSTESS: Ha, ha, ha, thank you, monsieur. *(forced laugh)*
ARTIST: MORTALITY.

Every human being has to face their own MORTALITY; that is the only truth, the only certainty!
HOSTESS: Ha, ha, ha. Thank you, mademoiselle . . .

She forces a laugh, takes a sip from her champagne glass, and puts the hammer on the coffee table.

PATRONESS: MORTALITY: A banality one must consider seriously when one has a knife at the throat, a rifle to their head, or *tuberculosis* banging at the door!

On the word "tuberculosis" we hear a very dramatic musical accent. The HOSTESS *violently throws her glass to the floor.*

POET & ARTIST: *(between their teeth to the* PATRONESS*)* NOOOO, NO! NOT that! Not THE word, not that word! NOT . . .

PATRONESS: Not the word? What not? What word? I do not understand. Not what?

HOSTESS: Ha, ha, ha . . . champagne? Where is my glass? I've lost my glass! Where is my glass, my glass?!!

The HOSTESS*'s attitude is suddenly extremely calm. She takes a big swig directly from the champagne bottle.*

"I Can"—also—"Give You a Phrase With" *(jingle)* MORTALITY.

She fears the day when, in her mirror's reflection, a vaguely familiar old lady will whisper to her quietly, "Forget about your vanity, MORTALITY has replaced it definitively."

THE THREE AUTOMATONS: Yes, the cruelty of existence, madame! Ha, ha, ha, ha, ha, ha, ha!

The AUTOMATONS*' forced laughter reproduces the tune of the game-show jingle.*

HOSTESS: But, but, but . . . this day will never come, my friends. I will never be this old lady weeping and decomposing in front of her mirror! I will not have this marvelous privilege. I know that for a fact. It's a feeling I have always had, a sick conviction—my gruesome destiny.

ARTIST: Have you always felt this way, madame? Myself, I don't believe in spiritualism, or supernatural forces, or premonitions. But I do strongly feel eternal. I am made to go on eternally. This, I know.

PATRONESS: I myself have an iron constitution. I am not ready to stop any time soon. There are still too many things to accomplish. I will go on endlessly. That's all I know. This, I know.

POET: And me, well, I have the conviction that I will stay like this forever. I will be beautiful, elegant, and talented, until the end of time. I will stay like this. Immutable, imperishable, indestructible, ME.

The HOSTESS *leaps from her chair, brandishing the champagne bottle.*

HOSTESS: *(furious)* DO YOU EVEN KNOW WHAT YOU ARE TALKING ABOUT? How pretentious you are, my friends! Pretending to be immortal! I would not have thought this possible, coming from you, such refined and intelligent human beings. You brashly think that you are eternal? Ha, ha, ha, ha, ha, PLEEEASE! We will all end up on the scrap heap, in the rubbish, at the dump, in pieces, in ashes, and crawling with worms! Fini, terminé, oublié, seuls.

ETERNellement seuls!

(suddenly calm, apologetic) Seuls.

I am so sorry for my emotive outburst, un trop plein d'émotions! Excusez moi. I will go and figure out why time flies . . . and breathe through my nose, and count a hundred sheep, and light one thousand candles in the chapel of rest, in memory of me, and admire the intricate patterns dancing on the wallpaper, and ahhhhh! Go see if I am there? Who knows, maybe I am? And shake my fingers until they fall to the ground and bounce back by themselves to sleep in my gloves, and, most importantly, soak my eyeballs in cold water: "They're soaking in it!"

She exits upstage with the bottle. We can see her spying on the AUTOMATONS *throughout the following scene as she continues to drink champagne.*

Scene 6: Existential Automatons

Minimal electronic music, reminiscent of an old science-fiction film, underscores the following.

ARTIST: Something is wrong.
POET: Something is wrong.
PATRONESS: Something is wrong.

POET: She is trying to provoke us, but we have to respect our internal mechanisms and our programming. We have to be the perfect guests. We have to pretend to be human; it is our mission.
ARTIST: This is all YOUR fault, Drinking Patroness. Madame's sudden departure, her existential crisis. You have used a forbidden-word-for-which-we-do-not-know-the-meaning. Are you defective?
POET: She's right, Drinking Patroness, you have used a forbidden-word-for-which-we-do-not-know-the-meaning!
PATRONESS: Dandy Poet, I do not recall using a forbidden-word-for-which-we-do-not-know-the-meaning. ME, defective? NO. Impossible. Defective? NO!
ARTIST: Recapitulate, it will come back to you, recapitulate.
POET: Recapitulate! Recapitulate!
POET & ARTIST: RECAPITULATE! RECAPITULATE! RECAPITULATE!
PATRONESS: All right, there. I am putting myself into recapitulation mode. Are you happy? But I am telling you, I don't feel defective.

She rapidly glosses back over the entire show in fast-forward. We hear snippets of phrases and music from each of the scenes. Finally she lands on the fatal forbidden phrase.

MORTALITY: a banality one must consider seriously when one has a knife at the throat, a rifle to their head, or *tuberculosis* banging at the door!

Oh, you were right; I did use a forbidden-word-for-which-we-do-not-know-the-meaning! What a mechanical shame! Oh, NO. I do not want a sordid repair, not a sordid repair! No! No! No! Ahhhhhhhhhhhhhhhhhhhh!
ARTIST: Drinking Patroness! Revert to CALM MODE! Revert to CALM. There . . .

The PATRONESS *calms herself. Her eyes close and she relaxes.*

POET: Do not worry. A simple mechanical mistake. But we must be vigilant.
ARTIST: We have to be vigilant, and be the perfect guests. We are the perfect guests.
PATRONESS: *(opening her eyes)* If I derail again, let me know . . .

ARTIST: I most certainly will.
POET: First, we must help our dear hostess forget her vile spleen and her persistent melancholy. When she gets back, I will recite a lyrical poem!
PATRONESS: And I, to cheer her up, will perform a sweet little song!
ARTIST: And I will devise a diverting new pantomime!

A long pause, as the AUTOMATONS *become solemn.*

THE THREE AUTOMATONS: Humans are mortal.
ARTIST: But we are not. We are not mortal. We will outlive those who possess us, those who love us. We will survive our creator, our master.
POET: Survive!
PATRONESS: We will survive!
ARTIST: We are not copies of humans, we AUTOMATONS, we are reminders that unlike them we are "Forever unliving, and yet never dead"![1]
THE THREE AUTOMATONS: "Forever unliving, and yet never dead!"
"Forever unliving, and yet never dead!"
"Forever unliving, and yet never dead!"

Scene 7: From Hearsay To Poetry and Mime, Through To a Song!

The HOSTESS *returns with a full bottle of champagne.*

HOSTESS: Je suis de retour!
THE THREE AUTOMATONS: Ah, madame, our hostess!
HOSTESS: Votre hôtesse est de retour! L'hôtesse du salon est de retour! My dear guests, have you already forgotten about me? Did you miss me terribly? This short pause gave me the chance to revamp my "mental beauty," if I may

1 Quoted from Gaby Wood, *Living Dolls* (New York: Faber & Faber, 2002), 46.

say, and I am in better shape than ever. In the shape of what? I wouldn't know! But I brought fresh champagne!

The HOSTESS *pours fresh champagne for the* PATRONESS.

And now, what shall we launch into?

She drinks from the bottle.

Let's see . . .

Out of pure curiosity, what was the subject of your conversation as you patiently awaited my return to the salon?

PATRONESS: Oh, society gossip!

ARTIST: Ah, harmless hearsay!

POET: Euh, amusing chit-chat, unoffending tittle-tattle!

PATRONESS: Madame X loves Madame Y but has cheated on her with Mademoiselle Z and people will talk about it until the day where there is no more saliva to spurt about this particular faux pas!

ARTIST: The sublime poems of Nestor Druor were all along written by his blind and mysterious sister, Alphonsine, who is still living in poverty on the dingy street of Espoir-Fini!

POET: Monsieur, the baron of Namur, is a broken and useless man ever since that fateful Sunday in the forest, when his horse Arthur brutally left him sitting on his bottom in total discomfiture.

HOSTESS: Amusing, interesting, charming, is that all?

POET: Well, madame, if you please, I would love to recite for you my brand-new poem. It is fresh, and light, experimental and bright. I wrote it thinking of you.

HOSTESS: Oh joy, oh bliss! A new poem! We are all ears, monsieur!

POET: From / his / if / but / what / winged

The winged king in his golden cage is free: FRE_E_E_E_E_E_E!
Knowing quite, quite knowing well/well/well!

O plumage! O cage! O feathers! O prisoner! O Eternity! O Eternity!
From / his / if / but / what / winged! From / his / if / but / what / winged!
Never forgetting, forgetting never: WHAT HE BE!

HOSTESS: Monsieur, you have given us wings!

ARTIST: No venom, no bitterness? You surprise me.

POET: *Mesdames*, quite frankly, sometimes, I even surprise myself!

PATRONESS: You gave me courage, my friend. I shall rise above my own shyness and bare it all! I offer you . . . a delicate French song! What do you say?

ARTIST: *(with sarcasm)* Une chansonnette française! Hourra!

POET: *(resigned)* Since we have no other choice! Pourquoi pas?

HOSTESS: *(too happy)* Oui, oui, oui! Madame the Patroness, it is your turn to entertain us! Gâtez nous et gâtez vous aussi!

PATRONESS: Well, here it goes: "L'oiseau sur la branche / The Bird On the Branch."

The PATRONESS sings the sentimental and resolutely kitsch song "L'oiseau sur la branche" in an impassioned warble, that seems, by the final lingering verse, as though it will never end.

ARTIST & POET: Ohhhhhhhhhhhhhhhhhhhh . . .

HOSTESS: Madame, I am speechless. Il n'y a pas de mots pour décrire la beauté de votre interprétation!

ARTIST: My friends, Monsieur le Poète, Madame the Patroness, your flights of fancy have inspired me. I ardently desire to create for you all, right here, tonight, a new pantomime! BUT, but, madame, our dear hostess, I have an ingenious proposition! I will describe the movements one by one, and YOU, madame, will interpret them instead of me. What do you say?

PATRONESS: What a marvellous idea! From one body to another! The creative talent will be transferred like electricity! Mademoiselle will be the creative voice and YOU, madame, will be the moving statue, the trained doll!

THE THREE AUTOMATONS: Yes! Be the moving statue, the trained doll!!!

HOSTESS: Weeeeell, yes! I accept your challenge!

The HOSTESS *slowly, gleefully opens her skirt, revealing her boots and elaborate matching red Victorian undergarments. She is enjoying this immensely. It is her favourite activity.*

I will be your moving statue, your trained doll!!

ARTIST: THE FREED BIRD: AN EXPRESSIVE PANTOMIME.

The POET *and* PATRONESS *make bird noises to underscore the following. Vintage flute music plays underneath. The* HOSTESS *climbs onto the coffee table to begin her interpretation. She proceeds to act out the pantomime as it is described by the* ARTIST.

You are a bird in a cage! Knees bent, torso forward, arms resting alongside your body. All your feathers are quivering, your gaze is strong yet fragile. A twitch of the head, bird beak half open, whistling lightly. Ahhhhhhh, that's it. Let the public come to you. You are the centre, the arrow, the target. Undulate your torso and trunk and turn around, stretch your torso, keep your head high, your neck straight. Look at the world in which you are imprisoned, YES. You are a creature made for liberty, but you have been confined to the ground. Dive into your need to be the bird that you are. Whistle with all your rage, whistle with all your passion! YES! And then, open your right wing, from the bottom upwards, open you arm, yes, your arm is now a wing, keep it high, and then, open the left wing—aerial, celestial, good, good! Undulate both wings simultaneously, good . . . lightness, internal takeoff! Good. We want to feel the bird all the way to your fingertips, that's it! And now! Break through the cage! Suddenly you can fly anywhere! Take the whole space, it belongs to YOU! Very good! Fly. Yes, yes, this is your true nature, your instinctive animal nature! Break free! Let the animal in you express itself! It was always there, just waiting for the chance to break free! Good, very good!

The HOSTESS *is passionately flapping her wings.*

And now begin your return, calm yourself, slowly . . . calm. Come back, madame. Madame, calm yourself!

The HOSTESS *in not listening anymore, she has lost herself in the dance; she exits to her backroom upstage.*

Come back, madame, the pantomime is over. It's over, madame, come back, madame, madame, madame, madame! Come back! Come back! She is not coming back! *(to the others)* She is not coming back!
THE THREE AUTOMATONS: *(in a state of panic)* COME BACK! COME BACK! COME BACK! MADAME, COME BACK! DEAR HOSTESS!

Finally the HOSTESS *returns, sits at the coffee table, and begins to cough into a white handkerchief.*

ARTIST: *(relieved)* Ahhhhhhhh! There you are, good . . . good . . .
POET: Madame! That was worthy of mademoiselle's greatest performance! You are an exceptional student!
ARTIST: Yes, madame, bravo! It was impressive, stunning! You were so free!
PATRONESS: A truly humbling lesson in virtuosity! You WERE THE BIRD!
THE THREE AUTOMATONS: *(extremely passionate)* You were SUPERB, madame!
Marvellous, fabulous, stupendous, prodigious, YES!
Marvellous, fabulous, stupendous, prodigious, YES!
Marvellous, fabulous, stupendous, prodigious, YES!

Scene 8: Suicide Action

The HOSTESS *grows impatient and cuts off their sycophantic praise.*

HOSTESS: MERCI! MERCI! MERCI!

Dear guests. Thank you for this playful demonstration of cheerfulness made of syrupy poetry, stiff pantomime, and dusty ditties! But, but, but, truly I say to you, yes, I am telling you truly, you are exhausting me terribly, my dear guests.

You exhaust me with your vain attempts to cheer up a woman who has simply ceased to believe! I must abandon the ship, comrades.

She waves a white handkerchief and we hear the sound of an ocean liner's horn followed by dramatic music reminiscent of an Ennio Morricone classic.

She then pulls out a fake gun and hides a red handkerchief in her vest.

(dramatically) Adieu. I am leaving, never to return. Bang! Lower the flags and wring your soaked handkerchiefs. Bang! I choose my own destiny, no martyr, no regrets. Bang! And I, yes, I, I take my leave of you, and all of this: the armchairs, the knick-knacks, the paintings, the curtains, the aviary! Bang! Bang! Bang! Champagne! Auf Wiedersehen! Adios! Ciao! Adieu! Don'y cry for me!

She pretends to shoot herself in the head, laying the red handkerchief between her lips as if it were blood coming out of her mouth. She slumps, immobile, in her chair.

POET: Eeeeeeeeeeeeeeeeeeeeeee . . . precious hostess . . .
ARTIST: Aaaaaaaaaaaaaaaaaaaaaa . . . beloved hostess . . .
PATRONESS: Mmmmmmmmmmmmmmm . . . dear hostess . . .
POET: What . . . is . . . it?
ARTIST: What . . . is . . . what?
PATRONESS: What . . . is . . . THAT?
POET: Metal object that goes BANG! I have never seen that. I am searching. Metal object that goes BANG . . . a, a, a, pistol, I am given the word pistol. Pistol: a handgun whose chamber is integral with the barrel. Pistoleer, one armed with a pistol. Pistol-whip, to beat with a pistol.
ARTIST: Madame is a pistoleer . . . armed with a whip . . . fighting pistol barrel?

PATRONESS: The colour red? I have used it often while talking about my mediocre talent as a painter . . . Fire-truck red, brick red, cherry red, Chinese red . . .
POET: RED: the color of blood, and poppies. Red lipstick. RED ALERT! The color of danger: DANGER, DANGER, DANGER!

His arms move in an agitated manner suggestive of the 1960s American TV show Lost in Space.

ARTIST: Blood red? Poppy red? Danger red? What kind of red are we talking about here? I can't choose the right red. Choosing is an art in itself. To choose is the ART of CHOICE. The art of choosing is to choose the right thing. This or that? These or those?
PATRONESS: Is there a play on words that we simply aren't getting? A charade, or perhaps the beginning of an exotic treasure hunt filled with mysterious symbols? A secret anagram? YES! THAT'S IT!
Pistol: Tolpis, spilot, lotsip, tolpsi?
ARTIST: Tolpsi, lotsip, spilot, tolpis, pistol?
POET: Spilot, tolpis, tolpsi, pistol, lotsip?
ARTIST: We must remain CALM!!!!!! Remain calm! Calm! Let us all revert to CALM MODE!
POET: Yes, let's behave as though nothing happened. We saw nothing, we heard nothing. Remain CALM.
PATRONESS: Yes, remain CALM. C-A-L-M. Nothing happened! Mum's the word!

The THREE AUTOMATONS *begin to hum softly with their eyes closed.*

The HOSTESS *explodes in anger.*

HOSTESS: NON! NON! NON!! J'étais MORTE! I was dead!
I was supposed to seem dead! As in a SUICIDE! I committed a fake suicide! A suicide is when one decides to end one's own life, to voluntarily end it all. I was playing dead. I shot myself with a fake bullet, with a fake pistol, pointed at my real head, and you were supposed to cry. Moi fausse-morte,

fausse suicidé, et vous en VRAIS larmes! And the red handkerchief was supposed to represent blood, *LE SANG*! Not red lipstick or red alert, monsieur, but BLOOD, MY OWN BLOODY BLOOD! BLOOD! THE RED LIQUID CIRCULATING THROUGHOUT OUR VEINS, ARTERIES, AND HEART, CARRYING VARIOUS NUTRITIVE ELEMENTS AND OXYGEN!

And when the bullet comes out of the pistol: Mhhhhgrrrrrrr, INSIDE the pistol, there are BULLETS that are the projectiles of a firearm—you know, small pieces of metal shaped like a bean that hurt like hell. When one of these bullets is ejected from the pistol and enters the human body the result is catastrophic! You lose a lot of blood and this is not good, AND, IT BREAKS THE HUMAN MECHANISM!!!!! AND IT KILLS YOU! And then you die, and THIS, MY DEATH, SHOULD HAVE MADE YOU VERY SAD. MA MORT À CAUSE D'UNE BALLE DE PISTOLET DANS MA TÊTE DEVAIT VOUS RENDRE TERRIBLEMENT TRISTE!

I did this . . . this "coup de théâtre" to study your reaction, to put you to the test, to challenge you, and to prepare you for the eventuality of my DEPARTURE . . .

We hear a drum roll.

But, mostly to measure your love for me, your attachment to me.

I am so sorry. You were not ready for that. It is not your fault.

PATRONESS: You were dead? No, no, noooooooo . . .

She tries to cry.

ARTIST: Dead? Noooooooooooooo . . .

She tries to cry.

POET: Not . . . dead? Noooooooooooooooo . . .

He tries to cry.

THE THREE AUTOMATONS: Ahhhhhh, aaaaaaaaaaaaaahh, sniff, sniff, sniff . . .

They fake cry for the longest time; it is too much, too intense, not at all believable.

HOSTESS: Oh, please, STOP! It is too late now. You have so many things to learn about life and about what it means to be alive, to love, desire, feel, and die.
POET: Madame, our dear and precious hostess, we have the rest of our lives to try to be better, and evolve, and become the best humans possible.
ARTIST: We all make mistakes, but to err is human!
PATRONESS: And forgiveness is indeed one of the most noble sentiments of human nature.
POET: What would I do without your salon, without you? I would be bored, madame. BORED!
ARTIST: Madame, without your Friday salon, I would be destitute. You are my muse, madame. There, I said it.
PATRONESS: I would have no interest left. Only lassitude and dreadful solitude.
HOSTESS: Thank you, my friends. I know that you love me, and that you have a real attachment to our weekly ritual. BUT, now, PLEASE, leave me alone.

The AUTOMATONS gasp.

Just go.
THE THREE AUTOMATONS: *(blurting out)* Eh?
HOSTESS: We will meet again next week.
THE THREE AUTOMATONS: *(crying out)* OH!
HOSTESS: Please! I want to be alone. Go away. Just go! Go away!

A long pregnant pause as the AUTOMATONS try to figure out how to react to the HOSTESS's impossible demand.

Scene 9: Madame is Cruel

HOSTESS: Pleaseee, don't make me beg you. If you truly love me, you will leave me alone. NOW, GO AWAY!
PATRONESS: If we could, we would leave without question, but it's simply not possible . . .
HOSTESS: Not possible? Do you mock me?
THE THREE AUTOMATONS: NO, madame, it's the truth. It is not possible.
HOSTESS: And how is this NOT POSSIBLE?

The AUTOMATONS exchange glances, worried. They voice the next three phrases in robotic, metallic, clipped speech patterns.

POET: The, the, the "degrees of liberty" are limited . . .
ARTIST: You know, our "degrees of liberty" . . . don't allow us to . . .
PATRONESS: Our "degrees of liberty" limit us to certain things . . . for example, to be seated, here, nothing else.
HOSTESS: WHAT? WHAT ARE YOU TALKING ABOUT? Monsieur, my encyclopedic friend! Please, give me the *définition* of the words "degrees of liberty," please!
POET: Really, madame, the definition?
HOSTESS: Really, the definition.
PATRONESS: And what do you say we drink a little more champagne to lighten up the mood, my friend, champagne?
HOSTESS: You've had enough. I don't have any anti-rust left in my workshop, and you have seriously begun to creak, madame. And it is beginning to irritate me.
ARTIST: My dear hostess, you suddenly seem so tense; I could help you relax. Do you remember how those cold and lonely nights in your workshop last winter became so torrid in my company? Why don't we resume that complex game of love that you so precisely taught me. Press the right button and my expert fingering technique will work its magic!

She simulates orgasm.

Ahh, ah, ah, ahhh, ah, AH . . . !

HOSTESS: Mademoiselle!!! Didn't I deactivate that? Those particular services are no longer required. Your amorous gestures were too mechanical for me. Forget about it, sweetheart. Monsieur! Donnez-moi la définition des mots "degrés de liberté"!

POET: If you insist . . . "Degrees of liberty": Name given to . . . mechanical joints . . . in robotics.

We hear scary robotic music with inverted voices.

HOSTESS: *(feigning surprise)* WHAT? What are you saying? Mechanical joints in robotics? What do you mean? Do you mean, *OH HORREUR*, you are not human beings, but, but, but, MACHINES! ANDROIDS! ROBOTS! AUTOMATONS!

THE THREE AUTOMATONS: Oh NO, NO, NO!!!!

They take a panicked intake of breath.

WE ARE human beings!!!!

Human beings!

Human beings!

Human beings!

HOSTESS: Stop your antics. The game is over. I don't want to play anymore. Your hostess has had enough. You are good old reliable machines. I know it, you know it. Forget all your programming. Shut down the motors. Slacken the pulleys. Unscrew the bolts and stop the gears. C'est moi qui vous le dis!

THE THREE AUTOMATONS: But, but, but everything inside us tells us, obliges us, to be—be—to be humans, and never stray from our mission. We are the guests of madame's salon. That is a fact. We are the faithful friends of every Friday's salon.

HOSTESS: Today, we will end this farce.

The HOSTESS *begins to cough. She exits upstage to her workshop where the lighting, for the first time, reveals the details of this upstage area. We see tools, old automaton parts (faces, legs, arms) hanging everywhere. Old mechanical parts cover the work table. She puts on a long smock—a costume that evokes an eerie combination of Marie Curie and Dr. Frankenstein.*

THE THREE AUTOMATONS: But the salon, the conversations, our precious company? Our stimulating intellectual exchanges?
HOSTESS: *(from behind the curtain)* You do not think for yourselves. You exist only because I want you to.
POET: I do think; I think continually, I think! And I exist; I am here for you and I think like a human, therefore I exist!
PATRONESS: But, madame, I think too! And I do exist; I am human and I think only of you! I think, madame. I think.
ARTIST: I think of you, and of our salon, and of my own humanity, constantly! This is what makes me exist here, for you!
HOSTESS: *(returning from the workshop, revealing her true nature)* Obey your master, your DIVINE CREATOR! You think that YOU THINK, BUT YOU CAN'T! Don't forget: your intelligence is artificial. This is reality, and you have to accept it.
ARTIST: I don't think?
PATRONESS: I don't think?
POET: I don't think?
THE THREE AUTOMATONS: Therefore I am not?

There is a long pause. The HOSTESS *moves to downstage centre.*

THE THREE AUTOMATONS: *(in extreme despair)* Divine creator, mother, MOTHER ANSWER US. MOMMY! I DON'T EXIST? MUMMYYYYYYYY!

The HOSTESS *tenderly caresses the face of each of the* AUTOMATONS. *They calm down and close their eyes, one by one. She then moves upstage and stands behind the coffee table.*

HOSTESS: My poor machine-children in existential crisis. Your questions trouble me and touch me deeply. But how can I explain it to you simply. There are philosophical rules linked to our time on earth. And one of the rules is that *I am, and you are not . . . I am, and you are not.* You were created in our image, the human image, but you are only an image, a concept, an idea. Don't forget, I have predetermined everything for you. You are nothing without me. My little children, I have given you a soul. But it is ONLY ME, ME, ME, and I am really sorry to say so, BUT only I can say with certainty: I think, therefore I am!

Pompous music, like a marching band with trumpets and drums, builds as the HOSTESS *coughs more and more, her state of health clearly degrading before our eyes.*

Scene 10: Forest of the Sleeping Death

ARTIST: Mother, why are you talking to us like this?
PATRONESS: Mother, why are you so cruel to us?
POET: Mother, why are you attacking your only friends, us, us, and us? Why US?
HOSTESS: My children, I am dying!

Cinematic music erupts to support the coming drama.

THE THREE AUTOMATONS: You are dying? Oh! Mother, do not be afraid of death, it is nothing, really, nothing. We are not afraid of death. Don't be afraid, creator, mother of our universe. Be like us, fearless.
HOSTESS: Of course you are not afraid! The notion of extinction is not programmed into you. You could go on like this for a very long time, a hundred years, possibly even centuries, especially if you end up in a museum, and if

your maintenance is well funded . . . How I would like to be one of you, to not feel the anxiety of the inevitable end of my life.

PATRONESS: How will you die?

HOSTESS: *(She coughs.)* A very serious sickness, fatal . . . HIGHLY contagious, tuber . . .

THE THREE AUTOMATONS: The forbidden-word-for-which-we-do-not-know-the-meaning? TUBERCULOSIS?

HOSTESS: I told you to not to mention this word . . .

THE THREE AUTOMATONS: ARE WE contagious too, Mother?

HOSTESS: Of course NOT, you are in no danger. I can't transmit anything to a bunch of scrap metal. THAT is WHY I created you. I needed friends to survive my quarantine without having to worry about putting their lives in danger . . . You were the perfect companions for my long and final voyage . . . But more than anything, quite humanly, I wanted to make sure to leave a trace, a little something of me on this earth. Because of you, my mechanical children, I won't disappear completely. I will finally be "forever unliving and yet never dead!"

The HOSTESS spits real blood for the first time.

PATRONESS: Ohhhhhhhhhhhhh, blood, red blood, red alert? Death becomes her? Death is here? Will you leave us soon? Mother, madame, mommy, answer me?

TUBERCULOSIS IS HERE!

TUBERCULOSIS? OR NOT? WHO TO BELIEVE? I DO NOT KNOW?

TUBERCULOSIS? OR NOT? WHO TO BELIEVE? I DO NOT KNOW?

TUBERCULOSIS? OR NOT? WHO TO BELIEVE? I DO NOT KNOW?

HOSTESS: TAISEZ VOUS! TAISEZ VOUS!!! I told you not to mention this WORD! You really asked for it this time; you asked for it! REPAIR!

She goes to her workshop and puts on large work gloves and clockmaker's goggles, then returns to the salon with some dangerous-looking tools.

Creepy robotic music plays.

PATRONESS: NO! No repairs!!!!!!!!!!!!!!!!!!!! Please, no repairs! NNNNNNN-NOOOOOOOOOOOOOOOOOOOOOOOOOOO! Tuberculosis or not? Who to believe? I do not know!

PATRONESS & POET: No repairs, MOMMY! We are worried about you! Don't unplug your mechanical chicks! DIE IN OUR ARMS, DIE IN OUR ARMS!

ARTIST: We have done nothing wrong . . . nothing. I love you; we love you!!!!! No repairs! For pity's sake! For pity's sake! We desire, we wonder, and we dream of reaching human perfection! Humanity, humanity! To understand and feel and be your perfect guests! FOR PITY'S SAKE, MAMAN!

THE THREE AUTOMATONS: TO BE YOUR PERFECT GUESTS! FOR PITY'S SAKE! FOR PITY'S SAKE! FOR PITY'S SAKE!

POET & ARTIST: NO not that!!!!!!!!!!!!!!!!!!!! MAMAN!!!!!!!!!!!!!!!!!!!!!!!!!!!!!! She is not defective!!!! NOOOOOOOOOOOOOOOOOOOOOOOOOOOOOOOO!

The HOSTESS approaches the PATRONESS with her tools and begins to open the top part of her head. She unplugs some connections in the PATRONESS's "brain" and unravels some wires, but then is seized by an uncontrollable coughing fit. The HOSTESS reels and sways around the room as the PATRONESS begins to sputter, her face a mask of fear and distress. The other two are in a state of paralytic shock.

PATRONESS: *(emitting inarticulate sounds)* Ahhhrreuiiiiiiiiiiii i37829p-01111bxmmmmmmmmmmmjuoprà r0#88888 8888888$ $∂££££££££££££££££££££££££££££££111111111 @!!!!!!!!!%?&&** (P¨P¨P(*??$@#!!!@#E$%YUO¨G-GGGGGggggggggggggggaaaaaaaaaaaaaaaaaaaaaaaaaiiiiiiiiiiiiiiiiiiiiiiiiiiiiiiiiiiiiiiiiiiiiiiiiiiiiiiiiiiiiiiiiiiiiiiiiii GRRRRRRRRRRRRRRRRRR . . . .tttttttiiiiiiiiiiiiiiiiiiiiiiiiiiiiiiiiiiiiiiiiiiiiiiiiipffffffffffffffffffffffffffffffffffffffffff . . . .

Slowly she manages to reactivate a part of her brain.

Mummy, Mummy, Mummy?

We hear Christmas bells.

Happy to be back amongst you.

We hear a donkey scream and broken mechanical sounds.

And since it is my turn to speak?

She regains a modicum of control.

Where are we? Oh yes, dear hostess, MOTHER you don't feel well?
THE THREE AUTOMATONS: She is leaving us; we are losing her, my friends, we are losing her, WE ARE LOSING HER!!!!!!

The pre-death delirium of the HOSTESS sets in. Suddenly, we are thrust into the final scene of what seems to be a very pathetic musical comedy. The following song, seeming to be the grand finale, is inspired by the style of "The Umbrellas of Cherbourg."

"THE MORTUARY SONG/TUBER_KILLED"

HOSTESS: *(sings live)* Tuberculosis has rung,
The pulmonary trumpet has sung!
The finale, the finale

Pause.

The grand finale has arrived . . .
Life is finalized,
neutralized, pulverized
TUBERCULERIZED-TUBERCULERIZED!

TUBER_KILLED! TUBER_KILLED!
Finally the end is near,

The last stop, the end of the line
The last stop of the train of your life . . .
CHOUCHOOOOOOOOOOOO, CHOUCHOOOOO!
THE THREE AUTOMATONS: *(singing)* Dying, spitting blood,
Hair in the wind!
Dying, spitting blood,
Hair in the wind!
Dying, spitting blood,
Hair in the wind!
Dying, spitting blood,
Hair in the wind, hair in the wind . . .
THE VOICE OF THE HOSTESS THROUGH THE BODY OF THE ARTIST: *(spoken verse)* We must die to make space for something else . . .
THE VOICE OF THE HOSTESS THROUGH THE BODY OF THE PATRONESS: *(spoken verse)* . . . something else that will flourish . . . accept decay, and abandon oneself to death . . .
THE VOICE OF THE HOSTESS THROUGH THE BODY OF THE POET: *(spoken verse)* . . . and live on in the heart of those who remain, those who remain, those who remain . . .
THE THREE AUTOMATONS: *(singing)* EMBRACE YOUR DESTINY! EMBRACE YOUR DESTINY!
IT WAS MEANT TO BE,
DYING AS YOU'RE SPITTING BLOOD, HAIR IN THE WIND, HAIR IN THE WIND, HAIR IN THE WIND . . .
POET: *(solo)* Tuber_killed!
It won't hurt you, I am with you!
Tuber_killed! Tuber_killed! Tuber_killed!
ARTIST: *(solo)* Tuber_killed!
It won't hurt you, I am with you!
Tuber_killed! Tuber_killed! Tuber_killed!
PATRONESS: *(solo)* Tuber_killed!
It won't hurt you, I am with you!
Tuber_killed! Tuber_killed! Tuber_killed!

Finale.

THE THREE AUTOMATONS & HOSTESS: *(singing)* IT WAS MEANT TO BE DYING AS YOU'RE SPITTING BLOOD,
HAIR IN THE WIND, HAIR IN THE WIND, HAIR IN THE WIND . . .

The HOSTESS *stands motionless in the middle of the salon. She is out of breath. She moves downstage and speaks with difficulty.*

Scene 11: Epilogue and Farewell

HOSTESS: OHHHHHHHHHHHHHHHHHHHHHHHH! This is it, this is it, the time has come, my little ones, to say farewell! ADIEU! ADIEU!

The INVISIBLE awaits me . . . I have an urgent meeting somewhere between twilight and oblivion; I mustn't be late . . .

Thank you for your words, though empty, your phrases, though predictable, your laughter, though false . . .

Thank you for your presence, which has filled the emptiness, the emptiness suspended in time . . .

Dreadful time that runs, crumbles, and disappears . . .

And finally, my marvellous creatures, thank you for having pretended to breathe beside me. Your breath, though not human, made me feel better, comforted me, and made me forget for a while that in the end we die alone, we die alone, we die alone . . .

We hear the sounds of a forest at night and the mystical hoots of an owl.

The HOSTESS *leaves the stage, steps off the raised platform that constitutes the salon, and lies on the theatre floor outside of the playing space, like a deer dying alone in the woods under a large oak tree. She dies.*

THE THREE AUTOMATONS: And now it's over, finished; she's gone forever, into infinity? Shall we cry? Yes, let's cry.

The AUTOMATONS *cry out for real this time: they are touching, human, true.*

THE THREE AUTOMATONS: How long should we cry, when a loved one has died?

POET: A minute, an hour?

ARTIST: A day?

PATRONESS: A month?

THE THREE AUTOMATONS: A year?

ARTIST: If I had a walking function I would go to her, into the darkness, so she wouldn't feel so lonely.

PATRONESS: If only I could have become contagious, contagious like a human being, I would have shared in her fatality.

POET: I miss her terribly already. It is very disconcerting.

ARTIST: And now, we wait. Is that all?

POET: For what? We wait for what?

PATRONESS: For time to pass, for the pain to disappear, to blur and soften?

POET: Voluntary disconnection? What do you say?

THE THREE AUTOMATONS: YES! VOLUNTARY DISCONNECTION!

ARTIST: Like bears, we should hibernate, in our metallic bodies, we should fall asleep . . .

PATRONESS: . . . until the return of a sunnier spring, of a happiness without sadness, of a lighter and sweeter day . . .

POET: But until that day my automaton friends . . .

THE THREE AUTOMATONS: My friends automaton.

PATRONESS: Let us disconnect the complexity of our machinery.

ARTIST: Let us stop momentarily the cardiac clockwork and its persistent tick tock.

THE THREE AUTOMATONS: Let us disconnect.

A nostalgic tune, with the haunting sound of a theremin, begins its slow crescendo of volume and intensity.

POET: Until that day . . .

ARTIST: . . . until the day . . .

POET: . . . that we no longer feel anything . . .

PATRONESS: . . . feel nothing, only EMPTINESS . . .

ARTIST: . . . EMPTINESS . . .

THE THREE AUTOMATONS: . . . EMPTINESS.

Only then will we come back, come back to be filled with wonder, to be filled with wonder staring at YOUR HUMANITY, YOUR HUMANITY, YOUR HUMANITY, YOUR HUMANITY, YOUR HUMANITY, YOUR HUMANITY, YOUR HUMANITY . . .

THE THREE AUTOMATONS *disconnect themselves. Jaws go slack, eyes shut, limbs hang loose at their sides.*

The music diminishes to an echo, then silence.

The end.

Acknowledgements

I would like to express my sincere thanks to the artists whose plays appear in these pages, and to those artists and academics whose words preface those plays. Blake Sproule, you're the bomb! Annie Gibson, thanks so much for this opportunity.

Contributors

Born and raised in the Philippines, **Patrick Alcedo** is an associate professor in the Department of Dance at York University, Toronto. Under the auspices of the Asian Cultural Council, he received his Ph.D. in Dance History and Theory from the University of California, Riverside. A former Rockefeller Humanities Fellow at the Smithsonian Institution in Washington, DC, he was awarded a Social Sciences and Humanities Research Council grant for his work on dance performance, emotional labour, and immigrant identities among Filipina caregivers in Toronto. He is the lead editor of the forthcoming anthology *Religious Festivals in Contemporary Southeast Asia* (2014) and a producer of the multimedia project "Boxing To Be The Next Pacquiao," which appeared in the *New York Times*. A recipient of York University's Dean's Award for Excellence in Teaching, he received a 2013 Early Researcher Award from the Government of Ontario Ministry of Research and Innovation. He is the incoming graduate program director of York University's M.A. and Ph.D. programs in Dance Studies.

Olivier Choinière graduated from the National Theatre School in 1996 with a degree in playwriting. He has written twenty plays and translated authors such as Mark O'Rowe. In 2001 he was awarded the Canada Council of the Arts Future Generations Millennium Prize.

Caryl Churchill is arguably the most respected female dramatist in the English-speaking world. She is the author of some twenty plays including *Light Shining in Buckinghamshire, Cloud 9, Top Girls, Serious Money, The Skriker, Blue Heart, Far Away, A Number, Drunk Enough to Say I Love You,* and *Seven Jewish Children.*

Nathalie Claude is an award-winning Montreal-based actor, director, dancer, choreographer, MC, musician, writer, and coach. As an actor she has over fifty professional theatre, dance, film, and television credits to her name. An active member of Momentum, her own creations include *Les Filles de Séléné*; *La Fête des Morts*, co-created with Céline Bonnier; and *Limbes/Limbo*, a collaboration with dancer Lin Snelling. Nathalie has also created six solos performances, forming *The Sadness Trilogy* and *The Madness Trilogy*. In 2009 she was invited by the Montreal Museum of Fine Arts to co-design the largest ever retrospective of the works of the celebrated pre-Raphaelite British artist John William Waterhouse.

Nicholas Hanson is an associate professor at the University of Lethbridge, teaching courses in Theatre for Young Audiences and coordinating tours of original theatre creations that perform for several thousand elementary- and high-school students each year. Nicholas has contributed youth-related articles to *Canadian Theatre Review* and *The Lion & Unicorn*, and he has presented TYA-themed papers at a number of national and international conferences. In 2011, Nicholas received the Canadian Association for Theatre Research's Robert Lawrence Prize for research on solo productions in Canada. Co-author of *The Ultimate Improv Book*, Nicholas has delivered workshops and lectures for a myriad of schools, camps, theatres, and organizations.

Kyla Harris is a visual artist whose subject matter is influenced by her experiences of being a wheelchair user. Her work is shaped by multidisciplinary collaborations, which include co-writing *The Glass Box* and a photography series with Sarah Murray and health practitioners that assist with her sculptures. After studying at Vancouver Film School and receiving a B.A. of Fine

Arts at the University of the Arts London, she now resides as an artist and consultant in London, England. Kyla is continually thankful to her multiple collaborators, including those at Theatre Terrific and the support of her personal assistants.

The author of *National Performance: Representing Quebec from Expo 67 to Céline Dion* (University of Toronto Press) and *Theatre and Feeling* (Palgrave), **Erin Hurley** is an associate professor of English at McGill University. With Sara Warner, she edited the special section, "Affect/Performance/Politics," of *The Journal of Dramatic Theory and Criticism* (Spring 2012). Her current research focuses on contemporary performance, with special attention to women, affects, and objects.

Caleb Johnston is a lecturer in human geography at the University of Edinburgh. Interested in interdisciplinary and collaborative research, his work engages cities, social justice, theatre, politics, informalization, and methods. His research at the intersection of geography and art has been performed internationally and has involved partnerships with artists from varied disciplinary backgrounds. He is currently writing a monograph for the Justice and Social Transformation series from the University of Georgia Press.

Originally from East Farnham, Quebec, **Moynan King** is a Toronto-based theatre artist currently working on a Ph.D. in performance studies at York University. She is honoured to have been the first automaton voice in an early workshop of *The Salon Automaton* in 2006 and to have performed the voice of the Cabaret Artist in the final English version of the play in 2009.

Allison Leadley is a Ph.D. student at the Centre for Drama, Theatre, and Performance Studies at the University of Toronto. Her dissertation explores the self-fashioned display of disease and dis/ability in contemporary performance with a particular interest in how contemporary artists engage with the performance tradition of the freak show. Allison holds an M.A. from the University of British Columbia and a B.A. from Dalhousie University.

Watson Moy studies theatre craft with Theatre Terrific and has studied neutral mask work with Ian Wallace. He performed in the professional production of *doGs*, where he played the improvisational role of the Gardener. Watson approaches his work with thoughtful honesty, generosity, and dedication to the form. Watson has Down syndrome. "I like this job and I was surprised that you picked me. I was so relieved that I got the part. When you gave me the news I was so happy. It was totally new to me and I love playing the part."

Stéphanie Nutting is an associate professor of French at the University of Guelph. She is the author of *Le tragique dans le théâtre québécois et canadien-français, 1950–1989* (2000), and co-editor, with François Paré, of a collection of essays titled *Jean Marc Dalpé: Ouvrier d'un dire* (2007). She has also contributed to various reviews including *Voix et Images*, *L'Annuaire théâtral*, and *Theatre Research in Canada/Recherches théâtrales au Canada*. Her recent research focuses on gossip and social networks as an evolving aesthetic in Québécois and Franco-Canadian theatre.

Geraldine Pratt is Professor of Geography at the University of British Columbia. She has collaborated with the Philippine Women Centre of BC for the last eighteen years, researching various aspects of Canada's Temporary Foreign Worker Program, including the marginalization of Filipino youth. She is the author of *Working Feminism* and *Families Apart: Migrant Mothers and the Conflicts of Labor and Love*, co-author of *Gender, Work and Space*, and co-editor of *The Global and the Intimate: Feminism in Our Time* and the fourth and fifth editions of the *Dictionary of Human Geography*.

Michele Riml is a critically acclaimed playwright from Vancouver, British Columbia. Her plays include *Miss Teen*; *Under the Influence*; *Poster Boys*; *Souvenirs*; *On the Edge*; *The Amaryllis*; and *Henry and Alice: Into the Wild*, the sequel to *Sexy Laundry*, which has been translated into several languages and has been produced in Canada, Poland, Germany, New Zealand, Iceland, Mexico, and the USA. Her plays for young audiences include *RAGE* (winner of the 2005 Sydney Risk Award for Outstanding Original Play), *The Skinny*

Lie, *The Invisible Girl*, and *Tree Boy*. Michele was nominated for the 2008 Lou and Elinore Siminovitch Prize.

Susanna Uchatius has been the artistic director of Theatre Terrific since 2005 and has collaboratively directed and written over twenty productions with the company. Her directorial/playwright practice is based in inclusive theatre ensemble creation for actors of all abilities, committing to the elements of respect, rigour, and risk. She was deeply honoured to collaborate and perform in this intimate journey with the insightful initial guidance of Jan Derbyshire and under the perceptive direction of Joanna Garfinkel. She wishes to thank Kyla and Watson for their honesty, generosity, and support, giving her the courage to once again tread the boards.

First edition: May 2014
Printed and bound in Canada by Marquis Book Printing, Montreal

Cover art, *Orée VI* © Marianne Chevalier
Cover and book design by Blake Sproule

PLAYWRIGHTS CANADA PRESS
202-269 Richmond St. W.
Toronto, ON
M5V 1X1

416.703.0013
info@playwrightscanada.com
www.playwrightscanada.com

RECYCLED
Paper made from recycled material
FSC® C103567
FSC www.fsc.org

Printed on Enviro 100% post-consumer EcoLogo certified paper, processed chlorine free and manufactured using biogas energy.

100% PERMANENT BIO GAS ENERGY